Chapter features

Studying can be a daunting prospect, particularly when you have lots of other commitments. This Workbook is full of useful features, explained in the key below, designed to help you get the most out of your studies and maximise your chances of exam success.

Key to icons

Key term

Central concepts are highlighted and clearly defined in the Key terms feature. Key terms are also listed in bold in the Index, for quick and easy reference.

Formula to learn

This boxed feature will highlight important formula which you need to learn for your exam.

PER alert

This feature identifies when something you are reading will also be useful for your PER requirement (see 'The PER alert' section above for more details).

Real world examples

These will give real examples to help demonstrate the concepts you are reading about.

Illustration

Illustrations walk through how to apply key knowledge and techniques step by step.

Activity

Activities give you essential practice of techniques covered in the chapter.

Exercise

Exercises suggest tasks which can be done to further your understanding.

Essential reading

Links to the Essential reading are given throughout the chapter. The Essential reading is included in the free eBook, accessed via the Exam Success Site (see inside cover for details on how to access this).

At the end of each chapter you will find a Knowledge diagnostic, which is a summary of the main learning points from the chapter to allow you to check you have understood the key concepts. You will also find a Further study guidance which contains suggestions for ways in which you can continue your learning and enhance your understanding. This can include: recommendations for question practice from the Further question practice and solutions, to test your understanding of the topics in the Chapter; suggestions for further reading which can be done, such as technical articles; and ideas for your own research.

Introduction to the Essential reading

The digital eBook version of the Workbook contains additional content, selected to enhance your studies. Consisting of revision materials and further explanations of complex areas (including illustrations and activities), it is designed to aid your understanding of key topics which are covered in the main printed chapters of the Workbook. The Essential reading section of the eBook also includes further illustrations of complex areas.

To access the digital eBook version of the BPP Workbook, follow the instructions which can be found on the inside cover; you'll be able to access your eBook, plus download the BPP eBook mobile app on multiple devices, including smartphones and tablets.

A summary of the content of the Essential reading is given below.

Chapter		Summary of Essential reading content
1	Strategic management accounting	• Characteristics of planning and control at strategic and operational levels in organisations • Relationship between strategic plans and short-term, localised decisions • Overview of performance management systems, including performance pyramid and balanced scorecard • Porter's five forces model and its application to performance management. Also includes potential problems with the model • Using the BCG matrix in performance management, and potential problems with the model
2	Performance hierarchy	• Objectives, and issues to consider in relation to objectives, in the performance hierarchy • Operational performance – characteristics of operational performance, and the significance of operations for organisations • Recap of planning and control at strategic level and operational level • Sources of critical success factors (CSFs)
3	Performance management and control	• Characteristics of different approaches to budgeting (incremental; zero-based; rolling; fixed; flexible; activity-based) • Variances – types of variances, and possible reasons why variances occur • Illustration showing the use of a flexed budget in order to analyse variances • Controllability – highlighting the importance of distinguishing a manager's performance from a division's performance, including a detailed illustration of this
4	Organisational change, environmental and ethical issues	• Characteristics of service industries, and the importance of employee motivation and customer satisfaction in service industries • Porter's value chain – activities in the chain, and linkages between them • Business process re-engineering (BPR) – discussion of characteristics and principles of BPR, as well as potential problems with it

ACCA

Strategic Professional

Advanced Performance Management (APM)

Workbook

For exams in September 2021, December 2021, March 2022 and June 2022

BPP
LEARNING
MEDIA

Third edition 2021

ISBN 9781 5097 3755 0

Previous ISBN 9781 5097 8292 5

ISBN (for internal use only): 9781 5097 3754 3

e-ISBN 9781 5097 3853 3

British Library Cataloguing-in-Publication Data

A catalogue record for this book is available from the British Library.

Published by

BPP Learning Media Ltd

BPP House, Aldine Place

142–144 Uxbridge Road

London W12 8AA

learningmedia.bpp.com

Printed in the United Kingdom

> Your learning materials, published by BPP Learning Media Ltd, are printed on paper sourced from sustainable, managed forests.

The contents of this book are intended as a guide and not professional advice. Although every effort has been made to ensure that the contents of this book are correct at the time of going to press, BPP Learning Media makes no warranty that the information in this book is accurate or complete and accept no liability for any loss or damage suffered by any person acting or refraining from acting as a result of the material in this book.

Contains public sector information licensed under the Open Government Licence v3.0.

We are grateful to the Association of Chartered Certified Accountants for permission to reproduce past examination questions and extracts from the syllabus. The suggested solutions in the practice answer bank have been prepared by BPP Learning Media Ltd, except where otherwise stated.

Contents

Helping you to pass

BPP Learning Media – ACCA Approved Content Provider

As an ACCA Approved Content Provider, BPP Learning Media gives you the opportunity to use study materials reviewed by the ACCA examining team. By incorporating the examining team's comments and suggestions regarding the depth and breadth of syllabus coverage, the BPP Learning Media Workbook provides excellent, ACCA-approved support for your studies.

These materials are reviewed by the ACCA examining team. The objective of the review is to ensure that the material properly covers the syllabus and study guide outcomes, used by the examining team in setting the exams, in the appropriate breadth and depth. The review does not ensure that every eventuality, combination or application of examinable topics is addressed by the ACCA Approved Content. Nor does the review comprise a detailed technical check of the content as the Approved Content Provider has its own quality assurance processes in place in this respect.

BPP Learning Media do everything possible to ensure the material is accurate and up to date when sending to print. In the event that any errors are found after the print date, they are uploaded to the following website: www.bpp.com/learningmedia/Errata.

The PER alert

Before you can qualify as an ACCA member, you not only have to pass all your exams but also fulfil a three-year practical experience requirement (PER). To help you to recognise areas of the syllabus that you might be able to apply in the workplace to achieve different performance objectives, we have introduced the 'PER alert' feature (see the next section). You will find this feature throughout the Workbook to remind you that what you are learning to pass your ACCA exams is equally useful to the fulfilment of the PER requirement. Your achievement of the PER should be recorded in your online My Experience record.

Chapter		Summary of Essential reading content
		• The influence of structure, culture and strategy on the way performance is measured
		• The need for information systems, and the impact of the competitive environment on management accounting information
		• Stakeholders and their relationship with organisations
5	Impact of risk and uncertainty	• Breakeven analysis and margin of safety (brought forward knowledge from *Performance Management*)
		• Value of perfect information (brought forward knowledge from *Performance Management*)
6	Performance measurement systems and reports	• Characteristics to consider when evaluating management accounting information
		• Lean information systems. Further explanation on:
		- The characteristic of 'lean'
		- Applications of lean to management information systems
		- The 5S concept, for implementing lean principles
		- Difficulties with implementing lean principles
		• Impact of human behaviour on the design of management accounting systems, and ways of presenting information
		• Sources of management information, and the costs and benefits of obtaining data from internal/external sources
		• Knowledge management systems
		• Big data. Further explanation of:
		- The ways organisations can use big data
		- The implications of big data for accountants
		• Potential issues with numerical data
		• Avoiding information overload in reports
		• Integrated reporting, and its implications for management accountants
7	Strategic performance measures in the private sector	• Assumed knowledge, brought forward from *Performance Management*:
		- Profit ratios
		- Liquidity ratios
		- Gearing ratios
		- Investor ratios
		- The importance of measuring liquidity as well as profitability
		• Modified internal rate of return (MIRR), and the importance of distinguishing between the return phase and the investment phase of a project
8	Divisional performance and transfer pricing issues	• Importance of negotiation in transfer pricing, and issues arising from transfer pricing in an international context
9	Strategic performance measures in not-for-profit	• Value for money, and issues relating to measuring economy, efficiency and effectiveness

BPP LEARNING MEDIA

Chapter	Summary of Essential reading content
organisations	• Undesirable outcomes arising from the use of targets
10 Non-financial performance indicators	• Disadvantages of focusing solely on financial performance • The importance of the interaction between financial and non-financial performance indicators • The risk of manipulation of performance indicators • Indicators of product/service quality • The importance of branding, and its potential impact on organisational performance
11 The role of quality in performance management systems	• Just-in-time (JIT): characteristics of JIT systems • Target costing process, and the implications of target costing • Kaizen costing process; contrast between Kaizen costing and standard costing • Importance of continuous improvement • Key principles of total quality management (TQM) • Costs of quality, and the contrast between the traditional view of costs of quality and the TQM approach • Importance of quality for managing performance • Quality and information – characteristics of good information • Six Sigma – DMAIC project phases; organising Six Sigma projects
12 Performance measurement and strategic HRM issues	• The role of appraisals in performance management • Approaches to measuring employees' performance • Reward systems: performance-related pay and share options • Control mechanisms in relation to employee performance • Hopwood's management styles, and the importance of context in determining an appropriate management style
13 Alternative views of performance measurement and management	• Balanced scorecard – potential issues with using the balanced scorecard • Value-based management (VBM) – potential issues related to using value-based management
14 Strategic performance issues in complex business structures	• Performance management issues in multinational companies
15 Predicting and preventing corporate failure	• Reminder of working capital ratios • Industry life cycle, and its implications for portfolio management • Performance improvement strategies; in particular, turnaround strategies

Introduction to Advanced Performance Management (APM)

Overall aim of the syllabus

This exam requires students to apply relevant knowledge and skills, and to exercise professional judgement in selecting and applying strategic management accounting techniques in different business contexts and to contribute to the planning, control and evaluation of the performance of an organisation, and to its strategic and operational development.

Brought forward knowledge

The Advanced Performance Management syllabus includes a number of topics which were covered in Performance Management but develops them further, and requires candidates to be able to apply them to more complex scenarios in the exam.

The syllabus

The broad syllabus headings are:

A	Strategic planning and control
B	Impact of risk and uncertainty on organisational performance
C	Performance management information systems and developments in technology
D	Strategic performance measurement
E	Performance evaluation and corporate failure
F	Employability and technology skills

Main capabilities

On successful completion of this exam, you should be able to:

A	Use strategic planning and control models to plan and monitor organisational performance
B	Assess the impact of risk and uncertainty on organisational performance
C	Identify and evaluate the design features of effective performance management information and monitoring systems, and recognise the impact of developments in technology on performance measurement and management systems
D	Apply appropriate strategic performance measurement techniques in evaluating and improving organisational performance
E	Advise clients and senior management on strategic business performance evaluation and on recognising vulnerability to corporate failure

Links with other exams

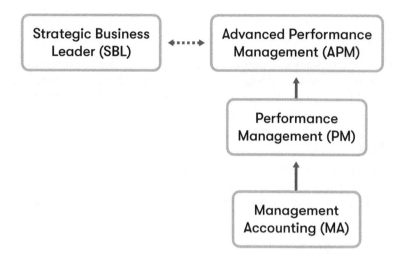

The diagram shows where direct (solid line arrows) and indirect (dashed line arrows) links exist between this exam and other exams preceding or following it.

The Advanced Performance Management (APM) syllabus assumes knowledge acquired in Performance Management (PM), and develops and applies this further and in greater depth.

Achieving ACCA's Study Guide Learning Outcomes

This BPP Workbook covers all the Advanced Performance Management (APM) syllabus learning outcomes. The tables below show in which chapter(s) each area of the syllabus is covered.

A	Strategic planning and control	

A1	Strategic management accounting	Chapter 1
A2	Performance hierarchy	Chapter 2
A3	Performance management and control of the organisation	Chapter 3
A4	Changes in business structure and management accounting	Chapter 4
A5	Environmental, social and governance factors	Chapter 4

B	Impact of risk and uncertainty on organisational performance	

B1	The impact of risk and uncertainty on performance management	Chapter 5

C	Performance management information systems and developments in technology	

C1	Performance management information systems	Chapter 6
C2	Sources of management information	Chapter 6
C3	Recording and processing systems and technologies	Chapter 6
C4	Data analytics	Chapter 6

| C5 | Management reports | Chapter 6 |

D. Strategic performance measurement

D1	Strategic performance measures in the private sector	Chapter 7
D2	Divisional performance and transfer pricing issues	Chapter 8
D3	Strategic performance measures in not-for-profit organisations	Chapter 9
D4	Non-financial performance indicators	Chapter 10
D5	The role of quality in management information and performance measurement systems	Chapter 11
D6	Performance measurement and strategic human resource management issues	Chapter 12
D7	Other behavioural aspects of performance management	Chapter 12

E. Interpreting financial statements for different stakeholders

E1	Alternative views of performance measurement and management	Chapter 13
E2	Strategic performance issues in complex business structures	Chapter 14
E3	Predicting and preventing corporate failure	Chapter 15

F. Employability and technology skills

F1	Use computer technology to efficiently access and manipulate relevant information.	Exam skill
F2	Work on relevant response options, using available functions and technology, as would be required in the workplace.	Exam skill
F3	Navigate windows and computer screens to create and amend responses to exam requirements, using appropriate tools.	Exam skill
F4	Present data and information effectively, using the appropriate tools.	Exam skill

Syllabus section F is new and is present in the syllabus for all ACCA professional exams; it reflects the skills needed in a computer-based exam and has no specific detailed syllabus content. This area is covered in the exam success skills section later in this introduction.

The complete syllabus and study guide can be found by visiting the exam resource finder on the ACCA website: www.accaglobal.com/gb/en.html.

The exam

Computer-based exams

With effect from the March 2020 sitting, ACCA have commenced the launch of computer-based exams (CBEs) for this exam with the aim of rolling out into all markets internationally over a short period. Paper-based examinations (PBE) will be run in parallel while the CBEs are phased in. BPP materials have been designed to support you, whichever exam option you choose. For more information on these changes, when they will be implemented and to access Specimen Exams in the Strategic Professional CBE software, please visit the ACCA website. Please note that the Strategic Professional CBE software has more functionality than you will have seen in the Applied Skills exams.

www.accaglobal.com/gb/en/student/exam-support-resources/strategic-professional-specimen-exams-cbe.html

Approach to examining the syllabus

The Advanced Performance Management syllabus is assessed by a 3 hour 15 minute exam. The pass mark is 50%. All questions in the exam are compulsory.

You will be expected to demonstrate an integrated knowledge of the syllabus topics, and an ability to apply your knowledge understanding of the subject to strategic and operational issues relevant to the organisation identified in the question scenario, in order to be able to add value to senior management in that organisation.

Format of the exam		Marks
Section A	**One compulsory scenario-based question**, totalling **50 marks**, but typically **comprising four or five requirements** relating to the same scenario information. The case study scenario will be based on an organisation in a particular business context, and will include the organisation's mission and strategic objectives. You will be expected to assess the methods by which the organisation is controlling, managing and measuring performance in order to achieve its objectives. This assessment could include an evaluation of the organisation's performance report, its information systems, new strategies or projects, and its performance management and measurement systems. You could be expected to undertake calculations, draw comparisons against relevant information where appropriate, and be prepared to offer recommendations as needed. You should expect to see Section A of the exam focus on a **range of issues from across syllabus sections A, C and D**, although the issues will vary depending on the business context of the organisation in the scenario. The detail of the question's requirements will (from September 2019 onwards) be **embedded in the scenario**. The 'requirements' at the end of the scenario then ask you to respond as you have been instructed in the scenario. Therefore, you will need to refer back to the detailed requirements in the scenario in order to answer each part of the question.	50 (incl. four professional marks)
Section B	**Two compulsory 25-mark questions** These questions are more likely to assess a range of discrete subject areas from the main syllabus section headings. However, they will still require evaluation and synthesis of information contained within a scenario, and the application of this information to the question requirements. Although one subject area is likely to be emphasised in each Section B question, you should not assume that questions will be solely	50

Format of the exam	Marks
about content from a single subject area. One of the Section B questions will come **mainly from syllabus section E**. The other question can come from **any other syllabus section**.	
	100

Analysis of past exams

The table below provides details of when each element of the syllabus has been examined in the ten most recent sittings and the Section (A or B) in which each element was examined.

Note that in exams before June 2018 there were three questions in Section B (of which two had to be answered) so five questions in total are referenced for those exams.

*		Sept/Dec 2020	Mar/June 2020	Sept/Dec 2019	Mar/June 2019	Dec 2018	Sept 2018	Mar/June 2018	Sept/Dec 2017
	STRATEGIC PLANNING AND CONTROL								
1	Strategic management accounting					A, B			B
2	Performance hierarchy	A		A	A		A		
3	Performance management and control				B				
4	Organisational change, environmental and ethical issues	B		A			B	A	
	IMPACT OF RISK AND UNCERTAINTY ON ORGANISATIONAL PERFORMANCE								
5	Impact of risk and uncertainty			B		B			B
	PERFORMANCE MEASUREMENT SYSTEMS AND DESIGN								
6	Performance management systems and design	B	A	A		A	B	A, B	A
	STRATEGIC PERFORMANCE MEASUREMENT								
7	Strategic performance measures in the private sector		A	A					B
8	Divisional performance and transfer pricing issues		B	A				B	
9	Not-for-profit organisations	A							B

*		Sept/Dec 2020	Mar/June 2020	Sept/Dec 2019	Mar/June 2019	Dec 2018	Sept 2018	Mar/June 2018	Sept/Dec 2017
10	Non-financial performance indicators	A					A		
11	The role of quality in performance management systems		B		A	B			A
12	Performance management and strategic HR issues						A		B
	PERFORMANCE EVALUATION AND CORPORATE FAILURE								
13	Alternative views of performance measurement and management		B	B	B	B	A	B	
14	Strategic performance issues in complex business structures	B						B	
15	Predicting and preventing corporate failure						B	B	

IMPORTANT! The table above gives a broad idea of how frequently major topics in the syllabus are examined. It should **not** be used to question spot and predict, for example, that Topic X will not be examined because it came up two sittings ago. The examining team's reports indicate that they are well aware that some students try to question spot. They avoid predictable patterns and may, for example, examine the same topic two sittings in a row, particularly if there has been a recent change in legislation.

Essential skills areas to be successful in Advanced Performance Management (APM)

We think there are three areas you should develop in order to achieve exam success in APM:

(a) Knowledge application

(b) Specific APM skills

(c) Exam success skills

These are shown in the diagram below.

Specific APM skills

These are the skills specific to APM that we think you need to develop in order to pass the exam.

In this Workbook, there are five **Skills Checkpoints** which define each skill and show how it is applied in answering a question. A brief summary of each skill is given below.

Skill 1: Creating information from data

One of the themes in the APM syllabus is that accountants are increasingly expected to act as 'internal business consultants'. An important aspect of this role is in interpreting the **meaning** of data, ie **creating information from data.**

In any part of the exam you may be given data (or calculations) that have already been prepared by a more junior accountant and your role will be to analyse that data and interpret what it means for the organisation in the scenario.

ACCA's examining team have noted (in past exams) that where data has been provided for analysis, **candidates have often failed to add any value in their analysis of that data.**

A step-by-step technique for ensuring that **analysis of data creates useful information**, and therefore **adds value**, is outlined below:

Step 1	Consider the 'big picture'; ie the **main issues** facing the organisation as presented in the scenario of the question.
Step 2	Plan to categorise your analysis into a **small number** of **relevant categories**. When relevant, plan to use ratio analysis to add meaning to

	the data provided.
Step 3	Complete your answer by discussing the data and any further numerical analysis (eg ratios) by reference to the 'big picture' issues identified in Step **1. Avoid statements that simply describe the data,** without adding any value in terms of analysis.

Skills Checkpoint 1 covers this technique in detail through application to an exam-standard question.

Skill 2: Creating a coherent performance management framework

In the exam, it is highly like you will need to assess the methods by which an organisation is controlling, managing and measuring performance, in order to achieve its objectives.

An important part of this could be in assessing whether the organisation has a coherent performance management framework (for example, whether the key performance indicators it measures will help it achieve its mission and objectives) and recommend ways the framework could be improved.

Key steps in developing and applying this skill are outlined below:

Step 1	Identify an organisation's mission and/or objectives in the question scenario, to get an understanding of the aspects of performance which are important to the organisation.
Step 2	Identify whether the aspects of performance being measured/monitored (eg CSFs; KPIs) relate to key areas of performance, and help to support the organisation in achieving its mission and objectives. (Could the measures used be improved?)
Step 3	If you are asked to recommend KPIs or CSFs, make sure these relate to mission, objectives etc. and make use of data provided in the scenario.

Skills Checkpoint 2 covers this technique in detail through application to an exam-standard question.

Skill 3: Evaluating performance management reports

An important element of creating a coherent performance management framework is ensuring that performance reports show how well an organisation is performing in the areas which are strategically significant for it. Exam questions can often require you to evaluate a performance report, and this requires you to assess the report to see if it provides relevant information about appropriate areas of performance, in a way that is easy for users to understand, and which enables them to take effective control action

A step-by-step technique for evaluating performance management reports is outlined below.

Step 1	Where a question includes a significant table of data, read the requirements carefully to make sure that you understand clearly whether a question requires you to analyse the performance of an **organisation**, or of the **performance report** itself.
Step 2	Where a question requires analysis of the performance report, make sure that you clearly understand the mission, strategy and objectives of a company (from the main body of the scenario) and carefully consider the degree to which the performance report gives visibility to these strategic factors.
Step 3	Also consider other practical factors such as the structure, clarity and level of detail of the report, and whether it distorts the meaning of data. Where relevant to the requirement, look for positive as well as negative features of the report.

Step 4	Complete your answer plan and write up your answer. If you are asked to recommend improvements, make sure these relate specifically to the organisation in the scenario and its context, rather than being generic points.

Skills Checkpoint 3 covers this technique in detail through application to an exam-standard question.

Skill 4: Critical analysis

The overall aim of the APM syllabus highlights that candidates should be able to exercise professional judgement in selecting and applying strategic management accounting techniques in different business contexts. As such, it is important to critically analyse the techniques that you study, for example to consider whether a certain technique would be appropriate for an organisation to use in a certain situation or not.

This skill requires you not only to understand the techniques, but also to appreciate their potential advantages or disadvantages. Just because an organisation in a question scenario is thinking about introducing a new technique does not necessarily mean that technique is appropriate for the organisation.

The skill of critical analysis can potentially be applied to any syllabus area in APM, and can be an important ingredient in developing a discussion that addresses the question scenario in a way that adds value.

A step-by-step technique for critical analysis is outlined below.

Step 1	Analyse the scenario and requirements. Ensure that you recognise the possibility that using a critical approach in your analysis can be a useful way of 'adding value'.
Step 2	Plan your answer. Without adopting a hyper-critical approach, ensure your answer is balanced, in terms of identifying the potential benefits **and** limitations of techniques that are being used or recommended.
Step 3	As you write your answer, try wherever possible to apply your analysis to the scenario, instead of simply writing about criticisms (or benefits) in generic, technical terms.

Skills Checkpoint 4 covers this technique in detail through application to an exam-standard question.

Skill 5: Addressing the scenario

All of the questions in the APM exam will be scenario-based.

It is **vital** that you use the information in the scenario to ensure that the discussion points that you are making in your answer are 'relevant'. The discussion parts of a question – applying your knowledge to the scenario – will normally account for the majority of the marks available.

Although you need to have a good underlying knowledge of a number of theories and frameworks, in the APM exam you will primarily be tested on your **ability to apply** your theoretical knowledge to the scenario in question, not your ability to simply recite it. The APM ACCA Examining Team often comment that candidates who repeat memorised material 'will probably score only between 20% and 30%...'.

A good, professional-level answer needs to go beyond the mere repetition of how a technique works and focus on relating it to the entity's specific environment, as identified in the question scenario.

The skill of addressing the scenario is the most important of the APM specific sills. It is relevant to every syllabus area, and **every question** in the APM exam.

A step-by-step technique for addressing the scenario is outlined below.

Step 1	Allow at least 20% of your allotted time for analysing the scenario and the requirements. Begin by analysing the requirements so that you know what you are looking for when you read the scenario.
Step 2	Prepare an answer plan using key words from the requirements as headings. Complete your answer plan by working through each paragraph of the question identifying specific points that are relevant to the scenario and requirement, to make sure you generate enough points to score a pass mark.
Step 3	As you write your answer, explain what you mean – in one (or two) sentence(s) – and then explain **why this matters in the given scenario**. This should result in a series of short paragraphs that address the specific context of the scenario. Avoid quoting theory at length.

Skills Checkpoint 5 covers this technique in detail through application to an exam-standard question.

Exam success skills

Passing the APM exam requires more than applying syllabus knowledge and demonstrating the specific APM skills; it also requires the development of excellent exam technique through question practice.

We consider the following six skills to be vital for exam success. The Skills Checkpoints show how each of these skills can be applied in the exam.

1 Exam success skill 1

Managing information

Questions in the exam will present you with a lot of information. The skill is how you handle this information to make the best use of your time. The key is determining how you will approach the exam and then actively reading the questions.

Advice on developing this skill

To avoid being overwhelmed by the quantity of information provided, you must take an **active approach** to reading each question.

Active reading means focussing on the question's requirements first, highlighting key verbs such as 'evaluate', 'analyse', 'explain', 'discuss', to ensure you answer the question properly. Then, now that you have an understanding of what the question will require you to do, read the rest of the question, highlighting important and relevant information, and making notes of any relevant technical information you think you will need.

Computer-based exam

In a computer-based exam (CBE) the **highlighter tool** provided in the toolbar at the top of the screen offers a range of colours:

This allows you to choose **different colours to answer different aspects to a question**. For example, if a question asked you to discuss the pros and cons of an issue then you could choose a different colour for highlighting pros and cons within the relevant section of a question.

The **strikethrough function** allows you to delete areas of a question that you have dealt with – this can be useful in managing information if you are dealing with numerical questions because it can allow you to ensure that all numerical areas have been accounted for in your answer (although this is of limited use in the APM exam).

The CBE also allows you to **resize windows** by clicking on the bottom right-hand corner of the window as highlighted in the following section:

This functionality allows you to **display a number of windows at the same time**, so this could allow you review:

- the question requirements and the exhibit relating to that requirement, at the same time; or
- the window containing your answer (whether a word processing or spreadsheet document) and the exhibit relating to that requirement, at the same time.

2 Exam success skill 2

Correct interpretation of the requirements

The active verb used often dictates the approach that written answers should take (eg 'explain', 'discuss', 'evaluate'). It is important you identify and use the verb to define your approach. The **correct interpretation of the requirements** skill means correctly producing only what is being asked for by a requirement. Anything not required will not earn marks.

Advice on developing this skill

This skill can be developed by analysing question requirements and applying this process:

Step 1	Read the requirement
	Firstly, read the requirement a couple of times slowly and carefully and **highlight the active verbs.** Use the active verbs to define what you plan to do. Make sure you identify any sub-requirements within a requirement; this is **often signalled by the use of the word 'and'** within a requirement.
	Important active verbs for APM include the following.
	Advise
	This requires you to provide someone with useful information, or to tell them what you think they should do based on a consideration of the issues presented in a scenario.
	Analyse
	This requires you to break an issue into separate parts and discuss, examine, or interpret each part. This may require you to give reasons for the current situation or what has happened.
	Apply
	This requires you to put a concept into action by applying it to the scenario in a relevant way.

BPP LEARNING MEDIA

Assess

This requires you to judge the importance or estimate the nature, quality or significance of an issue.

Discuss

This will require you to consider and debate/argue about the pros and cons of an issue.

Evaluate

This will require you to present a 'balanced' discussion of an issue looking at both the positive and negative issues. Where numbers feature in a question, an evaluation will require you to use the numbers provided to create a value from which a judgement can be made.

Explain

This involves making an idea clear and could require you to, for example, show logically how a concept is developed or to give the reason for an event.

Illustrate

This will require you to give concrete examples, normally drawn from the question's scenario.

Recommend

If you are asked to 'recommend' then you are expected to use details presented in the scenario to create a logical and justified course of action.

In APM – particularly in Section A questions – **the detailed aspects of a requirement are often embedded in the scenario**. For example, in the scenario, the CEO may ask you analyse or evaluate something, and then the requirement will ask you to respond to the CEO's instruction. Therefore, the initial requirement by itself may not provide a complete understanding of a question's requirement (although it is a useful starting point).

| Step 2 | **Read the rest of the question** |
| | By reading the requirement first, you will have an idea of what you are looking out for as you read through the scenario and any exhibits. This is a great time saver and means you don't end up having to read the whole question in full twice. You should do this in an active way – see Exam success skill 1: Managing Information. |

| Step 3 | **Read the requirement again** |
| | Read the requirement again to remind yourself of the exact wording before starting your written answer. This will capture any misinterpretation of the requirements or any missed requirements entirely. This should become a habit in your approach and, with repeated practice, you will find the focus, relevance and depth of your answer plan will improve. |

3 Exam success skill 3

Answer planning: Priorities, structure and logic

This skill requires the planning of the key aspects of an answer which accurately and completely responds to the requirement.

Advice on developing this skill

Everyone will have a preferred style for an answer plan. For example, it may be a mind map or bullet-pointed lists. Choose the approach that you feel most comfortable with, or, if you are not sure, try out different approaches for different questions until you have found your preferred style.

In a **computer-based exam** you can use the copy and paste functions to **copy the question requirements to the beginning of your answer**. This will allow you to ensure that your answer plan addresses all parts of the question requirements.

You can also **copy the question requirements to the main body of your answer**. This will allow you to create sub-headings for your answer, again ensuring that your answer addresses all parts of the question requirements.

Copying and pasting simply involves highlighting the relevant information and either right clicking to access the copy and paste functions, or alternatively using Ctrl C to copy and Ctrl V to paste.

4 Exam success skill 4

Efficient numerical analysis

This skill aims to maximise the marks awarded by making clear to the marker the process of arriving at your answer. This is achieved by laying out an answer such that, even if you make a few errors, you can still score subsequent marks for follow-on calculations. It is vital that you do not lose marks purely because the marker cannot follow what you have done.

Advice on developing this skill

This skill can be developed by applying the following process:

Step 1	**Use a standard proforma working where relevant** If answers can be laid out in a standard proforma then always plan to do so. This will help the marker to understand your working and allocate the marks easily. It will also help you to work through the figures in a methodical and time-efficient way.
Step 2	**Show your workings** Keep your workings as clear and simple as possible and ensure they are cross-referenced to the main part of your answer. Where it helps, provide brief narrative explanations to help the marker understand the steps in the calculation. This means that if a mistake is made you do not lose any subsequent marks for follow-on calculations.
Step 3	**Keep moving!** It is important to remember that, in an exam situation, it can sometimes be difficult to get every number 100% correct. The key is therefore ensuring you do not spend too long on any single calculation. If you are struggling with a solution then make a sensible assumption, state it and move on.

In a **computer-based exam** (CBE) it is important to **show the marker where numbers have come from**, ie it is not sensible to perform the calculations on a calculator and then manually transfer them to the spreadsheet. The marker also needs to be able to see **what the numbers are intended to mean**. For example, in the following spreadsheet the marker can see that the highlighted calculation in cell K9 is calculated as I9/G2 because this is what is recorded in the spreadsheet cell (as shown in the first row) and can also see from the headings in cells C9 and K4 that this is meant to be a measure of the appraisal costs as a % of sales.

	A	B	C	D	E	F	G	H	I	J	K	L	M
1		Cost of quality report											
2					Sales		4500						
3													
4		Cost of conformance					$000s		$000s		% sales		
5			Prevention costs										
6					Maintenance		8		8		0.18%		
7													
8					Quality audit		2						
9			Appraisal costs		QC supervisor		35		37		0.82%		
10												1.00%	

If the workings are visible in the cell, as shown here, then there is **less need to show detailed workings**. It will still sometimes be helpful to produce workings because they can reduce the likelihood of errors being made (if calculations are complex).

In a **computer-based exam** (CBE) you can also use useful spreadsheet short-cuts to improve the efficiency of numerical analysis. For APM useful short-cuts include the ability to calculate totals and averages and also to calculate NPV, IRR and MIRR.

Further details are given in the following table.

Function	Guidance & examples
Sum	=SUM(A1:A10) adds all the numbers in spreadsheet cells A1 to A10.
Average	=AVERAGE(A1:A10) averages the numbers in spreadsheet cells A1 to A10.
NPV	Net present value is based on future cash flows, assuming that the first cash flow is in one year's time. For example, if the future cash flows from a project arise over five years and need to be discounted at 10% then the formula could be as follows: =NPV(0.1, B10:F10) This would give the present value of cash flows from time period 1-5. The cash outflow in time 0 would then need to be deducted to calculate the net present value.
IRR	Internal rate of return is based on future cash flows, looking at cash outflows and inflows in each year of a project, from time 0 onwards. For example, to identify the internal rate of return of the future cash flows from a project arising over five years then the formula could be as follows: =IRR(A10:F10)
MIRR	Modified internal rate of return is based on future cash flows (looking at cash outflows and inflows) in each year of a project, from time 0 onwards. The formula is =MIRR (values, finance rate, reinvestment rate). The finance rate and reinvestment rate will normally be the same. For example, to identify the MIRR of the future cash flows from a project arising over five years (involving time periods 0-5), where the cost of capital to be applied to cash outflows (the finance rate) and cash inflows (reinvestment rate) is 10%, then the formula could be as follows: =MIRR(A10:F10, 0.1, 0.1)

Where numerical calculations require commentary then this can be provided in a word processing document with a **reference to calculations provided within the spreadsheet**.

5 Exam success skill 5

Effective writing and presentation

Written answers should be presented so that the marker can clearly see the points you are making, presented in the format specified in the question. The skill is to provide efficient written

BPP
LEARNING
MEDIA

answers with sufficient breadth of points that answer the question, in the right depth, in the time available.

Advice on developing Effective writing and presentation

Step 1	**Use headings**
	Using the headings and sub-headings from your answer plan will give your answer structure, order and logic. This will ensure your answer links back to the requirement and is clearly signposted, making it easier for the marker to understand the different points you are making. Underlining your headings will also help the marker.
Step 2	**Write your answer in short, but full, sentences**
	Use short, punchy sentences with the aim that every sentence should say something different and generate marks. Write in full sentences, ensuring your style is professional.

For APM there are four professional marks in question 1 of the exam:

These can be obtained by providing:

(a) A suitable, simple, heading to the answer (eg a simple report format) and use of headings / sub-headings (eg linked to the requirements) throughout the report: 1 mark is normally given for this

(b) A short introduction paragraph outlining the structure of the report: 1 mark is normally given for this

(c) A clear well-structured answer (eg referencing spreadsheet calculations where appropriate) presented in a concise, practical (as opposed to academic) way that adds value and addresses the given requirements: 2 marks are normally given for this

6 Exam success skill 6

Good time management

This skill means planning your time across all the requirements so that all tasks have been attempted at the end of the 3 hours 15 minutes available and actively checking on time during your exam. This is so that you can flex your approach and prioritise requirements which, in your judgement, will generate the maximum marks in the available time remaining.

Advice on developing this skill

The exam is 3 hours 15 minutes long, which translates to 1.95 minutes per mark. Therefore a 10-mark requirement should be allocated a maximum of 20 minutes to complete your answer before you move on to the next task. At the beginning of a question, work out the amount of time you should be spending on each requirement. If you take the approach of spending 10–15 minutes reading and planning at the start of the exam, adjust the time allocated to each question accordingly; eg if you allocate 15 minutes to reading, then you will have 3 hours remaining, which is 1.8 minutes per mark.

In APM it is **crucial to spend time on planning before starting to write your answer**. This allows time for a candidate to immerse themselves in the question scenarios.

Planning time can be built into time management by amending the 1.95 minutes per mark approach to allow for planning time. The total time for planning your answer should be about 20% of the total time you would allocate to a question. This means that for a section A question planning time would be 50 marks × 1.95 × 0.2 = (approximately) 20 minutes and for a section B question planning time would be 25 marks × 1.95 × 0.2 = 10 minutes.

Allowing 20% of time for planning means allocating 80% of the time for writing so the 1.95 minutes per mark approach becomes ie 0.8 × 1.95 = 1.56 minutes per mark for writing your answer.

Keep an eye on the clock

Aim to attempt all requirements, but be ready to be ruthless and move on if your answer is not going as planned. The challenge for many is sticking to planned timings. Be aware this is difficult to achieve in the early stages of your studies and be ready to let this skill develop over time.

If you find yourself running short on time and know that a full answer is not possible in the time you have, consider recreating your plan in overview form and then add key terms and details as time allows. Remember, some marks may be available, for example, simply stating a conclusion which you don't have time to justify in full.

Question practice

Question practice is a core part of learning new topic areas. When you practise questions, you should focus on improving the Exam success skills – personal to your needs – by obtaining feedback or through a process of self-assessment.

If sitting this exam as a computer-based exam, practising as many exam-style questions as possible in the ACCA CBE practice platform will be the key to passing this exam. You should attempt questions under **timed conditions** and ensure you produce full answers to the discussion parts as well as doing the calculations. Also ensure that you attempt all mock exams under exam conditions.

ACCA have launched a free on-demand resource designed to mirror the live exam experience helping you to become more familiar with the exam format. You can access the platform via the Study Support Resources section of the ACCA website navigating to the CBE question practice section and logging in with your myACCA credentials.

Strategic management accounting

Learning objectives

On completion of this chapter, you should be able to:

	Syllabus reference no.
Explain the role of strategic performance management in strategic planning and control.	A1(a)
Discuss the role of performance measurement in checking progress towards the corporate objectives.	A1(b)
Compare planning and control between the strategic and operational levels within a business entity.	A1(c)
Discuss the scope for potential conflict between strategic business plans and short-term localised decisions.	A1(d)
Evaluate how models such as SWOT analysis, PEST, Boston Consulting Group, balanced scorecard, Porter's generic strategies, and five forces may assist in the performance management process.	A1(e)
Apply and evaluate the methods of benchmarking performance.	A1(f)

Exam context

Advanced Performance Management (APM) is a Strategic Professional level exam, so 'knowledge' of models and frameworks alone will not be sufficient to pass the exam. Instead, you need to be prepared to assess how organisations can use the frameworks covered in this chapter to manage their performance – and potentially also to highlight limitations in the frameworks which could reduce their value to organisations.

In syllabus area A1 the Study Guide mentions, by name, six models which could assist the performance management process (SWOT analysis, the BCG matrix, balanced scorecard (covered in Chapter 13), Porter's generic strategies, Porter's five forces and PEST analysis), so you should be prepared for these models to be specifically examined. As the primary focus of APM is 'performance management', you will need to think how managers could use the models to help them understand an organisation's current performance, to identify key areas of performance to measure, or to evaluate the suitability of different performance measures in a given context. However, APM is not primarily concerned with questions around evaluating different strategies, or making strategic choices (as might be the case in *Strategic Business Leader*).

Chapter overview

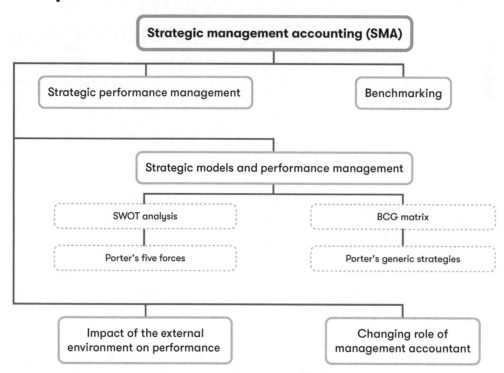

1 Strategic performance management

PER alert

Performance objective 3 (PO 3) – Strategy and innovation – requires that you 'contribute to the wider business strategy of your organisation through your personal and team objectives, identifying innovative business solutions to improve organisational performance by making or recommending business process changes and improvements.'

Although business strategy is not the primary focus for APM (in the way that it is for *Strategic Business Leader*) trying to 'improve organisational performance' is an absolutely fundamental part of performance management.

Similarly, the skills you need to demonstrate in order to achieve PO 3 include developing 'financial acumen and sound business judgement, in order to anticipate potential business problems and recognise weaknesses that need to be addressed, recommending appropriate solutions'. Again, the concept of identifying potential problems or weaknesses and recommending solutions to them is a key theme throughout APM so keep this Performance objective in mind as you are studying for your APM exam.

1.1 Planning and control

Robert Anthony (*Anthony, 1965*) classified the information used at different management levels for planning, control and decision making into three tiers: **strategic planning**, **management control** and **operational control**.

KEY TERM

Strategic planning: The process of deciding on objectives of the organisation, on changes in those objectives, on the resources used to attain those objectives, and on the strategies that are to govern the acquisition, use and disposition of those resources.

Management (or tactical) control: The process by which managers ensure that resources are obtained and used effectively and efficiently in the process of achieving an organisation's objectives.

Operational control: The process of ensuring that specific tasks are carried out effectively and efficiently.

This idea of a hierarchy between **strategic and operational levels** is an important theme in APM because:

- An organisation needs to perform well at operational level in order to achieve its strategic objectives; and
- To achieve strategic objectives, it is important that the objectives and goals at operational level are aligned to meeting those strategic objectives.

For example, if an organisation's underlying strategy is based on differentiating itself from competitors through the quality of service it provides its customers, then it needs to ensure that its customer-facing staff deliver the necessary high quality of service to all its customers on a day-to-day basis (ie at operational level).

1.2 Potential conflicts between strategic and operational decisions

If strategies are to be successfully implemented there must be a clear link between **strategic planning and operational planning**; this may be absent due to:

(a) **Unrealistic plans** – plans could be **over-ambitious**, eg planned market share based on unrealistically high forecasts of production capacity. Unrealistic plans may lead to overworking operational staff, leading to mistakes, quality issues, and possibly lost sales.

(b) **Poor communications** – if operational managers are unaware of strategic planning goals this could lead to inconsistent goals at different levels in an organisation, eg operational managers focusing on quality, whereas strategic plans are based on a low cost base.

BPP
LEARNING
MEDIA

(c) **Inadequate performance measurement** – meaning that managers will not know whether the organisation is performing well in the areas that contribute to competitive advantage.

Essential reading

See Chapter 1 Section 1 of the Essential reading for more detail about the contrast between planning and control at the strategic and operational levels within a business entity.

Also see Chapter 1 Section 2 of the Essential reading which highlights the scope for potential conflict between strategic business plans and short-term localised decisions.

The Essential reading is available as an Appendix of the digital edition of the Workbook.

1.3 Performance management in strategic planning and control

The underlying aim of performance management is to improve an organisation's performance and ensure that its goals and objectives are achieved. This means that an organisation must first have established its goals and objectives, in order to then assess whether they are being met.

Therefore, there is a need for planning (to define goals and objectives) and control (to assess if plans are working as intended).

Performance management can be seen as a set of processes, often supported by technology, which enable organisations to plan and control effectively.

Performance management systems: The systems in an organisation by which the performance of that organisation is measured, controlled and improved.

1.4 Strategic management accounting (SMA)

The aim of strategic management accounting (SMA) is to provide information that is relevant to the process of **strategic** planning and control.

SMA is sometimes described as **modern performance measurement**. In a **dynamic** (rapidly changing) business environment, it is important to develop information that:

(a) Is linked to the corporation's strategy;

(b) Is forward-looking;

(c) Monitors changes to the environment; and

(d) Includes a mix of financial and non-financial information.

Strategic management accounting (SMA): A form of management accounting in which emphasis is placed on information about factors **external** to the organisation as well as on **non-financial** and internally generated information.

Traditional management accounting is more concerned with the achievement of **internal financial** performance targets (eg budget).

Activity 1: Training Co

Training Co operates a network of accounting training centres throughout Europe, the US and Australia. The business intends to enter developing markets in order to drive growth and has now decided to enter Country X, which is 7,500 kilometres from Training Co's UK headquarters.

In its present form, the management accounting information provided by Training Co's Finance function is largely internally focused, covering areas such as cost and revenue variances. However, the board has suggested it will now require more externally focused management information in light of the move into Country X.

Required

Advise the board how strategic management accounting could help to support the implementation of Training Co's strategy.

(5 marks)

Solution

1.4.1 Hierarchy of performance measures

In reality, SMA will need to be supplemented by:

- **Tactical information**: to facilitate planning and control for **shorter time periods** (eg one year ahead)
- **Operational information**: to facilitate day-to-day decision making

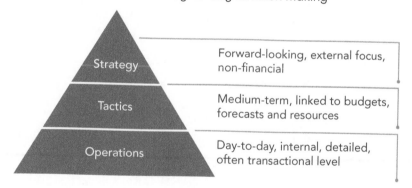

Activity 2: Hydra

Hydra is a bicycle retailer which has a significant presence in the south of England. Each location has a manager who is responsible for day-to-day operations and is supported by an administrative assistant. All other staff at each location are involved in retailing operations.

The directors of Hydra are currently preparing a financial evaluation of an investment of $2 million in a new IT system for submission to its bank. They are concerned that sub-optimal decisions are being made because the current system doesn't provide appropriate information throughout the firm.

Required

Discuss the three levels of information (strategic, tactical, and operational) required to assist in decision making at Hydra, and recommend (with justification) two examples of information which could be provided at each level. **(10 marks)**

Solution

1.4.2 Performance measurement and performance management

Performance measurement is an essential **part of performance management**, and in later chapters you will come across many different types of performance measures.

However, **performance management is more than simply measuring**; in order to manage a company to help it to achieve its corporate objectives it is also necessary to:

(a) Take effective **control action**: this requires effective budgetary control and appropriate information systems

(b) Improve **business processes**: eg information systems, environmental management, transfer pricing, quality management, reward systems

These areas are the focus of many of the later chapters in this Workbook.

Essential reading

See Chapter 1 Section 3 of the Essential reading for more detail on performance management systems, and the importance of linking performance information across different hierarchical levels in an organisation.

The Essential reading is available as an Appendix of the digital edition of the Workbook.

2 Benchmarking

Benchmarking is an example of the application of SMA, in that it can be used to provide performance measures that are strategically important.

> **Benchmarking:** The establishment, through data collection, of targets and comparators, which will allow relative levels of performance (and particularly underperformance) to be identified in relation to best practice. The aim is that adopting identified best practices will lead to an improvement in performance levels.

The source of data used in benchmarking could be **internal** or **external**.

External benchmarking includes **industry** benchmarking and **functional** benchmarking.

2.1 Types of benchmarking

You will need to be able to apply a variety of different types of benchmarking in exam questions. The majority of the marks awarded will be for making relevant comments about the application of benchmarking.

Type of benchmarking	
Internal Compares one operating unit or function with similar ones in the same organisation	• Typically easier to do than comparing performance with external organisations (especially if other organisations are unwilling to share data).
	• But are business units really similar? Benchmarking information will be less relevant if units are diversified.
	• Also, internal benchmarking alone is unlikely to lead to innovative or best practice solutions, because there is no scope to learn from other external organisations.
	• Internal focus may mean that an organisation might not pay sufficient attention to competitors' performance. (However, an organisation's competitive advantage depends on performance relative to competitors.)
External – industry competitor	• If the organisation can match a competitor's performance in an area which was previously a source of competitive advantage for

Type of benchmarking	
Compares an organisation's performance against that of direct competitors	them, then the organisation removes its rival's competitive advantage. • But how feasible will it be to get information about the competitor? Competitors are unlikely to disclose commercially sensitive information, or information about key processes. • If information can be obtained about competitors, is it current, or has the organisation only been able to find historical information?
External – industry, non-competitor Particularly relevant for not-for-profit organisations (eg exam success rates in schools)	• Because organisations are not direct competitors, they should be more willing to exchange data than would be the case with competitor benchmarking. • The aim is that poorer performers will be motivated to improve performance compared to top performers. • However, need to recognise inherent reasons for difference in performance (eg exam results may reflect the socio-economic backgrounds and abilities of pupils, as much as the teaching they receive).
External – functional Compare functions to 'best-in-class' practitioners, regardless of their industry	• The aim is to help organisations to find new, innovative ways to perform activities to create competitive advantage. • Because the comparator is not a competitor, there should be less resistance to sharing data than would be the case in relation to competitor benchmarking. • However, need to recognise that differences in systems, processes and strategy between the 'best in class' practitioner and the organisation carrying out the benchmarking may make it harder to implement improvements identified in the benchmarking exercise.

Activity 3: Subsequent Co

Subsequent is a fashion retailer, which distributes through a portfolio of 105 stores and through catalogue and online channels. In response to increasingly difficult trading conditions, Subsequent's board has requested a report benchmarking the business against its main competitor, Cavity. The preliminary calculations have been completed by a junior analyst; you have been asked by the finance director to analyse these figures. A sample of the report is provided below.

	Cavity		Subsequent	
	20X3	20X4	20X3	20X4
Revenue ($m)	2,100	1,900	1,950	2,000
Profit ($m)	290	190	330	250
No. of stores	160	180	100	105
Revenue per store ($m)	13.1	10.6	19.5	19.0
Change year on year				
Revenue	–	–9.5%	–	+2.6%
Profit	–	–34.5%	–	–24.2%
No. of stores	–	+12.5%	–	+5.0%

Required

Evaluate the method of benchmarking used, and the performance of Subsequent Co using the data prepared by the analyst. **(10 marks)**

Solution

2.2 Stage of benchmarking

It is important to read the requirement for benchmarking questions very carefully; you may not actually be asked to evaluate the benchmarked performance of the organisation. You may, for example, be required to evaluate the benchmarking process itself, or to evaluate the completeness of a benchmarking exercise. In such a situation you might need to identify what further benchmarking information would be useful or what further steps to take in the benchmarking process.

Kaiser Associates, a consultancy company, divided benchmarking into **seven steps** (*Kaiser, 1988*). The table below outlines the steps, and also how these might be applied to a scenario in an exam question:

	Description	**Application to the scenario**
Step 1	**Set objectives** and determine the areas to benchmark.	Has the scenario outlined the objective of the exercise, eg to reduce admin costs or increase revenues?
Step 2	Establish **key performance measures** or performance drivers which will be measured during the benchmarking exercise. Priority should be given to benchmarking the areas of performance which are most important to an organisation's success (its critical success factors).	Have all the calculations been provided, or does the question require you to calculate additional measures or performance indicators? Are the areas being benchmarked the ones which are most important to the organisation's success? Are there other areas which might be more appropriate to benchmark?
Step 3	**Select organisations** to compare performance against.	Is the organisation comparing against a close competitor or another suitably similar organisation? Could the choice of comparators affect the usefulness/validity of the figures being compared against?
Step 4	**Measure** own and others' performance, using the measures identified in Step 2 above.	Is it plausible to measure competitors' performance? Is the data widely available?
Step 5	**Compare** performances, and identify gaps between the performance of your own organisation and those of the comparator organisations.	You may be asked to complete this stage in the requirements: 'Analyse the organisation's benchmarked position'.
Step 6	Design and implement an **improvement programme** to close the performance gaps identified. An important element of this step will also be analysing **how** the comparator organisations achieve superior performance, then assessing whether similar processes and techniques could be introduced into your own organisation.	Is there narrative information in the scenario that describes how the competitor is able to achieve higher revenues or lower costs? Is it practical to implement these changes into the organisation in the scenario? How quickly could this happen?
Step 7	**Monitor** improvements. Benchmarking shouldn't be seen just as a one-off process; its value to an organisation comes from the ongoing improvements in performance which result from the initial comparisons (Steps 4 and 5 above).	A post-project review may be required; who should conduct it and can you make reference to people in the scenario.

3 Strategic models and performance management

Strategic models can be useful in helping an organisation identify the key aspects of its performance which need **measuring and managing**.

3.1 SWOT analysis

> **SWOT analysis:** A critical assessment of the strengths and weaknesses, opportunities and threats affecting an entity, in order to establish its strategic position prior to developing a strategic plan.

SWOT analysis requires assessment of internal and external factors.

Strengths and weaknesses	Involves consideration of **internal factors**.
Opportunities and threats	Involves consideration of **external factors**.

3.1.1 SWOT analysis in performance management

How can SWOT analysis help the performance management process (ie how can it help to improve performance and ensure goals/objectives are met)?

- **Identifying weaknesses and threats** – Issues which need to be addressed, either within the organisation (weaknesses) or in the external environment (threats).
- **Identifying strengths and opportunities** – Factors that may give the organisation potential to grow (opportunities) through exploiting its own strengths.
- **Maintaining strengths** – Having identified its strengths, an organisation must ensure it continues to perform well in these areas to maintain competitive advantage over its rivals.
- **Identifying critical success factors (CSFs)** – What are the key areas in which an organisation needs to perform well in order to achieve its goals? (**Note.** CSFs are discussed in more detail in Chapter 2.)
- **Determining information needs** – Is the organisation measuring performance in the areas which SWOT has identified as being important?
- **Evaluate targets** – Are targets realistic and achievable in the context for the opportunities available and given the threats an organisation faces?

3.2 Porter's five forces

Porter's five forces model (*Porter, 1980*) suggests that five key forces determine the profitability of an **industry**; the stronger the competitive forces are, the lower the level of industry profits. Analysing the forces can help firms develop plans to mitigate the forces; eg if buyer power is strong, action may be taken to reduce buyer power by differentiating a firm from its rivals.

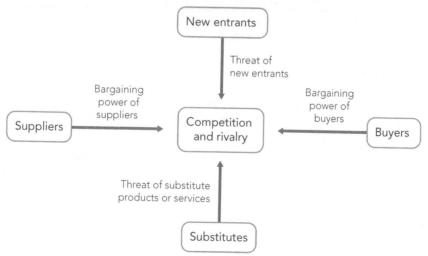

3.2.1 Porter's five forces and performance management

Analysing the five forces can also help firms identify performance measures which could be particularly important. Some general performance metrics which a firm might consider are:

New entrants	• % revenue from products protected by patents • % revenue from long-term customer contracts • Brand value • Entry costs • Market share
Suppliers	• Cost of suppliers' product relative to overall cost (high bargaining power if a major part of overall cost) • Degree of market concentration (eg % share of largest ten firms) • Level of discounts offered to customers • Switching costs
Competition and rivalry	• Market growth • Market share • Marketing expenditure • Industry league tables on price and quality
Buyers	• Number of buyers • Size of buyers • % total sales attributable to largest customers • Level of discounts offered to customers • Market share • Switching costs
Substitutes	• Relative price/performance of substitutes • Growth rates of substitute markets

3.2.2 Potential issues with Porter's five forces model

Although the five forces model can be useful in assessing the impact that competition is having on the profitability of an industry, there are limitations with the model.

- The model focuses on the profitability of an industry, so underplays the extent to which the capabilities of individual firms can influence their profitability within an industry.
- It is not always easy to identify what industry a firm operates in. For example, some large firms might operate across more than one market or industry.

Essential reading

See Chapter 1 Section 4 of the Essential reading for more detail on the use of Porter's five forces model in the context of performance management – including potential issues and limitations to be aware of when using the model.

The Essential reading is available as an Appendix of the digital edition of the Workbook.

Activity 4: Flash Co

Flash Co is a well-known sports goods manufacturer which sells its branded products worldwide. The Marketing Director has applied Porter's five forces and reached the following conclusions:

*   **Threat of entry**: Low, as Flash Co's size presents a large entry barrier.
*   **Power of buyers**: Very important as customers worldwide have much choice from different competitors.
*   **Power of suppliers**: Little threat. Most of Flash Co's material suppliers are small and Flash could easily find alternative sources of these. Labour is relatively cheap as most of Flash's production facilities are based in developing countries.
*   **Substitutes**: Low, as there is little by way of a substitute for sports goods.
*   **Competitive rivalry**: A major threat due to the constant launch of new products in this competitive industry.

Required

Evaluate the five forces acting on Flash Co to determine if you agree with the Marketing Director's conclusions. Suggest and justify two performance indicators to assess the strength of each of the forces.
(15 marks)

Solution

3.3 BCG Matrix

The BCG matrix (*Boston Consulting Group, 1970*) examines the interrelationships between the range of products/services offered by an organisation in terms of the **strength** of their position within the market, and the **market's attractiveness** as measured by its capacity for growth.

Analysis can take place at two levels:

(a) **Product/service level**: The brands or products/services offered by the firm are examined to determine their current position and prospects.

(b) **Corporate level**: The strategic business units of the diversified firm are examined for their interrelationships and balance.

The BCG matrix classifies products and/or services in terms of potential cash generation and cash expenditure requirements. The matrix presupposes that there are only two factors that directly influence competitive position:

(a) The **growth rate** of the market segment the organisation serves (this is likely to slow over time due to the impact of the product life cycle); and

(b) The **relative market share** of the segment held by the organisation (ie the organisation's market share **compared to the market share of its largest competitor**). A relative market share of >1 indicates that a product or business unit is the market leader.

		Relative market share	
		High	Low
Market growth	High	Stars	Question marks
	Low	Cash cows	Dogs

Note. As a guide, 10% is often used as the dividing line between high and low market growth.

(a) **Stars** are products or services with a high relative market share in a high growth market.

   In the short term, they require expenditure in excess of cash generated to maintain relative market position. However, they promise high returns in the future.

(b) A **question mark** is a product in a high growth market, but holding a relatively low market share.

   Considerable expenditure may be required to turn a question mark into a rising star; consequently they tend to be poor cash generators and show a negative cash flow.

(c) **Cash cows** hold a high share of a low growth, mature market.

They generate more cash than they incur, and so can finance the growth of rising stars and question marks.

(d) A **dog** is a product with a low share of a low growth market.

Often they are cash cows fallen on hard times, and unless the trend can be reversed (classified as a war horse) they should be allowed to die, or be killed off.

3.3.1 Uses of BCG analysis

Internal balance should be checked.

(a) Proper distribution of resources between products, eg largest should be stars or cash cows.

(b) Sufficient cash flows from cash cows repay finance and permit investment in question marks and stars.

(c) There should be sufficient successor products (and services) to replace declining stars and cash cows.

Assess trends by mapping matrix at regular intervals and superimposing on earlier matrices to reveal direction and momentum of each product.

Evaluate competitors by creation of portfolios based on their products or business divisions.

Evaluate risk by adjusting portfolio to reflect impact of hypothetical scenarios or changes in key environmental variables. This can be accomplished by sensitivity analysis.

3.3.2 The BCG matrix and performance measures

The different characteristics of business units in each of the quadrants means that different financial performance measures are likely to be appropriate, depending on the business unit's position in the matrix.

Metrics for business units in high growth markets (eg stars, question marks) should be based on **growth**, eg revenue growth, profit growth and (relative) market share are likely to be important.

On the other hand, metrics for business units in low growth markets (in particular, cash cows) should focus more on **margins and cash generation**. For cash cows and dogs, cost control is likely to be an important issue in preserving profits, indicating a need for performance measures looking at cost and cost control.

Essential reading

See Chapter 1 Section 5 of the Essential reading for more detail on using the BCG matrix in the context of performance management – including the issues and limitations organisations could face when using the matrix. This is an **important** area to review.

The Essential reading is available as an Appendix of the digital edition of the Workbook.

Activity 5: DEF Co

DEF Co is a large company which has three divisions: a restaurants division, a pubs division and a casino division.

The company's management accountant has prepared the revenue information about the divisions.

	Revenue	
	Current actual $m	3-yr forecast $m
Restaurants		
DEF	95	100
Market sector	10,200	10,350
Market leader	295	305
Pubs		
DEF	425	420
Market sector	9,500	9,550
Market leader (DEF)	425	420
Casino		
DEF	150	195
Market sector	1,800	2,200
Market leader	250	290

Required

Analyse the divisions according to how they fit into the BCG matrix and comment on which performance indicators may be relevant for each division.

(9 marks)

Solution

3.4 Porter's generic strategies

Michael Porter (1980) argues that, to compete successfully, a firm needs to either be the lowest cost producer (cost leadership strategy), or to differentiate its products from competitors' products in a way which customers value (differentiation strategy).

KEY TERM

> **Cost leadership:** A strategy in which a firm seeks to be the lowest cost producer in the industry as a whole.
>
> **Differentiation:** A strategy in which a firm seeks to gain a competitive advantage through the particular characteristics of its products or processes.

Porter argues that if a firm tries to combine different generic strategies it risks losing its competitive advantage and becoming '**stuck in the middle**'.

Cost leadership and differentiation are industry-wide strategies. However, a firm could also adopt a **focus strategy**, restricting its activities to a segment of the market and pursuing a strategy of cost leadership or differentiation within its chosen market niche. Focusing on a specific niche could be due to either a lack of resources, a strategy to minimise costs or to differentiate effectively.

3.4.1 Implications for performance management

Cost leadership

(a) **Financial control** is likely to be crucial. There may be an emphasis on variance analysis, and a focus on **maximising efficiency** and **reducing waste**.

(b) Production facilities are likely to be set up to obtain economies of scale and to mass produce goods wherever possible. Firms may try to exploit the **learning curve effect**. By producing more items than its rivals, a firm can achieve lower average costs.

(c) May also encourage **kaizen costing**/continuous improvement (see Chapter 11), and **benchmarking**.

Chapter 4 also considers the impact of a cost leadership strategy on a firm's value chain.

Differentiation

Although a firm pursuing a differentiation strategy will still need to monitor its costs, it will also be very important for the firm to measure its performance in those areas which **differentiate** its product or service from competitors (eg product features, product quality, brand image, quality of service, speed of delivery).

These characteristics are often **non-financial**, which means that firms will need non-financial performance measures, linked to these characteristics (in effect, its critical success factors – see Chapter 2).

A firm pursuing a differentiation strategy needs to **select performance indicators which underpin the areas of performance which differentiate it from its competitors.**

3.5 Balanced scorecard

The syllabus identifies that you may need to evaluate how the balanced scorecard can assist in the performance management process. We will look at the balanced scorecard (*Kaplan & Norton, 1996a*) in more detail in Chapter 13.

However, key features of the scorecard to note in terms of the performance management process are:

- It links strategic elements (eg mission, objectives) to operational elements (targets, key performance indicators).

- It highlights the need to consider performance from a range of perspectives: eg customers and business process, not just financial. The balance between **non-financial measures** and financial measures in the scorecard is important.

4 The impact of the external environment on performance

Performance measurement and performance management usually focus on how well an individual organisation is performing. Analysis of performance needs to consider the environment in which a firm operates, because this can affect its performance.

4.1 Industry environment

As Porter's five forces (*Porter, 1980*) – discussed earlier – suggests, the level of competition in an industry affects its ability to sustain profits. In turn, the performance of firms operating in that industry could also be affected by the strength of the different competitive forces.

The significance of Porter's model for assessing an organisation's own performance is that it reminds us that the organisation's **performance needs to be assessed in the context of its industry**. For example, if a government is about to deregulate an industry, it is likely that there will be a number of new entrants into the industry. This could lead to the pre-existing organisations in the industry reducing their prices to deal with the threat from the new entrants, which could in turn lead to lower margins and profitability.

Simply looking at the firm's results (lower margins and profitability) might suggest that there are problems with the firm's operational processes which have led to a decline in performance. However, considering the external environment will help explain the reasons for the lower margins and profitability, especially if the other pre-existing organisations in the industry have experienced similar reductions in margins and profitability.

4.2 Macro-environment

The wider business environment ('macro-environment') can also have a significant impact on an organisation's performance. The business environment can be analysed using **PEST analysis.**

4.2.1 Political environment

There are many ways in which the **political climate** can have a direct bearing on performance:

(a) Is consumer spending affected by government spending and **taxation** decisions (eg changes to income tax, or sales tax)?

(b) Is the government's corporation tax policy affecting the returns to an organisation?

(c) Might **regulations** and **legislation** affect growth and profits in the industry (such as minimum product quality standards or minimum wage legislation)?

4.2.2 Economic environment

There are also many ways in which the economic environment can impact performance:

(a) Is the economy growing or shrinking?

(b) Is a high **inflation** pushing up production costs?

(c) Have changes in **interest rates** affected consumer spending (and demand for products)? Have changes in interest rates affected the cost of borrowing (and investment)?

More generally, could movements in interest rates affect a company's interest cover and its ability to service its debt?

(d) Have changes in **exchange rates** affected the competitiveness of a firm's exports, or affected the price of imported components they need to use in a manufacturing process?

4.2.3 Social factors

Different **culture**, **tastes** and **lifestyles** can influence the level of demand for a product in different parts of the world. Equally, changes in consumer tastes can lead to changes in the demand for products over time.

4.2.4 Technological factors

Technological change can affect an organisation's activities in a number of ways:

(a) The type of products or services that are made and sold (eg the development of electric cars, or autonomous vehicles)

(b) The way in which products are made (eg increased automation) or sold, in particular, the growth of e-commerce

(c) The way in which firms are structured (eg the increase of network and virtual organisations; the increase of remote working)

(d) The way firms communicate with customers and suppliers

(e) The amount and type of data firms capture (eg big data) and the way they use that data for decision making (eg predictive analytics)

External factors identified through PEST analysis represent potential opportunities and threats for an organisation. An organisation's ability to respond more quickly, or more effectively, than its rivals to opportunities and threats could help give it a competitive advantage over its rivals, thereby helping it improve performance.

PER alert

One of the elements which supports Performance objective 14 – Monitor performance – is the need to 'Advise on the external influences affecting performance' of a department or a business.

Models such as PEST analysis and Porter's five forces could be very useful frameworks for identifying or assessing external influences which could be affecting performance.

5 Changing role of the management accountant

5.1 Modern view

Management accountancy is now often seen as a key driver of improved strategic performance, not just as a mechanism for imposing short-term control. In other words, there has been a shift from **performance measurement** to performance management, ie acting as **internal business consultants**.

Growing numbers of management accountants spend the majority of their time as internal consultants or business analysts. They spend less time preparing standardised reports but more time analysing and interpreting information. Many no longer work in an 'accounting department' but are based in the operating departments with which they work, meaning they are increasingly involved with the operations of their business, and more actively involved in decision making.

Chapter summary

Strategic management accounting (SMA)

Strategic performance management

- Levels of management: **strategic, tactical, operational**
- Need for **congruence** between levels; but potential for conflict between strategic and operational
- **Performance management systems** are the systems in an organisation by which the performance of an organisation is measured, controlled and improved
- SMA is a modern approach to performance measurement that emphasises the importance of information that is:
  - Relevant to an organisation's **strategy**
  - Monitoring an organisation's environment ie **external**
  - A mix of **financial** and **non-financial**

Benchmarking

- Internal
- Industry (competitive; non-competitive)
- Functional
- Stages
  - Set objectives
  - Choose key performance measures
  - Select benchmark partners
  - Measure performance
    ◦ Compare performance
  - Implement improvements
  - Monitor improvements
- Advantages
  - Innovate
  - Change
  - Learn
- Disadvantages
  - Reactive
  - Difficulty in obtaining information
  - Choosing activities

Strategic models and performance management

SWOT analysis

- Internal: strengths; weaknesses
- External: opportunities; threats
- Identifying S, W, O, T can help identify key aspects of performance which need measuring

Porter's five forces

- Threat of new entrants
- Bargaining power of suppliers
- Bargaining power of customers
- Threat of substitutes
- Competition and rivalry
- Strength of the forces determine the level of profits which can be sustained in an industry
- May need to either:
  - Take decisions to mitigate forces; or
  - Measure the strength of each force

BCG matrix

- Relative market share: Used to indicate company's strength
- Growth rate: Used to indicate **market attractiveness**
- Ignores other factors affecting strength (brand, strength in niche market) and attractiveness

	Relative market share	
	High	Low
Market growth High	Star	Question mark
Market growth Low	Cash cow	Dog

Porter's generic strategies

- Cost leadership
- Differentiation
- The type of strategy being pursued influences which areas of performance are most important (eg cost control vs quality) and therefore which need to be measured and monitored

Impact of the external environment on performance

- PEST analysis: Macro-environment
- Porter's five forces: Industry environment
- When assessing an organisation's performance, need to consider environmental factors as well as internal ones

Changing role of management accountant

- Role changing to 'internal business consultant'
- Accountants' role moving away from a focus solely on financial control
- Becoming more of an internal consultant or business partner

Knowledge diagnostic

1. Strategic performance management

Performance management systems help an organisation measure how well it is performing against its goals and objectives, and to identify where performance can be improved in order to help the organisation achieve those goals and objectives.

The information used for planning and control can be classified into three tiers: strategic, tactical and operational. The hierarchy between strategic and operational is an important theme in performance management.

If strategies are to be successfully implemented, there needs to be a clear link between strategic and operational plans. The controls and performance measures in place at operational level need to be properly aligned with strategic goals and objectives. However, this is often absent due to unrealistic plans, poor communication and inadequate performance measurement.

2. Strategic management accounting (SMA)

Strategic management accounting (SMA) can be used to support the entire process of planning and control, because it considers factors external to an organisation, as well as internally generated information, and because it considers non-financial information as well as financial.

SMA techniques are essential for effective performance management and are covered across the APM course.

3. Benchmarking

Benchmarking enables comparison of performance between functions or between firms. Benchmarking can help identify and evaluate areas of underperformance, so that steps can be taken to improve performance in those areas.

However, benchmarking is more useful for helping firms 'catch up' rather than innovating or developing competitive advantage.

It can sometimes be difficult to establish which firm is operating the best approach and is therefore the one against which comparisons should be drawn. Similarly, it can be difficult to obtain information about competitors' performance to compare against.

4. Strategic models and performance management

SWOT analysis helps an organisation identify its own strengths and weaknesses, as well as the opportunities and threats it faces. This can help it evaluate strategic options it could pursue. However, SWOT analysis can also help an organisation identify key aspects of performance which need measuring – eg monitoring performance in areas of strength to ensure they remain sources of competitive advantage.

Porter's five forces analyses the power of suppliers and customers, the intensity of competition in an industry, and the threats of new entrants and substitutes. Collectively, the strength of these forces determines the level of profit which can be sustained in an industry.

The **BCG matrix** positions an organisation's business units or products according to relative market share and market growth. This helps organisations assess the balance in their portfolios, and how these might change throughout product or industry life cycles.

Porter's generic strategies identify that, in order to be successful, firms should try to pursue a strategic of either cost leadership or differentiation. Financial control, especially cost control, is likely to be crucial for firms pursuing cost leadership. Non-financial factors (eg quality, service) are likely to be more important for firms pursuing a differentiation strategy, and this needs to be reflected in aspects of performance which firms measure.

5. Impact of the external environment on performance

Firms need to take account of a wide variety of external factors (eg political, economic) when assessing performance. PEST analysis can be a useful framework for assessing the opportunities and threats in the macro-environment, and the potential impact they could have on performance.

BPP LEARNING MEDIA

Porter's five forces model (see above) is a useful framework for analysing the industry environment, and the potential impact this has on the level of profits which a firm – or industry – can sustain.

6. Changing role of the management accountant

The role of the management accountant has changed, and continues to do so, because of changes in technology, management structure and competition. The focus of the management accountant's role is no longer purely on financial control, but accountants are increasingly becoming business partners for the operational managers they work with.

Further study guidance

Question practice

Now try the following from the Further question practice bank (available in the digital edition of the Workbook):

Q1 *SCC*

Q2 *Lithio Car*

Further reading

There is a Technical Article available on ACCA's website, called *Performance management models*, which discusses Porter's five forces and the BCG matrix in the context of performance management.

You are strongly advised to read this article in full as part of your preparation for the APM exam.

Activity answers

Activity 1: Training Co

Training Co will require an analysis of features of its new **market** as opposed to traditional management accounting information. Country X is likely to be very different to Training Co's domestic markets. Training Co's board will lack local knowledge and therefore be unable to make decisions without information on **external factors** such as:

- Where are the most desirable locations?
- What courses are suitable for this market? (Online? Day release? Weekend?)
- When should the course be run? (Are there public holidays, religious festivals etc to be avoided?)
- Who are the key local rivals, and what are their strengths and weaknesses?

Training Co's board will no doubt be familiar with its main competitors in its current markets; however, it will need to develop a familiarity with the incumbent competitors in Country X. Typically strategic management accounting will provide competitor information, which will help Training Co's board develop its pricing strategies and product offerings by positioning itself relative to the competition.

Activity 2: Hydra

Strategic information is required by the management of an organisation in order to enable management to take a **longer-term view** of the business and assess how the business may perform during that period. The length of this longer-term view will vary from one organisation to another, being very much dependent upon the nature of the business and the ability of those responsible for strategic direction to be able to scan the planning horizon.

Strategic information tends to be holistic and summarised in nature and would be used by management when, for example, undertaking SWOT analysis. In Hydra, **strategic information** might relate to the **development of new services** such as the provision of car parts (which could represent an opportunity for expansion and diversification). Other examples of strategic information could relate to the threats posed by Hydra's **competitors** or assessing the potential acquisition of a bicycle manufacturer in order to enhance customer value via improved efficiency and lower costs.

Tactical information is required in order to facilitate **management planning and control for shorter time periods** than strategic information. Such information relates to the tactics that management adopt in order to achieve a specific course of action.

For Hydra this might involve information to support consideration of whether to **open an additional outlet** in another part of the country, or whether to **employ additional staff** at each outlet in order to improve the quality of service provision to its customers.

Operational information relates to a very short timescale and is often used to determine immediate actions by those responsible for day-to-day management.

In Hydra, the manager at each location would require information relating to **the number of bicycles sold or serviced, and the number of complaints received** during a week. Operational information might be used within Hydra in order to determine whether staff are required to work overtime due to an unanticipated increase in demand, or whether operatives require further training due to excessive time being spent on servicing.

Activity 3: Subsequent Co

Method of benchmarking

Subsequent has used competitor benchmarking, comparing its performance against that of its main competitor, Cavity. This appears appropriate, given the board's concerns with the difficult trading conditions, because it will enable Subsequent to compare how well it is performing against Cavity under those conditions.

However, it might also be useful to compare Subsequent's performance against other retailers, to compare how well it is performing against the retail sector as a whole.

Performance

Although Subsequent's revenue increase of 2.6% seems unremarkable, this is an encouraging result in comparison to Cavity's poor revenue performance of –9.5%, which could indicate Subsequent has been able to take market share from its nearest competitor.

Subsequent has experienced a significant fall in profit, which may have been the result of offering significant discounts in order to grow or stabilise revenues. Since Cavity has experienced an even greater fall in profits this may be the case across the industry, perhaps as a result of adverse economic conditions.

Cavity has seen a dramatic increase in the number of stores; however, since revenue has fallen by 9.5% this may have caused significant operational disruption to its supply chain, resulting in poor stock availability and lost sales. In contrast Subsequent has a more modest increase in outlets and has been able to bring about modest increases in revenue.

Subsequent's revenue per store is significantly above Cavity; this may be as a result of larger store formats, which may be more cost effective, since Subsequent generates significantly more profit than Cavity from a similar revenue base. Also it may indicate that Subsequent has been more successful in generating online sales.

Activity 4: Flash Co

Tutorial note. You may have identified different performance indicators to the ones in the solution below. Provided you justify your selections, you will receive credit for relevant answers, even if they differ from the suggested solution.

Forces	Performance indicators
Threat of entry Low • Brands are significant barriers	• Customer loyalty – if customers are loyal to Flash, it will make it harder for new entrants to join the market. • Brand awareness – high brand awareness should help Flash attract customers (again making it harder for new entrants to join).
Power of buyers High • Retail stores • End users different powers Attracted by • Price • Quality • Fashion Lots of choice available	• Profit/product – customers with high bargaining power (eg large retail stores) may be more able to negotiate discounts. • Product quality/customer satisfaction scores – customers are attracted by quality; so maintaining high quality will mean that Flash has more scope to maintain a higher price (compared to lower quality brands).
Power of suppliers May be increasing • Depends if competition uses same suppliers • Some low-cost economies are being replaced by new ones/are exercising power through government and	• Number of suppliers – as Flash uses a large number of suppliers, and can switch easily, the bargaining power of suppliers will be low. • Proportion of cost – the amount Flash spends with a supplier (as a proportion of total cost, or of total revenue) could indicate the importance of that supplier and therefore their potential

Forces	Performance indicators
economic actions	bargaining power.
Substitutes May vary globally • Many exist – other casual clothing types • Fewer exist for serious sports players • New technologies may be included here	• Customer loyalty – if customers are loyal to Flash, then this should reduce the risk of them switching to substitute products. • Price of substitutes – the price of potential substitute products (compared to the price of Flash's products) could be a factor which influences customers' decisions about whether or not to switch to the substitute.
Competitive rivalry Probably high as many exist of similar size Little differentiation unless niche, eg: • Speedo swimwear • Skiing products	• New product launches – launching new products provides an opportunity for growth (for the company making the launch). • Market share – market share indicates how effectively Flash is maintaining its position in the market.

Activity 5: DEF Co

Restaurants

Relative market share is **low**; about 0.3 (95/295).

Market growth is also **low**. The market sector is only forecast to grow about 1.5% (150/10,200) over three years.

The restaurant division should be classified as a **dog**.

Performance indicators for business units in low growth markets should focus on **cash generation**.

Pubs

DEF is the market leader, so its relative share must be >1 (because the market leader's sales, by definition, must be higher than any other entity's). Therefore the pub division's relative market share is **high**.

However, market growth is very **low**. Forecast growth in the market sector is only about 0.5% (50/9,500) over three years, while DEF's own revenue is actually expected to decline slightly over the three years.

The pubs division should be classified as a **cash cow**.

Performance measures are likely to focus on profit margins and cost control.

Casino

Relative market share is 0.6 (150/250), so while it is still low it is not as **low** as the restaurant division's market share.

Market growth is **high**. The market sector is forecast to grow about 22% (400/1,800) over three years, and DEF's own casino division is forecast to grow even faster than the market.

The casino division is currently a **question mark**, although if it continues to outperform the market it has the potential to become a 'rising star'.

Performance indicators for business units in high growth markets are more likely to focus on **growth**, so revenue growth, profit growth and (relative) market share are likely to be important.

Skills checkpoint 1
Creating information from data

Overview

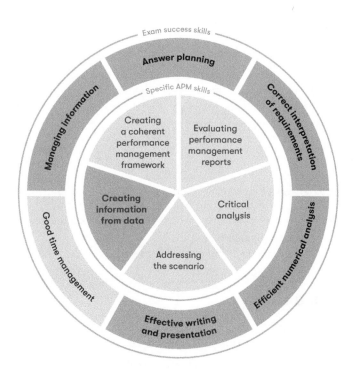

Introduction

An important theme in Section A of the APM syllabus, but one which also continues throughout the syllabus, is that accountants are increasingly expected to act as 'internal business consultants'. An important aspect of this role is in interpreting the **meaning** of data, ie **creating information from data.**

In any part of the exam you can expect to have to deal with calculations that have already been completed (ie data) and your role will be to analyse that data and interpret its meaning.

Sometimes, in the process of creating information from data, you may have to perform some additional calculations, such as comparing one number to another by means of a suitable ratio.

For example, in past exams, questions have involved interpreting data on:

- A company's competitive position against a benchmark
- The BCG matrix (relative market share and market growth)
- Variances
- Environmental performance
- Net present value (NPV) and probabilities
- Value for money performance measures

Many of these technical areas are covered later in your studies but the **general skill required in creating information from data** is covered here.

Where data is provided for analysis, a common problem is that candidates **fail to add any value** in their analysis of that data. This is the main issue we will address here.

APM Skill: Creating information from data

A step-by-step technique for ensuring that analysis of data creates useful information, and therefore adds value, is outlined below. Each step will be explained in more detail in the following sections, and illustrated by answering a requirement from a past exam in stages.

> **STEP 1:**
> Consider the 'big picture', ie the main issues facing the company as presented in the scenario of the question.

> **STEP 2:**
> Answer plan. Plan to categorise the analysis into a small number of relevant categories. Where relevant, plan to use ratio analysis to add meaning to the raw data provided.

> **STEP 3:**
> Complete your answer by discussing the data and any further numerical analysis (eg ratios) by reference to the 'big picture' issues identified in Step 1.
> Avoid statements that simply describe the data, eg costs have risen by 10%, without adding any value in terms of analysis.

Exam success skills

The following illustration is based on an extract from a past exam question, about an airline company called 'Amal'. This extract was worth 12 marks.

For this question, we will also focus on the following **exam success skills**:

- **Managing information.** It is easy to feel that the amount of information contained in scenario-based questions is overwhelming. **Active reading** is a useful technique to use to avoid this. This involves focusing on the requirement first, on the basis that until you have done this the detail in the question will have little meaning and will seem more intimidating as a result.

  Focus on the requirement, underlining the key verb or verbs to ensure you answer the question properly. Then read the rest of the question, underlining and annotating important and relevant information, and making notes of any relevant technical information you think you will need.

- **Correct interpretation of requirements.** At first glance, it looks like the following question just contains one requirement. However, on closer examination you will discover that it contains at least two sub-requirements. This is very common in the APM exam.

- **Answer planning.** Make sure that your answer will follow a logical structure and has a sense of which issues are most important in the context of the scenario.

- **Efficient numerical analysis.** Present clear workings with sensible and consistent roundings.

- **Effective writing and presentation.** It is often helpful to use sub-headings in your answer to provide your analysis with a structure. It is also helpful to present the results of any further calculations (eg ratios) in a summary table. Underline your headings and sub-headings and write in full sentences, ensuring your style is professional.

Skills activity

STEP 1 Consider the 'big picture' ie the **main issues** facing the organisation as presented in the scenario of the question. Start by reading the requirements to understand the scope of analysis required.

Required

Using the data provided, analyse[1] the three airlines[2] using appropriate[3] performance indicators and comment on your results.

(12 marks)

[1] Verb - refer to ACCA definition.

[2] So not just Amal — need to compare Amal with others.

[3] Judgement required here.

The key action verb is 'analyse'. This is defined by the ACCA as 'Break into separate parts and discuss, examine, or interpret each part'.

The verb 'comment' is asking you to remark or express an opinion, in a concise manner. So note you have to do two things here – 'analyse', then 'comment'.

To understand what measures might be appropriate we will now examine the scenario and look for 'big picture' issues (these are shown in the following analysis as call-out boxes).

Question – Amal (12 marks)

Company background and objectives

Amal Airline (Amal) is the national airline of Jayland. The airline's objective is to be the best premium global airline[4].

[4] This is a critical point – any performance measures should be supporting the company's core mission.

Recent events

Amal provides long- and short-haul services all over the world and is based at its hub at Jaycity airport. Amal has been hit by a worldwide reduction in air travel due to poor economic conditions[5]. The most recent financial results show a loss and this has caused the board to reconsider its position and take action to address the changed environment.

[5] This is the context for the analysis of performance.

Amal has **cut its dividend** in order to conserve cash and it is trying to rebuild profitability **by reducing costs by 14%.** The airline is capital intensive as it needs to maintain a large fleet of modern aircraft. The two major costs for the airline are staff and fuel[6]. In trying to renegotiate working conditions and pay, the management have angered the unionised workforce. There has already been some strike action by the unions representing the aircraft crew and ground staff and more is threatened.

[6] Utilisation of aircraft, staff costs and fuel costs will be important areas to control.

The board has also been considering taking advantage of new technology in aircraft engines by making a large investment ($450m) in new low-noise, fuel-efficient aircraft in an effort to reduce the environmental complaints[7] surrounding air travel and also cut costs.

[7] Environmental issues are a concern.

Performance analysis

The Chief Executive Officer (CEO) has provided the data for Amal and **two of its main competitors**[8] (shown in Appendix 1). **Kayland Air is a government-owned** and run airline in the **neighbouring country** of Kayland. It has a similar mix of business to Amal and targets a similar market. **Cheapo Air** is currently one of the most successful of the new privately owned airlines that have gained significant market share over the last 15 years by offering a **cheap but basic short-haul** service to customers in and around Jayland. Cheapo Air **subcontracts** many of its activities in order to remain flexible.

[8] The two companies used as a benchmark have different operational and geographical scope; and different objectives.

The CEO wants you to **calculate some suitable performance measures** and explain the results.

Appendix 1

Data provided by the CEO:
Data for the most recent calendar year

		Amal	Kayland Air	Cheapo Air
Passengers ('000)		23,649	38,272	35,624
Passenger kilometres (millions)		79,618	82,554	40,973
Revenue	$m	5,430	7,350	2,170

Data for the most recent calendar year

Costs		Amal	Kayland Air	Cheapo Air
Fuel	$m	1,480	1,823	535
Staff	$m	1,560	2,998	238
Staff numbers		32,501	56,065	5,372
Operating profit	$m	630	54	127
Number of aircraft		182	361	143
Average aircraft size (seats)		195	163	125
Seat kilometres (millions)		100,654	105,974	46,934

Note. A seat kilometre is generated for every one kilometre flown by an available seat on the company's aircraft.

Now we can move on to plan our approach.

STEP 2 Plan to categorise the analysis into a small number of relevant categories. Where relevant, plan to use ratio analysis to add meaning to the raw data provided.

Answer plan

Relevant categories and ratios using the data in the scenario could include:

Analysis

- Capacity:

  passengers vs No of aircraft × average size

- Staff costs:

  staff costs/staff numbers or revenue/staff numbers

- Fuel per km travelled also an environmental issue:

  fuel costs/seat kilometre

- Profit margin

Comment

- Recognise different nature of the three airlines as per 'big picture analysis'

STEP 3 Complete your answer by discussing the data and any further numerical analysis (eg ratios) by reference to the 'big picture' issues identified in Step 1.

Avoid statements that simply describe the data, eg costs have risen by 10%, without adding any value in terms of analysis.

Make sure you generate enough points for the marks available – there are 12 marks available, so assuming 50% maximum for calculations and 50% for discussion, and assuming each discussion point is worth 1 mark, then approximately four categories of ratio accompanied by relevant discussion should be sufficient for a good pass mark.

Solution

(a) Performance summary[9] for the three airlines:

[9] Calculations (identified in answer plan) laid out neatly with a column for each airline & clear workings.

	Amal	Kayland	Cheapo
Operating profit margin	630/5,430	54/7,350	127/2,170
	11.6%	0.7%	5.9%

	Amal	Kayland	Cheapo
Capacity utilisation (load factor)	79,619/100,654	82,554/105,974	40,973/46,934
	79.1%	77.9%	87.3%
Revenue/staff member ($'000)	5,430m/32,501	7,350m/56,065	2,170m/5,372
	167	131	404
Fuel cost/seat kilometre ($)	1,480m/100,654m	1,823m/105,974m	535m/46,934m
	0.015	0.017	0.011

Operating margin

Amal has the highest operating margin of the three airlines (11.6%), which suggests it is being run efficiently overall.[10]

We might expect Amal to achieve a relatively high margin because it appears to be pursuing a **differentiation strategy**. However, Kayland, which appears to be pursuing a similar strategy, generates an operating profit margin of less than 1%.

Capacity utilisation

By showing, on average, how full each airline's aircraft are this indicator shows how well the airlines are using their asset base[11] (ie their aircraft).

Amal and Kayland's performance is similar in this respect, but Cheapo's is significantly better. This is likely to be because Cheapo (a low-cost airline) is pursuing a **cost leadership** strategy. Amal might consider reducing its prices to try to improve capacity utilisation, but it needs to do so in the context of its overall strategy. If it reduces prices too much, it may end up compromising the quality and service it offers to passengers, but these elements are crucial to its strategy as a differentiator.

Revenue per staff member

This is an important measure in the context of the recent disputes over working conditions and pay[12].

[10] Use headings from answer plan & explain the numbers using the big picture information that you have identified in Step 1.

[11] Add value in the narrative – don't simply describe the data identified in Step 1.

[12] Add value by relating one part of the data to another identified in Step 1.

BPP LEARNING MEDIA

Amal's staff appear to be performing better than Kayland's, which in turn might strengthen their claims for a pay rise.

The comparison between Amal and Cheapo's performance for this measure may be less meaningful. Cheapo **outsources** many of its activities, meaning its staff numbers will be significantly lower than Amal which carries out the corresponding activities **in house**.

Fuel costs/environmental issues

The board's interest in new fuel-efficient aircraft indicates that reducing fuel costs is an important concern for Amal.

Again, Cheapo appears to be controlling its fuel costs better than Amal or Kayland. This might be because it has more **fuel-efficient planes**, which would support the board's argument for Amal investing in new aircraft. However, Cheapo may have negotiated more favourable fuel contracts with its suppliers, or be using lower grade fuel.

Other points to note:

- Important to avoid non-value adding simplistic unexplained statements such as 'Amal has a higher profit margin than either Kayland or Cheapo'.

- Many points could be made here; as long as they are relevant and show understanding of the big picture in the scenario they will score well.

Exam success skills diagnostic

Every time you complete a question, use the diagnostic below to assess how effectively you demonstrated the exam success skills in answering the question. The table has been completed below for the Amal activity, to give you an idea of how to complete the diagnostic.

Exam success skills	Your reflections/observations
Managing information	Did you understand that the performance of all three airlines needed to be assessed? Did you understand that Amal is following a differentiation strategy?
Correct interpretation of requirements	Did you understand that the performance of all three airlines needed to be assessed? Did you understand what was meant by the verbs 'analyse' and 'comment'?
Answer planning	Was your choice of technique influence by the 'big picture' issues that you spotted in the main body of the scenario?
Efficient numerical analysis	Did you present workings and final calculations clearly?
Effective writing and presentation	Did you use sub-headings in your answer to provide your analysis with a structure? Did you relate your written points back to the 'big picture' issues in the scenario?
Most important action points to apply to your next question	

Summary

A common complaint of the APM examining team comments on the real exam is that candidates often struggle to analyse a table of raw data in a way that 'adds value'. Adding value does not simply mean repeating the points from your calculations; but it requires you to add some insight and explanation to them.

For example, if you have calculated the operating profit for the airlines, you won't then add any value by repeating the profit margins in your analysis. Instead, you should focus on the potential reasons for, or the implications of, the difference in profit margins between the airlines.

As we have seen the key steps are to:

(a) Make sure that you understand the big picture from the scenario

(b) Structure your analysis into different categories, using **relevant** ratios where appropriate

(c) Explain key themes by analysing your numbers in the context of the big picture issues

These are the important steps in **creating information from data.**

This skill will be revisited frequently in your studies, and is revisited as part of the analysis presented in Skills Checkpoint 4.

2

Performance hierarchy

Learning objectives

On completion of this chapter, you should be able to:

	Syllabus reference no.
Discuss how the purpose, structure and content of a mission statement impacts on performance measurement and management.	A2(a)
Discuss how strategic objectives are cascaded down the organisation via the formulation of subsidiary performance objectives.	A2(b)
Apply critical success factor analysis in developing performance metrics from business objectives.	A2(c)
Identify and discuss the characteristics of operational performance.	A2(d)
Discuss the relative significance of planning activities as against controlling activities at different levels in the performance hierarchy.	A2(e)

Exam context

The primary focus of APM is on an organisation's performance rather than its strategy. Although this chapter covers important aspects of strategy – mission, objectives etc – you need to think about the implications of these in the context of performance management, rather than evaluating an organisation's strategies and objectives themselves.

In this chapter we will look at four important elements in performance management: mission statements, objectives, critical success factors (CSFs) and key performance indicators (KPIs).

ACCA's Syllabus and Study Guide for APM states that the 50-mark (Section A) question 'will include the organisation's mission statement and strategic objectives and candidates will be expected to be able to assess the methods by which the organisation is controlling, managing and measuring performance in order to achieve its objectives'.

The link between objectives, CSFs and KPIs which we cover in this chapter could be very important in this respect. For example, are the areas of performance which the organisation is measuring (through its KPIs) the most appropriate ones for helping it to achieve its objectives?

In order for organisations to achieve their corporate objectives, it is important that those objectives are cascaded down the organisation. Later, in Chapter 13, we will look at models that create a structure for doing this (eg Lynch and Cross's performance pyramid). The performance hierarchy we look at in this chapter provides the foundations for such models.

Chapter overview

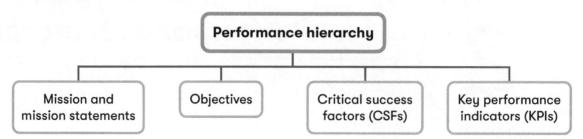

1 Mission and mission statements

PER alert

Performance Objective 13 (PO 13) – Plan and control performance – requires you to demonstrate that you plan business activities and control performance, making recommendations for improvement. One of the elements which demonstrate you have fulfilled PO 13 is that you 'contribute to setting objectives for the planning and control of business activities'.

Objectives, and the performance metrics developed from them, are important parts of this chapter. Identifying performance metrics and key performance indicators is a prerequisite to be able to evaluate performance. If an organisation hasn't set any performance targets then, by definition, it cannot subsequently measure whether it has achieved its targets or not.

1.1 Mission

An organisation's mission describes the organisation's basic **purpose**.

It has been argued (*Campbell et al, 1990*) that, in order to be effective, corporate mission must contain four elements:

1.2 Mission statements

Organisations often set out their missions in a mission statement.

Mission statement: Aims to provide employees and stakeholders with clarity about what the organisation is fundamentally there to do (*Johnson et al, 2017*).

Most mission statements will address some of the following aspects:

(a) The organisation's **reason for existence**

(b) The **identity** of the stakeholder groups for whom the organisation exists (such as shareholders, customers and employees) and the commitment made to these groups

(c) The **nature of the firm's business** (such as the products it makes or the services it provides, the markets it produces for, or the business areas in which it will operate)

(d) Ways of **competing** (eg quality, innovation, low prices; geographical spread of its operations) and **principles of business** (eg on non-discrimination or environmental issues)

1.3 Advantages and limitations of mission statements

The underlying aims of performance management are to ensure that an organisation meets its goals, and to identify areas where performance needs to be improved in order for it to do so.

By definition, an organisation must first have established its goals and objectives in order to assess how well it is performing in relation to them. By identifying an organisation's key purpose, a mission statement can also help to identify – at a high level – the aspects of performance which are important for an organisation, and therefore where its performance needs to be measured.

Advantages	Criticisms
Communicate the nature of the organisation to **stakeholders**	Are often full of **generalisations** or meaningless phrases (eg 'quality', 'best')
Communicate the desired **culture** and **behaviour**	May be **public relations** exercises rather than a true representation of the culture or goals of the organisation
Provide an underlying framework for **strategic planning**; ensure plans and activities are consistent with mission, developing **performance measures**	Have **little practical value** if they lack detailed objectives and programmes for implementation
Provide a focus for developing **performance measures**; ensure performance measures are linked to an organisation's purpose	May become obsolete if not updated for changes in the organisation or its environment

2 Objectives

Mission statements can help to identify an organisation's overall purpose, but in order to manage its performance, an organisation needs more **specific and measurable** objectives and targets.

Objectives should be quantifiable statements of what an organisation wants to achieve. It is important for organisations to set objectives because:

(a) They provide **guidance and direction**: what the organisation is trying to achieve (and how is it going to achieve this?)

(b) They facilitate **planning**; to determine how the goals will be achieved

(c) They help organisations **evaluate and control performance**: management can assess how the organisation is actually performing, compared to its objectives, and can then make any necessary adjustments

2.1 Hierarchy of objectives

The system of objectives ranges from high-level general objectives to lower-level goals for particular individuals in a clear structure.

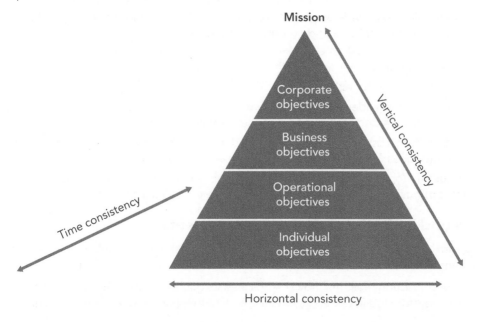

Essential reading

See Chapter 2 Section 1 of the Essential reading for more detail about objectives, including the relationship between corporate objectives and business unit objectives, and the importance of ensuring consistency ('congruence') between objectives.

See Chapter 2 Section 2 of the Essential reading for more detail about the characteristics of operational performance. Also, see Chapter 2 Section 3 of the Essential reading which highlights the differences in the nature of planning and control activities at strategic level compared to operational level.

The Essential reading is available as an Appendix of the digital edition of the Workbook.

Another important implication of the hierarchy of performance is that an organisation's ability to implement its strategies successfully ultimately depends on its **operational performance** and the way day-to-day activities are carried out.

3 Critical success factors (CSFs)

Once an organisation has identified its objectives, it also needs to identify the key factors and processes that will enable it to be successful and to achieve those objectives. These are its critical success factors (CSFs).

KEY TERM

> **Critical success factors (CSFs):** Those aspects of a product or service which are particularly valued by customers, and therefore at which a business must excel in order to outperform its competitors.

3.1 Sources of CSFs

CSFs can be identified by considering:

- A company's **mission**/strategy
- The **external environment** (eg from PEST analysis, or analysis of Porter's five forces)

CSFs don't only relate to internal processes or aspects of performance. For example, for a road transport company, the availability and price of fuel is likely to be vital for operational planning and could have a significant impact on financial performance.

Remember (from Chapter 1) SWOT analysis can be a source for identifying CSFs.

Essential reading

See Chapter 2 Section 4 of the Essential reading for more detail on potential sources of CSFs.
The Essential reading is available as an Appendix of the digital edition of the Workbook.

3.2 Types of CSF

We can identify two distinct types of CSF: monitoring and building.

(a) **Monitoring** – these have a relatively short-term focus, and are generally more **operational** in nature, and involve the scrutiny of **existing situations**, eg inventory availability, defect-free production.

(b) **Building** – these have a **longer-term focus**, and are typically **future orientated**. They will be important for helping an organisation **build strategic capabilities** so that it can adapt to changes in its external environment, eg innovating, launching new products or services; developing new competences.

4 Key performance indicators (KPIs)

Once an organisation has identified its CSFs, it also needs to know whether it is delivering on them. This is done by using key performance indicators (KPIs), which **measure** how well the organisation is performing against its CSFs.

> **Key performance indicators (KPIs):** The measures which are used to assess whether or not an organisation is achieving its critical success factors (CSFs). Effective KPIs focus on the processes and activities which are most important for achieving strategic objectives and performance targets.

KPIs should be designed to **address the key areas of performance identified by the CSFs,** to ensure that stepping stones to achieving corporate objectives are put in place.

KPI measures should be:

S – specific

M – measurable

A – attainable

R – relevant (ie addressing the CSFs or objectives)

T – time-bound

Example

We can illustrate the relationship between objectives, CSFs and KPIs by looking at an example of a supermarket company.

Let us assume the company has defined two of its **objectives** as follows:

(a) To ensure the loyalty of its customers ('to generate lifetime loyalty')

(b) To ensure its prices are at least 2% cheaper than the average of rival supermarkets ('to create value for customers')

The supermarket then needs to identify the **CSFs** which will help it achieve those objectives. These CSFs could be:

(a) Stocking the goods that customers most want to buy

(b) Making the shopping experience as pleasant as possible

(c) Refining internal processes to operate the business on a cost-effective basis

(d) Using economies of scale to source appropriate goods as cheaply as possible

Then in order to **measure how well it is performing against these CSFs,** the supermarket needs to set **KPIs.** Examples of KPIs could be:

- The proportion of goods taking more than a week to sell (relates to CSF 1)
- Results of customer feedback surveys (relates to CSF 2)
- Percentage of customers who are repeat customers (relates to CSF 2)
- Market share (relates to CSF 2)
- Cost measures and progress against savings targets (relates to CSF 3)
- Percentage of products cheaper than competitors (relates to CSF 4)
- Price of a 'basket of goods' compared to the price of the equivalent basket of goods at competitors (relates to CSF 4)

Activity 1: Sawton Hotel

The Sawton Hotel is a luxury hotel, situated on the edge of a seaside town in the south east of Britland. Like all of the other hotels in the area, the Sawton is privately owned, and is not part of a chain. The Sawton has a restaurant and a gym, which are for residents' use only.

Although the local area is popular with tourists, there is significant seasonal variation in demand for hotel rooms. As a result, the Sawton changes its room rates throughout the year, based on expected levels of demand, so that rates are higher in the peak summer months, and lower in the less busy winter months.

At the end of their stay, all customers are invited to complete a short survey asking them how satisfied they were with their stay, the reasons for this, and the likelihood that they will recommend the Sawton to their family and friends.

Feedback from these surveys shows that the comfort of the hotel's rooms, and the quality and efficiency of customer service are key factors influencing customer satisfaction. The surveys also indicate that guests' satisfactions have a significant impact on how likely they are to make repeat bookings and recommend the Sawton to their friends.

The Sawton has just appointed a new general manager who has expressed concern about the limited amount of management information available. In particular, he believes the Sawton should be monitoring its performance against key performance indicators (which it currently doesn't do).

Required

Recommend and justify two critical success factors (CSFs) for the Sawton Hotel, and two key performance indicators (KPIs) for each CSF.

(6 marks)

Solution

4.1 CSFs, KPIs and management information systems

CSFs and KPIs should influence the design of an entity's management information system (MIS) (as discussed in Chapter 6).

CSFs identify the key areas of performance, which management will need information about. However, this also has implications for an entity's management information systems:

- Can the current information systems provide the information required to measure performance in key areas (non-financial information, as well as financial)?
- What changes to the information systems might be required to ensure they can provide the information required?

Chapter summary

```
                        ┌─────────────────────────┐
                        │  Performance hierarchy  │
                        └─────────────────────────┘
```

Mission and mission statements

- **Mission:** An expression of an organisation's overall purpose
- Elements of mission:
  - Purpose
  - Strategy
  - Standards
  - Values
- **Mission statement aims** to provide employees and stakeholders with clarity about an organisation's fundamental purpose
- **But** can become a PR exercise, and have little practical value

Objectives

- **Objectives:**
  - Quantifiable statements of what an organisation wants to achieve
  - Derived from mission statement
- Benefits:
  - Provide guidance and direction
  - Facilitate planning
  - Basis for evaluating and controlling performance
- **Hierarchy of objectives**
  - The system of objectives ranges from high-level general objectives to lower-level goals for particular individuals in a clear structure
- Importance of **congruence** between objectives:
  - Horizontal
  - Vertical
  - Over time

Critical success factors (CSFs)

- **CSFs:** Areas where an organisation needs to excel in order to be successful and to achieve objectives
- **Sources** of CSFs:
  - Internal competences
  - External environment
- **Types** of CSF:
  - Monitoring
  - Building

Key performance indicators (KPIs)

- **KPIs:** Measures used to assess whether or not an organisation is achieving its CSFs
- To be effective, need to be linked to CSFs and objectives
- Can be financial and non-financial
- Should be 'SMART'

Knowledge diagnostic

1. Mission and mission statements

An organisation's mission should identify its overall purpose and scope. The 'elements' included in mission are: purpose, strategy, policies and standards of behaviour; values and culture.

An organisation's mission is expressed through its mission statement. A mission statement should be brief, flexible and distinctive, and should aim to provide employees and other key stakeholders with clarity about the organisation's fundamental purpose.

However, mission statements are not stated in quantifiable terms, and do not typically refer to time frames.

2. Objectives

Objectives should derive from an organisation's mission, but they should be more precise and quantifiable. Strategic objectives help translate mission into specific targets for an organisation to achieve.

High-level, strategic (or corporate) objectives should be supported by more detailed, subordinate objectives for individual divisions or departments within the organisation, and which can be used as a basis for tactical or operational-level decision making.

To be effective, objectives must be consistent throughout an organisation, and over time.

3. Relationship between objectives, CSFs and KPIs

Once an organisation has established its objectives, it needs to identify the key factors and processes that will enable it to achieve those objectives.

This highlights the importance of identifying CSFs and KPIs which are derived from the objectives, and which also – in turn – link back to the organisation's mission and strategy.

4. Critical success factors (CSFs)

CSFs are the aspects of performance which are particularly valued by customers, and therefore in which an organisation needs to excel in order to be successful and achieve its objectives.

5. Key performance indicators (KPIs)

KPIs are the measures which indicate whether or not an organisation is achieving the desired level of performance in relation to its CSFs. KPIs should derive from the CSFs and should be 'SMART'.

Further study guidance

Question practice

Now try the following from the Further question practice bank (available in the digital edition of the Workbook):

Q3 *Southside College*

Further reading

There is a Technical Article available on ACCA's website, called *Performance Indicators*, which illustrates the concepts of performance, objectives, CSFs, performance indicators and KPIs in more detail. The article also highlights some of the potential problems organisations face when designing performance indicators and measurement systems.

You are strongly advised to read this article in full as part of your preparation for the APM exam.

There is also a Technical Article available on ACCA's website called *Critical success factors*, which explores CSFs further.

We recommend you read this article as part of your preparation for the APM exam.

Activity answers

Activity 1: Sawton Hotel

> **Tutorial note.** You may have identified different CSFs or KPIs to the ones in the solution. Provided you justify your selections, you will receive credit for relevant answers, even if they differ from the suggested solution.

It will be important for the hotel to measure and monitor financial performance, but equally there are a number of key non-financial factors which will influence financial performance.

Critical success factor	Performance indicators
Maintaining occupancy rates: • Sawton needs to keep occupancy rates as high as possible, but needs to do so without reducing the room rate so far that this damages profitability.	• % room occupancy – this is the most immediate measure of occupancy rates. • Revenue per available room (REVPAR) – this measures the average revenue per room booked. If room rates are discounted too much (to try to boost occupancy) this will damage the perception of Sawton as a luxury hotel. Therefore, it will be important to monitor REVPAR, to ensure Sawton's pricing remains consistent with its overall strategy.
Maintaining high levels of customer satisfaction: • Customer satisfaction levels will influence how likely customers are to stay at the hotel again, and how likely they are to recommend it to their friends. Customer retention, and customer recommendations can both be very important in generating revenue.	• Number of repeat bookings – the number of repeat customers are an indicator of customer loyalty. Customers are only likely to make return visits if they have been satisfied with their previous stay. • Customer satisfaction ratings – Sawton collects feedback data from customers, so monitoring customer feedback (and, potentially, ratings on social media sites such as TripAdvisor) will help identify whether customer satisfaction levels are being maintained.

Performance management and control

Learning objectives

On completion of this chapter, you should be able to:

	Syllabus reference no.
Evaluate the strengths and weaknesses of alternative budgeting models and compare such techniques as fixed and flexible, rolling, activity-based, zero-based and incremental.	A3(a)
Evaluate different types of budget variances and how these relate to issues in planning and controlling organisations.	A3(b)

Exam context

Budgets are an important management (tactical) planning and control mechanism – setting performance targets for business units and managers to work towards, and then monitoring actual performance against those targets.

Actual revenues and costs can differ from budget figures for a wide variety of reasons, and budget variance analysis provides a way of exploring those differences. In many cases, variance analysis can identify issues which are affecting actual performance, but in some cases, variances may arise due to problems with the budgets themselves, and the assumptions made in them.

From your earlier studies (in particular *Performance Management* (PM) at Applied Skills level) you should be able to explain the different the different types of budget and the potential benefits and limitations of using different types of budget. However, it is important that you have a good understanding of these benefits and limitations, because in the APM exam you may be expected to apply it to a scenario in order to evaluate whether or not the type of budget an organisation is using is appropriate to its particular circumstances.

Similarly, you should be familiar (from PM) with how to calculate variances, and the difference between planning and operational variances. Being able to distinguish the extent to which variances are due to planning as opposed to operational issues is vital in assessing performance.

Chapter overview

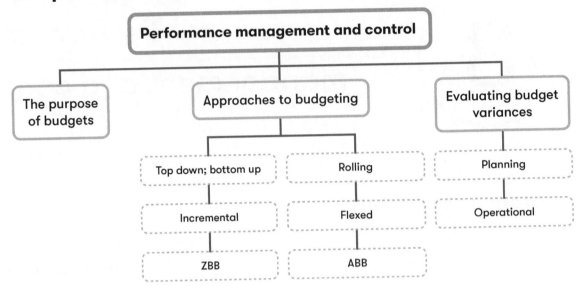

BPP
LEARNING
MEDIA

1 The purpose of budgets

Budgeting is one key method **to link strategy to operations**. Budgets provide greater detail about how plans will be implemented over time, and they communicate with and control lower-level employees.

The purpose of budgets can be summarised through the mnemonic 'PRIME':

Purpose	Benefits
Planning	Budget holders are forced to plan how to hit targets that should ensure that the organisation's **strategic plan** is achieved (eg for overall sales, margins, quality levels).
Responsibility	Budgets allocate responsibility, and specify which managers **control** which costs or revenues. (This is important; managers' performances should only be assessed in relation to aspects of performance they can control.)
Integration	Ensures that the planned activities of one business area **do not conflict** with another (eg avoid a situation in which the training budget is inadequate to support a planned increase in production).
Motivation	If managers and employees are **involved in setting budget targets**, this should increase their motivation in trying to achieve the targets. However, it is important budget targets are felt to be achievable, otherwise they could be demotivating.
Evaluation	Budgets allow trends in performance to be identified. For example, if actual revenue is consistently falling below budget, the **reasons for the variance can be investigated**, and action taken to correct the shortfall as necessary. In this respect, budgets act as a key performance control, and they can be used in relation to both **financial** performance (eg over sales, profits) and **non-financial** (eg error rates, customer satisfaction levels).

> **PER alert**
>
> One of the requirements of Performance objective 13 (PO 13) – Plan and control performance – is to 'co-ordinate, prepare and use budgets selecting suitable budgeting models'. Another element of PO 13 is to 'use appropriate techniques to assess and evaluate actual performance against plans'.
>
> In this chapter, we discuss the advantages and disadvantages of different budget models, and those advantages and disadvantages which could influence whether a particular budget model is suitable for your organisation or not. Similarly, variance analysis (which we discuss later in the chapter) is a key technique for assessing actual performance against plans.

2 Approaches to budgeting

Budgets are all designed to achieve the same end – better performance – but there are different approaches to budgeting, and it is important that the approach an organisation uses is appropriate to its context.

2.1 Top-down vs bottom-up budgeting

Top-down budgeting

- Budgets are prepared centrally by senior management.

  This should help to ensure budgets are co-ordinated across different departments, and are consistent with organisation's longer-term objectives.

  However, a significant drawback of top-down budgeting is that local budget holders do not participate in the budget-setting process. Instead, budgets are imposed on them, which could reduce their motivation to achieve budget targets (particularly if they think the targets are unrealistic).

Bottom-up budgeting

- Local managers prepare their own budgets, or at least participate in the process, prior to budgets being approved by senior management.

  Local managers should be motivated to achieve their budgets if they have been involved in setting them and may have better knowledge of the conditions their business units face. So, the resulting budget should be more realistic.

  However, this is time-consuming (for senior and local managers) and could lead to dysfunctional behaviour as local managers focus on the individual concerns of their business units rather than overall corporate objectives. Also, managers may create budgetary slack, and set targets which are too easy to achieve.

2.2 Alternative budget models

Essential reading

As noted at the start of this chapter, you should already be familiar with the characteristics of different budget models from earlier studies, so we do not cover them **in detail** here. However, Chapter 3 Section 1 of the Essential reading provides a reminder of the key features of different budget models.

The Essential reading is available as an Appendix of the digital edition of the Workbook.

Key advantages and disadvantages of different budget models

Approach	Advantages	Disadvantages
Incremental budgeting	Based on current performance, so relatively simple to prepare **Flexed** to actual activity levels to provide more meaningful control information	Encourages **slack** Does not consider alternatives or look for ways of improving performance
Zero-based budgeting (ZBB)	Responds to changes in the business environment Requires organisations to **analyse costs very closely**, so improves understanding of costs **Increased efficiency** helps to identify inefficient or obsolete processes Useful where cash is limited, eg not-for-profit organisations	Requires a lot of management **time and effort**, and training in the use of ZBB techniques Requires a participative approach, so may not be appropriate unless an organisation has a suitable culture Questioning of current practices and processes could be seen as threatening (especially for managers whose areas are subjected to ZBB)
Rolling	**Reduces the uncertainty** associated	Requires **time, effort and money** to

Approach	Advantages	Disadvantages
budgets	with budgeting in a **dynamic environment** since it is easier to predict what will happen in the short term The process of updating the budget means managers **identify current changes** (so can respond to these) Likely to be **more realistic** than a fixed annual budget drawn up prior to the start of the year, so will provide a better basis to appraise managers' performance	keep updating (if managers spend too long revising budgets, they will have less time to control and manage actual results) Managers may not see the value in continuous updating of budgets Constantly changing targets may be demotivating for managers and staff It may not be necessary to update budgets so regularly (eg in a stable operating environment)
Flexible budgets	Highlights costs of **unused capacity**, if output falls below budget It may be possible to plan for alternative uses of spare capacity if output falls short of budget	If there is a high degree of stability, the effort involved in flexible budgeting produces little extra benefit (fixed budgets can be adequate in such circumstances)
Activity-based budgets (ABB)	Recognises that **activities drive costs,** so encourages a focus on controlling and managing **cost drivers**	Require a lot of **time and effort** to prepare, so are suited to more complex organisations with multiple cost drivers May be difficult to identify clear, individual responsibilities for activities (and to determine accountability for performance of those activities)

2.3 Preparing budgets

Exam questions might require you to **prepare or analyse** a budget. The following activity is based on a past exam question.

Activity 1: Quench Co

Quench Co is a rapidly growing, non-alcoholic drinks company which currently uses a system of incremental budgeting. Quench Co has been receiving complaints from customers about late deliveries and poor quality control. Quench Co's managers have explained that they are working hard within the budget and capital constraints imposed by the board and have expressed a desire to be less controlled.

Quench Co's incremental budget for the current year is given below. You can assume that cost of sales and distribution costs are variable and administrative costs are fixed.

	Q1	Q2	Q3	Q4	Total
	$'000	$'000	$'000	$'000	$'000
Revenue	8,760	8,979	9,204	9,434	36,377
Cost of sales	4,818	4,939	5,062	5,189	20,008
Gross profit	3,942	4,040	4,142	4,245	16,369
Distribution costs	789	808	829	849	3,275
Administration costs	2,107	2,107	2,107	2,107	8,428
Operating profit	1,046	1,125	1,206	1,289	4,666

The actual figures for Quarter 1 (which has just completed) are:

	$'000
Revenue	8,966
Cost of sales	4,932
Gross profit	4,034
Distribution costs	807
Administration costs	2,107
Operating profit	1,120

On the basis of the Q1 results, sales volume growth of 3% per quarter is now expected.

Required

Recalculate the budget for Quench Co using rolling budgeting and assess the use of rolling budgets in this context.

(8 marks)

Solution

3 Evaluating budget variances

Budgets enable managers to manage by exception; that is, focus on areas where things are not going to plan (ie the exceptions). This is done by comparing the actual performance to the budgets to identify the **variances**.

However, the reason a budget is not achieved may sometimes be because the budget itself was unrealistic. If this is the case, the budget may need to be revised. Only realistic budgets can form a credible basis for control.

Essential reading

The *Performance Management* (PM) syllabus at Applied Skills level requires candidates to be able to calculate, identify the cause of, and explain planning and operational variances for: sales, materials and labour and also to be able to calculate a revised budget.

For this reason, these topics are assumed knowledge for *Advanced Performance Management*. However, we have included a brief recap of different types of variances in Chapter 3 Section 2 of the Essential reading.

Section 3 of the Essential reading also illustrates how flexed budgets need to be used in variance analysis when the actual volume of output differs from that anticipated in the budget.

The Essential reading is available as an Appendix of the digital edition of the Workbook.

3.1 Planning vs operating variances

When variances are reported in a system of budgetary control, it is often assumed that:
(a) The original budget is fairly accurate or reliable; and
(b) Any differences between actual results and the budget, measured as variances, are attributable to the manager who is responsible for that aspect of performance.

The manager responsible will then, typically, be expected to explain the reasons for any significant variances and, where appropriate, take measures to rectify problems causing an adverse variance.

However, changes in the external environment (eg a significant downturn in economic conditions) may mean that it is no longer realistic to compare performance to the original budget.

The external factors also mean that variances are (at least in part) due to changes that are outside the control of operational managers (ie due to planning factors). So, when reporting variances, a distinction needs to be made between planning and operational variances:

Planning variances
- Variances caused by problems in the original budget, or external factors which mean the original budget is no longer realistic.
- Operational managers should **not be held responsible** for these variances.

Operational variances

- Variances caused by difference between actual performance and a revised budget (adjusted for planning variances).
- These variances are within the operational manager's control, so the manager **should be held responsible and accountable for these.**

3.2 Revising a budget

If there has been a change in circumstances which is beyond the control of an organisation, but which makes the original budget unsuitable for use in performance management, then the budget should be **revised**.

However, a budget should **only be revised** for items that are **beyond the control** of the organisation. A budget must not be revised for operational issues. In some cases, it can be difficult to establish which variances are due to operational issues, and which are due to planning issues.

3.3 Advantages of revising the budget

Revising the budget:

(a) Highlights those variances which are **controllable** and those which are not

(b) Ensures that operational performance is appraised by reference to **realistic targets**

(c) Helps to improve the accuracy of **future budgets**

3.4 Disadvantages of revising the budget

The following are disadvantages of revising the budget:

(a) The revised budget may be **biased**. The budget might be revised in such a way that all reported operational variances become favourable, and the reason why actual results are worse than budget is attributable entirely to planning variances.

   In order to prevent manipulation and bias, revision should be based on independent and verifiable evidence that operational managers are not in a position to manipulate.

(b) Use of revised budget may **undermine original budget** as a target and as a motivator.

Activity 2: Anzo Co

Anzo Co makes a range of precision parts for two large vehicle manufacturers. The strategy of the business has been to be a leader in flexible, high-quality manufacturing.

The CEO has asked for your assistance in understanding the key variances from the latest operating statement and possible action to be taken as a result of these specific variances.

Operating statement (extract) for Anzo Co for 20X4

	Favourable	Adverse
	$'000	$'000
Sales variances		
Volume		1,050
Price	448	
Cost variances		
Total	1,063	

	Favourable	Adverse
	$'000	$'000
Detailed variances		
Cost variances		
Planning	660	
Operational	403	
Sales price variances		
Planning		180
Operational	628	

The budget profit for 20X4 was $17.5 million.

Required

Advise the CEO on the implications for performance management at Anzo Co of analysing variances into the planning and operational elements as shown above. **(8 marks)**

Solution

Essential reading

Controllability can be a particular issue when assessing a manager's performance because managers should only be held accountable for those aspects of performance they can control. The concept of controllability is covered in Chapter 8 but is introduced in the context of cost control in Chapter 3 Section 4 of the Essential reading.

The Essential reading is available as an Appendix of the digital edition of the Workbook.

Chapter summary

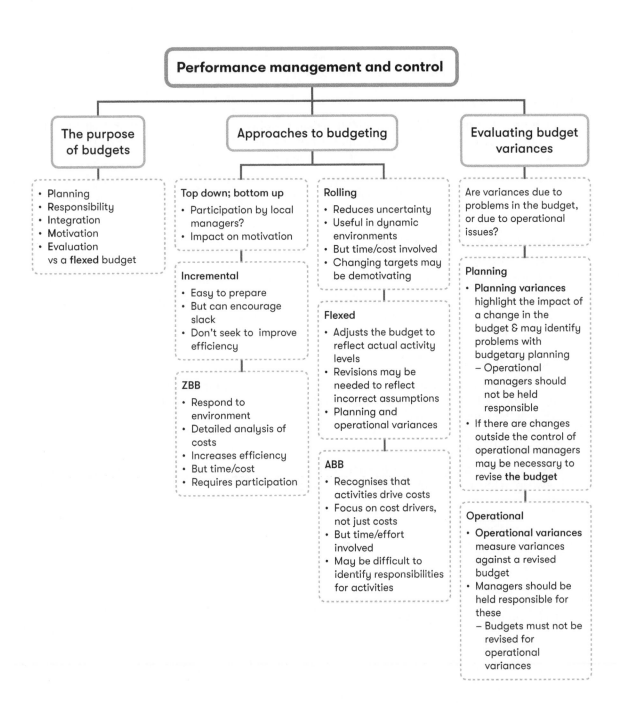

Performance management and control

The purpose of budgets

- Planning
- Responsibility
- Integration
- Motivation
- Evaluation
  vs a **flexed** budget

Approaches to budgeting

Top down; bottom up
- Participation by local managers?
- Impact on motivation

Incremental
- Easy to prepare
- But can encourage slack
- Don't seek to improve efficiency

ZBB
- Respond to environment
- Detailed analysis of costs
- Increases efficiency
- But time/cost
- Requires participation

Rolling
- Reduces uncertainty
- Useful in dynamic environments
- But time/cost involved
- Changing targets may be demotivating

Flexed
- Adjusts the budget to reflect actual activity levels
- Revisions may be needed to reflect incorrect assumptions
- Planning and operational variances

ABB
- Recognises that activities drive costs
- Focus on cost drivers, not just costs
- But time/effort involved
- May be difficult to identify responsibilities for activities

Evaluating budget variances

Are variances due to problems in the budget, or due to operational issues?

Planning
- **Planning variances** highlight the impact of a change in the budget & may identify problems with budgetary planning
  - Operational managers should not be held responsible
- If there are changes outside the control of operational managers may be necessary to revise **the budget**

Operational
- **Operational variances** measure variances against a revised budget
- Managers should be held responsible for these
  - Budgets must not be revised for operational variances

Knowledge diagnostic

1. Purpose of budgets

Budgets are designed to achieve better performance through planning, communication, motivation, performance evaluation and control.

2. Approaches to budgets

The type of budget model an organisation uses should reflect the context in which it operates. Traditional (incremental) budgeting models can criticised for their lack of flexibility to environmental factors and their ability to encourage inefficiency.

Zero-based models may be more appropriate for achieving cost control and rolling budgets may be appropriate in dynamic environments. But organisations need to consider the time and cost required by these types of budget.

3. Importance of variance analysis

Analysing the differences between actual results and expected results – and understanding the reasons for those differences – is a vital part of controlling performance.

However, it is inevitable that costs will vary as the volume of activity changes. Therefore, a flexible budget should be used for control purposes, if the volume of activity in a period is different to that originally planned.

4. Planning variances

Planning variances reflect error in the original budget, or changes to the assumptions in the original budget. If the original assumptions in the budget are no longer valid, it may be necessary to revise the budget.

5. Operational variances

Operational variances are those which are within a manager's control. They are the difference between actual performance and the revised budget.

Further study guidance

Question practice

Now try the following from the Further question practice bank (available in the digital edition of the Workbook):

Q4 *Kitch Co*

Activity answers

Activity 1: Quench Co

A rolling budget is one where the budget is kept up to date by adding another accounting period when the most recent one expires. The budget is then rerun using the new actual data as a basis.

For Quench Co, with its quarterly forecasting. This would work by adding another quarter to the budget and then rebudgeting for the next four quarters.

Rolling budgets are suitable when the business environment is changing rapidly (which is likely to be the case here) or when the business unit needs to be tightly controlled (which may not be valid here since managers are complaining about control).

The new budget at Quench Co would be:

	Current year					Next year
	Q1	Q2	Q3	Q4	Total	Q1
	$'000	$'000	$'000	$'000	$'000	$'000
Revenue	8,966	9,235	9,512	9,797	37,510	10,091
Cost of sales	4,932	5,080	5,232	5,389	20,633	5,551
Gross profit	4,034	4,155	4,280	4,408	16,877	4,540
Distribution costs	807	831	856	882	3,376	908
Administration costs	2,107	2,107	2,107	2,107	8,428	2,107
Operating profit	1,120	1,217	1,317	1,419	5,073	1,525

This is based on the assumptions that cost of sales and distribution costs increase in line with sales and that administration costs are fixed as in the original budget.

The budget now reflects the rapid growth of the division. Using rolling budgets like this will avoid the problem of managers trying to control costs using too small a budget and, as a result, choking off the growth of the business. This may explain some of the quality issues that Quench Co is experiencing.

The rolling budgets will require additional resources as they now have to be done each quarter rather than annually; but the benefits of giving management a clearer picture and more realistic targets outweigh this concern.

Poor budgeting is probably at the core of the manager's desire to be less controlled. Rolling budgets could be seen as a tightening of control, so it may also be worth considering changing the style of management control being used.

Note. Management control styles are discussed in more detail in Chapter 12 later.

Indicative marking scheme

Explanation of rolling budgets – up to 2 marks

Actual figures in Q1 – 1 mark

Revised budget figures for Q2–Q4 – 1 mark per item (revenue, cost of sales, distribution, admin) to a max of 4 marks

Inclusion of Q1 next year – 1 mark

Comments on the use of rolling budgets – 1 mark per point, max 3 marks

Activity 2: Anzo Co

Planning variances result from the assumptions or standards used in the original budget-setting process not being accurate. For example, if the original budget assumed that industry sales volumes would rise by 2%, but in fact they increased by 3%, the resulting sales volume variance should be treated as a favourable planning variance. So, a planning variance is the difference between the original budget and the budget as it would have been with the benefit of hindsight.

Operational variances are the differences between this 'revised' budget and actual performance. Operational variances result from the decisions of operational managers, rather than issues with the original budget-setting process.

Total cost variance

The total cost variance considers a number of costs together, and as such is hard to interpret or to act on. However, the total variance is over 5% of budget profit and as such should be investigated.

Although the variance is favourable there is the danger that the company is compromising on quality to drive down its input costs – perhaps as an attempt to deal with its adverse sales volume variance. If so, this would be potentially very damaging given Anzo's precision manufacturing strategy.

However, the favourable planning variance suggests that the budget costs have been set too high, and therefore most of the apparent cost improvements are due to this.

The budget-setting process should be reviewed to investigate whether there is an issue with managers padding their budgets by making overly conservative assumptions.

Sales price variance

The sales price variance indicates the extent to which sales prices were incorrectly estimated in the budget (planning variances) and how effective the sales managers have been in negotiating higher prices with customers (operational variances).

The adverse planning variance suggests that the original budget was too optimistic. The initial price-setting process should be examined, to identify why prices were budgeted too high. For example, market intelligence about the prices being set by competitors or the commercial situation of its customers may have been faulty.

However, the favourable operational variance suggests that the sales managers may have been quite successful in their price negotiations with customers.

We should also assess whether the higher prices indicated by the favourable operational variance are linked to the significant adverse sales volume variance.

Skills checkpoint 2

Creating a coherent performance management framework

Overview

Introduction

In Section A3 of the APM syllabus you are introduced to the idea of a 'performance hierarchy', ie the need for a **coherent performance management framework** starting from an organisation's mission statement, linking into critical success factors and then cascading down into key performance indicators.

This theme is revisited in later areas of the syllabus (for example, performance measurement models like Lynch & Cross's performance pyramid, or value-based management in Section E of the syllabus) and as a result could influence many questions in both sections of the exam.

In the APM exam you are expected have a strong skill base in terms of understanding mission statements, critical success factors and key performance indicators, and being able to apply these to the scenario presented in a question to assess whether an organisation has a **coherent performance management framework**, or to recommend ways its framework could be improved.

However, it is important to be aware that there may be legitimate criticisms to be made of this approach (especially over the usefulness of mission statements). Critical evaluation is encouraged at APM (where relevant to the question) and is covered in Skills Checkpoint 4.

APM Skill: Creating a coherent performance management framework

The key steps in applying this skill are outlined below and will be explained in more detail in the following sections, and illustrated by answering a requirement from the question 'CFD'.

> **STEP 1:**
>
> A good starting point in many APM questions is to identify the mission or objectives of an organisation. In Section A questions, an organisation's mission and/or objectives will normally be given. This will give you a feel for the organisation's strategy, and what is important to it. To help the organisation succeed, a coherent performance management framework, consistent with the mission and objectives, will be required.

> **STEP 2:**
>
> Creating a coherent framework will involve identifying areas that are critical to an organisation's strategic success; ie its critical success factors (CSFs). CSFs should be consistent with the organisation's mission and objectives, and could focus on day-to-day, operational issues as well as longer-term capabilities. CSFs may either be given in a question scenario, or you may need to suggest suitable ones.

> **STEP 3:**
>
> Questions may either require criticism of existing key performance indicators (KPIs) or the identification of new KPIs, often using a table of data (creating information from data is covered in Skills Checkpoint 1). Ensure that you choose KPIs that relate to CSFs/mission, and make use of data provided. Make the links between CSFs/KPIs and mission clear in your narrative answer.

Exam success skills

The following illustration is based on an extract from a past exam question, about a company called CFD (Care For Dogs). This extract was worth approximately 14 marks. Although this is not a recent exam question it provides a useful introduction to the skill of 'creating a coherent performance framework' - a skill that is commonly examined.

For this question, we will also focus on the following **exam success skills**:

- **Managing information.** It is easy to feel that the amount of information contained in scenario-based questions is overwhelming. **Active reading** is a useful technique to use to avoid this. This involves focusing on the requirement first, on the basis that until you have done this the detail in the question will have little meaning.

  Focus on the requirement(s), underlining the key verb or verbs to ensure you answer the question properly. Then read the rest of the question, underlining and annotating important and relevant information, and making notes of any relevant technical information you think you will need.

- **Correct interpretation of requirements.** Multi-part requirements are common in APM exam questions, so it is important to identify all aspects of the question. It is also important to consider the meaning of the verbs used in the exam question.

- **Effective writing and presentation.** It is often helpful to use key words from the requirement as headings in your answer. You may also wish to use sub-headings in your answer. Underline your headings and sub-headings, and write in full sentences, ensuring your style is professional.

- **Good time management.** Complete all requirements in the time available. APM marking schemes normally allocate 1 mark per relevant point made. So, while you need to explain your point and why it matters in the scenario, you should not write at length on a single point (unless there are many different aspects to that point that need to be explained).

Skills activity

Look at the requirements of the question in order to understand the scope of the question. Identify the mission of the company to understand the performance management approaches that are likely to be relevant.

Required

(a) Advise[13] the directors of CFD regarding the appropriateness of its mission statement.

                                                                    (4 marks)

[13] Key verb

(b) **Discuss**[14]**THREE** critical success factors for CFD, **and**[15] highlight a key performance indicator for each critical success factor.

                                                                    (7 marks)

[14] Key verb

[15] Multi-part requirement

(c) Excluding the number of complaints by clients, identify **and**[16] briefly **explain**[17]**THREE** quantitative non-financial performance measures that could be used to assess the 'quality of service' provided by CFD.

                                                                    (3 marks)
                                                              (Total = 14 marks)

[16] Multi-part requirement

[17] Key verb

The first key action verb is **'advise'**. This is asking you to express an opinion, explaining and justifying the basis for this opinion.

The second verb is **'discuss'**. This is defined by the ACCA as 'Consider and debate/argue about the pros and cons of an issue. Examine in detail by using arguments in favour or against'. In the context of part (b), the verb 'discuss' is asking you to examine your chosen CSFs in a critical way where appropriate.

The final verb is **'explain'**. This is defined by the ACCA as 'Make an idea clear. Show logically how a concept is developed. Give the reason for an event'. It is important here not to produce brief unexplained bullet points.

This is a 14-mark question and at 1.95 minutes a mark, it should take 27 minutes.

Assuming that you are spending approximately 20% of your time reading and planning, this time should be split approximately as follows:

• Reading and planning time – 5 minutes

- Writing up your answer – 22 minutes

- Writing time (1.95 × 0.8 = 1.56 mins per mark) breaks down into 6 minutes for part (a), 11 minutes for (b) and 5 minutes for part (c).

Next, read through the question, and where mission/CSFs/KPIs are featured take careful note of the company's mission and strategy. Make notes in the margins of the question.

Question – CFD (14 marks)

The Care For Dogs Company (CFD) is a very profitable organisation which was established in 1998. CFD offers accommodation, care and supervision for pet dogs owned by inhabitants of Barkland.

CFD provides temporary accommodation for dogs whose owners are unable to care for them due to holidays, work commitments, illness etc. As part of the service offered to dog owners, CFD collects and returns dogs at the beginning and end of all dog stays.

When CFD was formed, the directors created a mission statement which was 'to provide very high value for money to all of our clients'[18].

[18] Here is the mission statement. However, we know from the requirements that it may not be appropriate.

The directors have always attempted to manage CFD in a socially responsible manner[19]. Indeed, they are now considering the creation of a 'Dog Sanctuary' for homeless dogs which would involve an allocation of 20% of the total accommodation available for dogs to the Dog Sanctuary. The Dog Sanctuary would accommodate homeless dogs until a new owner was found for them. CFD would not receive any revenue whatsoever in respect of any homeless dog.

[19] Not consistent with the current mission statement?

STEP 2 Identifying critical success factors (CSFs) will depend on what areas you feel the mission statement should in fact be addressing.

CSFs should be consistent with the company's mission and could focus on day-to-day, operational issues as well as longer-term capabilities.

Question – CFD (14 marks)

The Care For Dogs Company (CFD) is a very profitable organisation which was established in 1998. CFD offers accommodation, care and supervision[20] for pet dogs owned by inhabitants of Barkland.

CFD provides temporary accommodation for dogs whose owners are unable to care for them due to holidays, work commitments, illness etc. As part of the service offered to dog owners, CFD collects and returns dogs at the beginning and end of all dog stays.

When CFD was formed, the directors created a mission statement which was 'to provide very high value for money to all of our clients'.

The directors have always attempted to manage CFD in a socially responsible manner. Indeed, they are now considering the creation of a 'Dog Sanctuary' for homeless dogs[21] which would involve an allocation of 20% of the total accommodation available for dogs to the Dog Sanctuary. The Dog Sanctuary would accommodate homeless dogs until a new owner was found for them. CFD would not receive any revenue whatsoever in respect of any homeless dog.

STEP 3 Ensure that you choose KPIs (or performance measures) that relate to CSFs and mission. Make the links between CSFs/KPIs and mission clear in your narrative answer.

Solution

(a) Appropriateness of the mission statement for CFD[22]

A mission is meant to capture the purpose of an entity, ie its reason for existence.[23]

Value for money involves providing a service in a way which is economical, efficient and effective, and so CFD's mission statement would appear to have accorded with its overall performance[24] (as it is highly profitable).

[20] What day to day competences will this require? And longer-term competences?

[21] Not consistent with the current mission statement?

[22] Use headings from the requirement.

[23] It is good to define your terms – but only briefly. Don't write in general terms about mission statements at length.

[24] 'Advice' does not have to be completely 'critical'.

Even so, the existing mission statement does not capture CFD's reason for existence, nor does it act as a guide to key stakeholders (such as employees). In order to do this it would need to mention the company's core strategy (high quality care?). In this sense it is not appropriate.

In addition, when CFD decided to open a homeless sanctuary for strays, as a free service[25], then value for money was not the driving force and so ceases to be an accurate reflection of its mission. Therefore the mission statement as it currently stands is certainly not appropriate, if it ever was.

(b) **CSFs** are the key factors and processes which enable an organisation to achieve its objectives and thereby achieve future success. In effect, CSFs highlight the areas in which it is crucial for an organisation to perform well in order for it to be successful.[26]

Key Performance Indicators (KPIs) are the **measures** which indicate whether or not CSFs are being achieved, and how well the organisation is performing. This idea of measurement is vital for KPIs. KPIs must be measurable, because otherwise an organisation will not be able to measure whether or not its CSFs are being achieved.

CFD is a service business and its CSFs are likely to relate to the quality of the services that it offers[27], and in particular to the features of those services which are valued by its customers.

(i) Maintaining a high standard of cleanliness of accommodation for the dogs at CFD.

If prospective clients come to visit CFD's kennels and the kennels look dirty and untidy, it is unlikely that the owners will want their pets to stay at CFD.[28]

[25] Apply each point to the scenario.

[26] Again start with a brief definition.

[27] Apply CSF to your understanding of the mission/strategy/values of CFD, as you understand them.

[28] Explain why your proposed measure matters in this scenario. Weaker answers fail to do this.

A KPI which could be used to measure cleanliness could be the number of cleans made per day or week of the dog kennels and common areas. However, this would not take into account the quality of the cleaning[29]. So customer assessment of cleanliness would be better.

[29] An element of critical analysis is appropriate in a 'discuss' question, where relevant.

(ii) Guaranteed safety of the dogs while in CFD's care.

Again, owners are not going to want to use CFD to care for their dogs unless they feel confident their dogs will be well looked after.

This could be measured by the number of accidents over a given period[30]. However this would not take into account the severity of accidents, so the number of major and minor accidents could be a better measure.

[30] Remember, you need to discuss each CSF, and then go on to identify a suitable performance measure for it.

(iii) An excellent health record.

This means no or minimal breakout of infections which would damage the reputation of the business. This could become particularly important if CFD does start accommodating homeless dogs, because if any of the homeless dogs have got infections or diseases it will need to ensure that none of these get transmitted to the pets in its care.

This could be measured by the number of dogs that fall ill during their time at CFD.

(c) **Three quantitative non-financial performance measures to assess quality of service**

- **Service availability.** This may be measured as the number of booking days lost through non-availability.

- Care taken of the dogs and the quality of the service experience.[31] This could be quantified by measuring the percentage of customers that are return bookings.

[31] Points should be relevant to the scenario and concise.

- **Prompt and reliable collection and return of dogs to their owners.** This is a key element of the service offered. This could be measured by logs of delivery and return of dogs safely and within the time promised.

Note. Other points could clearly be made. For example, a longer-term CSF would involve having highly trained staff. This could be measured be average length of employment of staff, or number of training days per staff member.

Exam success skills diagnostic

Every time you complete a question, use the diagnostic below to assess how effectively you demonstrated the exam success skills in answering the question. The table has been completed below for the CFD activity to give you an idea of how to complete the diagnostic.

Exam success skills	Your reflections/observations
Managing information	Did you read the requirements first so that you understood that the mission provided in the question was potentially not adequate, before reading the scenario?
Correct interpretation of requirements	Did you understand what was meant by the action verbs? Did you spot the requirement for three CSFs and three KPIs in part (b)?
Effective writing and presentation	Did you use headings (key words from requirements)? Did you use full sentences? Did you relate each of your points to the scenario?
Good time management	Did you allow yourself time to address all requirements?
Most important action points to apply to your next question	

Summary

A key principle underlying the APM syllabus is that effective performance management requires a coherent and logical performance management framework.

In order to help increase its chance of being successful, an organisation should have a clear sense of direction (mission; objectives), and an understanding of the areas it needs to perform well in in order to succeed, both now and in the future (CSFs). In turn, these CSFs should define the organisation's KPIs.

It is vital in APM that you are able to comment on an organisation's existing performance management framework, and recommend improvements to the elements of a performance hierarchy (objectives; CSFs; KPIs) in a way which would help the organisation identified in a question scenario to **create a coherent performance management framework.**

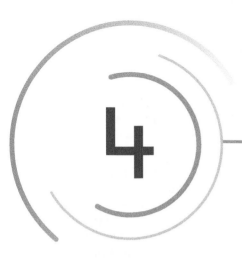

4 Organisational change, environmental and ethical issues

Learning objectives

On completion of this chapter, you should be able to:

	Syllabus reference no.
Identify and discuss the particular information needs of organisations adopting a functional, divisional or network form and the implications for performance management.	A4(a)
Assess the changes to management accounting systems to reflect the needs of modern service-orientated businesses compared with the needs of a traditional manufacturing industry.	A4(b)
Assess the influence of business process re-engineering on systems development and improvements in organisational performance.	A4(c)
Analyse the role that performance management systems play in business integration using models such as the value chain and McKinsey's 7Ss.	A4(d)
Discuss how changing an organisation's structure, culture and strategy will influence the adoption of new performance measurement methods and techniques.	A4(e)
Assess the need for businesses to continually refine and develop their management accounting and information systems if they are to maintain or improve their performance in an increasingly competitive and global market.	A4(f)
Discuss the ways in which stakeholder groups operate and how they influence an organisation and its performance measurement and performance management systems (eg using Mendelow's matrix).	A5(a)
Discuss the social and ethical issues that may impact on strategy formulation, and consequently, business performance (e.g. sustainability).	A5(b)
Discuss, evaluate and apply environmental management accounting using, for example, life cycle costing, input-output analysis and activity-based costing.	A5(c)

Exam context

One of the key themes in this chapter is the way the structure of an organisation affects **the information requirements** within that organisation, particularly in relation to the way that changing organisational structures could lead to changing information requirements. We also revisit this idea in Chapter 14 when we consider performance management issues in complex business structures.

Another important point to remember is that operational managers (rather than accountants alone) are making increasing use of management information for control and decision-making purposes, so an organisation's information systems need to be able to provide these users with the information they require. Accountants in business could be expected to contribute to the development of management accounting systems and internal reporting.

In Chapter 1, when we discussed strategic management accounting, we highlighted the importance of considering external as well as internal factors in planning and control. This chapter continues this idea: for example, by noting the potential influence that different **stakeholder** groups could have on an organisation's strategy and performance. The chapter also covers **environmental management accounting** which considers the (quite topical) issue of how organisations could measure their impact on the environment and how this could affect business decisions.

Alongside this, the chapter also looks at some important frameworks for analysing organisations' internal structure and operations – for example, **Porter's value chain**, **McKinsey's 7Ss**, and **business process re-engineering**.

Chapter overview

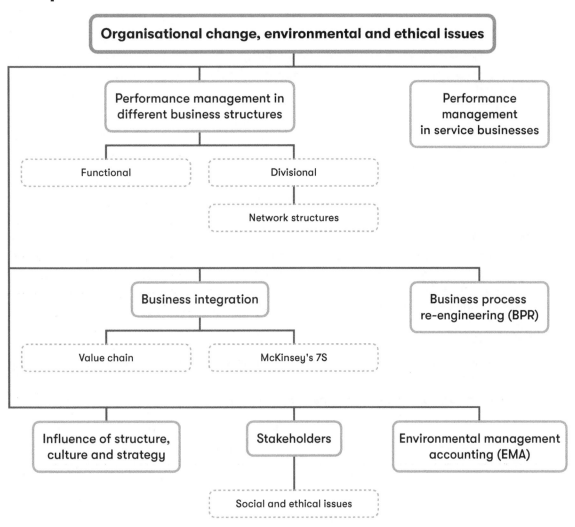

1 Performance management in different business structures

1.1 Functional

Functional departments are based on segregation of skills and responsibilities and are typically the first form of delegation. Planning and control in functional organisations tends to be **centralised**.

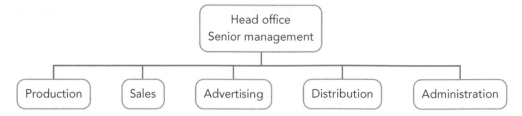

Information needs

- Information will be needed to support each **individual department**. This will often take the form of a variance report showing how efficiently departmental tasks are being carried out.

- However, the focus on individual departments can mean people **lack understanding of how an organisation works as a whole** (eg which products or markets are profitable).

1.2 Divisional

As businesses grow, they will need to devolve some power to lower-level managers and create autonomous divisions.

These may be based on **product ranges or market segments**.

Divisional performance measures will need to be created that reflect the areas that are **controllable** by divisional management. There will also be performance management issues arising from divisions trading with each other.

Both of these issues are covered later, in Chapter 8.

Information needs

- Divisional managers need a **clear understanding** of the **organisation's strategy** and objectives, in order to ensure their divisions perform in line with that strategy ('congruence').

- Divisional managers need **access to performance information** because they have a key role in budgeting and monitoring performance.

- Head office also needs information about **divisional performance** to assess whether divisions are performing in line with head office's objectives.

1.3 Network structures

Network organisations outsource many processes, on the basis that they can be done better or more cheaply externally, rather than 'in-house'.

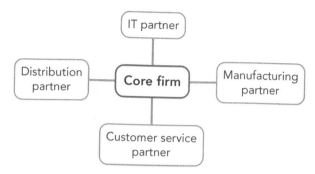

Success depends on the relationship between the 'core' organisation and its network partners.

Co-ordinating and controlling relationships with network partners is an important part of managers' roles in network structures. Performance management initiatives need to focus on improving performance across the whole **value network**. This is discussed further in Chapter 14.

Information characteristics and requirements

* The flow of information **between the network partners plays a key role in connecting the elements of the network.** Communication tends to be lateral (between network partners) rather than vertical. Information and advice are shared, rather than instructions and decisions being given. This is discussed further in Chapter 14.

* Access to **common data** for all network partners is vital (eg to avoid disputes around levels of performance shown by one partner's 'in-house' data which is different to another's). This is discussed further in Chapter 6.

2 Performance management in service businesses

It has been argued that performance management for modern service-based firms creates extra challenges (compared to traditional manufacturing) because services are:

Simultaneous: Production and consumption occur **at the same time.**

Heterogeneous: The service **varies** from day to day or employee to employee.

Intangible: No physical offering to assess customer value.

Perishable: Services only last for a period of time and **cannot be stored.** (Services also do **not** result in any **transfer of ownership.**)

As a result, it could be argued that performance management will need to adapt, for example:

(a) Information requirements of service businesses will be **broader than those of manufacturers**

(b) More **qualitative information** will be required concerning **customer satisfaction** and **employee morale**

(c) **Most of the expenses in service businesses are overheads,** making activity-based cost information more valuable

Activity 1: Service business

Using the example of a dentist's service, explain the characteristics that differentiate service businesses from manufacturing ones, using the following headings:

Simultaneous

Heterogenous

Intangible

Perishable

(6 marks)

Solution

Essential reading

See Chapter 4 Section 1 of the Essential reading for more detail about the characteristics of services, and the importance of maintaining customer satisfaction and employee motivation levels in service businesses.

The Essential reading is available as an Appendix of the digital edition of the Workbook.

---

3 Business integration

Whatever business structure is adopted, there needs to be **integration** between the parts of the business to ensure that **activities are co-ordinated**, and that the business **creates value**.

Performance management can be enhanced by the use of the **value chain** (*Porter, 1985*) or McKinsey's 7S model (*Peters & Waterman, 1982*) to enhance the **linkages between activities**.

3.1 Value chain

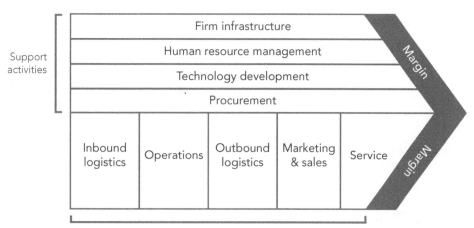

(Source: *Porter, 1985: p.46*)

(a) Activities in the value chain **affect one another**. For example, more costly product design or better quality production might reduce the need for after-sales service.

(b) Linkages require **co-ordination**. For example, just-in-time requires smooth functioning of operations, outbound logistics and service activities such as installation.

Essential reading

See Chapter 4 Section 2 of the Essential reading for more detail about Porter's value chain.

The Essential reading is available as an Appendix of the digital edition of the Workbook.

An organisation can use the value chain to **improve performance** in the following ways:

(a) Invent new or better ways to perform activities

(b) Combine activities in new or better ways

(c) Manage the linkages in its own value chain

(d) Manage the linkages in the value system with other companies

3.1.1 The value chain and performance management

Value chain analysis helps an organisation identify the activities which create value for its customers, and therefore those activities which it needs to perform more effectively than its competitors.

This has two important implications for performance management:

(a) The organisation needs to ensure that it is measuring its performance in **those key areas which create value for its customers** (ie its critical success factors).

(b) In order to assess how effectively it is performing activities and processes, an organisation **needs to compare its performance** against others. This suggests that **benchmarking** (see Chapter 1) could be useful here.

3.1.2 Value chain and Porter's generic strategies

Porter (1980) argues that, to compete successfully, a firm needs to either be the lowest cost producer (cost leadership strategy), or differentiate its products in a way which customers value (differentiation strategy). To be successful in such strategies, an organisation needs to ensure that the activities in its value chain are **consistent with each other**, and with its **strategy.**

Refer back to Chapter 1 (Section 3.4) for the implications for performance management of an organisation choosing a cost leadership or differentiation strategy.

Illustration 1: Value chain

How does the nature of the activities in the value chain for a fast food restaurant differ from those in a fine dining (eg Michelin-starred) restaurant? How do the differences in the nature of the activities reflect the different strategies the restaurants are pursuing?

Solution

The focus of the fast-food restaurants is likely to be on high volume, standardisation, and keeping costs low, while the fine dining restaurants focus on high quality, and customer experience.

3.2 McKinsey 7S model

McKinsey's 7S model (*Peters & Waterman, 1982*) provides another framework for looking at business integration.

The model was designed to show how the various aspects of a business relate to one another, and it characterises the aspects of the business as seven 'S's.

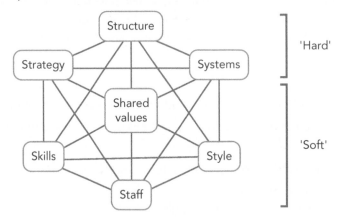

McKinsey 7S model (after *Peters & Waterman, 1982*)

The **'hard' elements** are relatively easily quantified and defined.

(1) **Structure**. This is the organisation structure (as discussed in Section 1).

(2) **Strategy**. How the organisation plans to outperform its competitors.

(3) **Systems**. These are the processes and procedures of the company, including the accounting, HR and management information systems.

Soft elements are equally important.

(4) **Style** refers to the way the company is managed by senior management, what they focus on, and how they conduct themselves.

(5) **Shared values** are the norms and standards that guide employee behaviour and create a sense of shared values.

(6) **Staff** refers to the type of employee recruited and how they are trained and motivated.

(7) **Skills** refer to those things that the organisation does well, ie its competences.

All elements, both hard and soft, **must be aligned for the organisation to be effective**.

For example, systems should be supported by skills, and strategy needs to be underpinned by appropriate shared values.

If an organisation identifies that some of the elements are not properly aligned, it can then assess what needs to change, before undertaking the necessary realignment.

4 Business process re-engineering (BPR)

The value chain and 7S models highlight that organisations deliver value to their customers through processes and activities. Improvements in key processes (ones linked directly to objectives or CSFs) are likely to lead to improved performance and competitiveness.

These are the processes which an organisation should look to improve in a business process re-engineering (BPR) exercise.

4.1 BPR

> **Business process re-engineering (BPR):** 'The fundamental rethinking and radical redesign of business processes to achieve dramatic improvements in ... critical measures of performance, such as cost, quality, service and speed' (*Hammer & Champy, 2001, p. 35*).

BPR seeks a **fundamental** redesign of business processes, to achieve **dramatic** improvements in performance. (A just-in-time (JIT) system, covered in Chapter 11, is an example of a re-engineered process.)

A **re-engineered process** has certain characteristics.

(a) Often several jobs are combined into one; this may require workers to be retrained

(b) Workers often make decisions

(c) The steps in the process are performed in a logical order

(d) Work is performed where it makes most sense

(e) Checks and controls may be reduced, and quality 'built-in'

Potential impact of BPR on organisations

- Work units change from functional departments to process teams
- Multi-skilling within process teams
- Performance measures concentrate on results rather than activities; process teams create 'value' which is measurable
- Organisational structures are de-layered; move from hierarchical to flat
- As a process is the work of a whole team, managing the process is the team's responsibility

Implications of BPR for accounting systems

- **Performance measurement** – As performance measures must be built around processes, not departments, this may affect the design of responsibility centres.
- **Reporting** – Need to identify where value is being added in processes, to ensure performance of key value-adding areas is monitored. New **KPIs** and new **variances** may have to be developed.
- **Structure** – The structure of the reporting system will depend on the organisational structure. Reports may need to be redesigned around processes rather than departments.

Essential reading

See Chapter 4 Section 3 of the Essential reading for more detail about BPR and some of the potential problems with it.

The Essential reading is available as an Appendix of the digital edition of the Workbook.

5 Influence of structure, culture and strategy

One of the consequences of business change (eg changing business structures, process re-engineering or the development of new technologies more generally) is that organisations may need to change the ways they measure performance.

Similarly, businesses may need to refine and develop their management accounting and information systems in order to maintain their performance in an increasingly competitive and global market.

Essential reading

See Chapter 4 Section 4 of the Essential reading for more detail about the influence of structure, culture and strategy on performance measurement methods.

Also, see Chapter 4 Section 5 of the Essential reading for more detail about the need to refine information systems as firms compete in global markets.

The Essential reading is available as an Appendix of the digital edition of the Workbook.

6 Stakeholders

> **Stakeholders:** Groups or individuals who have an interest in the strategy and activities of an organisation.

Organisations should take account of the interests of their key stakeholders when developing strategies and objectives.

Stakeholder group	Examples
Internal	Employees, management
Connected	Shareholders, customers, suppliers, lenders (banks)
External	Government, local community, pressure groups

In the context of performance management, it is important to consider how the interests and influence of different stakeholder groups can affect the organisation's performance (eg if key customers are unhappy about product quality, then an organisation will need to take action to improve product quality).

It could also be important to consider how the interests of key stakeholder groups influence the performance metrics the organisation chooses to measure (For example, is the organisation measuring the aspects of performance which its key stakeholders are interested in?).

Mendelow's (power/interest) matrix *(Mendelow, 1991)* can be used to **identify the key stakeholders**:

		Interest	
		Low	High
Power	Low	Minimal Effort	Keep Informed
	High	Keep Satisfied	Key Players

Stakeholders can influence the strategy adopted by an organisation, and its performance in relation to those strategies. Powerful stakeholders therefore require careful management.

The need to consider the objectives of different stakeholder groups is recognised in multi-dimensional performance measurement techniques, such as the balanced scorecard (covered in Chapter 13).

Essential reading

See Chapter 4 Section 6 of the Essential reading for more detail about stakeholders' needs from an organisation, and an organisation's needs from its stakeholders.

The Essential reading is available as an Appendix of the digital edition of the Workbook.

PER alert

Performance objective 2 – Stakeholder relationship management – requires that you develop and maintain productive relationships with stakeholders, and so some of the issues which we have discussed in this chapter (for example, around identifying an organisation's key stakeholders, what their interests are, and how this influences the organisation's strategy and performance) could equally be questions you need to address in the workplace.

6.1 Social and ethical issues

As a business attempts to improve its performance, its operations may adversely impact on its environment/staff/society as a whole (for example, increasing levels of production could lead to increased levels of pollution and emissions from a factory).

Social attitudes, and legal and political pressures, mean that organisations can no longer concentrate solely on short-term financial objectives, but need to consider their wider social obligations (eg to the environment, to suppliers and employees). This can be summarised in the concept of (corporate) **social responsibility**.

Ethics and social responsibility can affect strategy and performance:

- A socially and environmentally ethical approach to strategy can assist an organisation's ability to prosper in the long run
- Strong ethical policies can add value to a brand
- Conversely, failing to act ethically, or responsibly, can cause social, economic and environmental damage, and can undermine an organisation's long-term reputation and prospects

Implications for performance measurement

Organisations can no longer concentrate solely on financial performance (particularly short-term financial performance). They also need to pay greater attention to the impact that they have on society.

Consequently, they need performance measures which address social and environmental issues, as well as others which monitor short-term financial performance.

7 Environmental management accounting (EMA)

Environmental management accounting (EMA): The generation and analysis of both financial and non-financial information in order to support internal environmental management processes.

Managers have no incentive to reduce environment-related costs if they are not even aware of them. **EMA allows an organisation to identify environment-related costs and take steps to control them.** Such costs are often categorised into conventional costs, contingent costs and reputation costs.

Conventional costs	These costs include the cost of environmental costs associated with production of a good (eg energy) which often remain hidden within overheads.
Contingent costs	These are costs which are incurred in the future, for example, the decommissioning costs of a mine to return the land to its previous condition.
Reputation costs	Reputation costs are incurred where an organisation acts in a way which may cause harm to the environment, and include sales lost as a result of loss of reputation. Marketing managers aware of these reputation costs should focus their attention on the need to manage the risks of them occurring.

EMA is becoming more important for a number of reasons:

(a) Increasing profile of environmental issues

(b) Increased reputation, litigation or financial risk caused by poor behaviour

(c) Concern that conventional accounting and information systems do not identify or control environmental costs

(d) Environmental management is a key component of total quality management (avoidance of waste)

Suitable management accounting techniques for EMA include:

• Activity-based costing

• Life cycle costing

7.1 Activity-based costing (ABC)

More companies are now identifying and measuring direct environmental costs by revising allocation bases so as to separate out indirect environmental costs using ABC.

Using ABC, environmental costs are removed from overhead costs and traced to products and services by identifying the resources, activities and costs used to produce the output.

Removing environmental costs from overhead costs and accurately allocating them to specific products results in far fewer distortions in product costing and provides useful control information for environmental management.

Activity 2: Fantasia Co

Fantasia, a glass manufacturer, has identified the following activities and cost drivers relating to environmental costs:

Activities	$'000	Cost drivers	'000
Preventing air pollution	2,450	Waste emissions kg	7
Preventing water pollution	3,520	Waste water output m³	1,600
General waste recycling & disposal	2,520	Kg of general waste	3.0
Hazardous waste recycling & disposal	3,680	Kg of recycled waste	1.6
Monitoring environmental impact	275	Internal audit hours	1.1
Environmental training	835	Training time (hours)	0.5
R&D related to environment	7,420	R&D hours	140
Total	20,700		

Fantasia makes two products – Products A and B.

Currently environmental costs are a part of Fantasia's general overhead pool and apportioned per unit. Fantasia produces 82,000 units of Product A and 8,000 units of Product B.

An ABC analysis of this environmental data has been prepared by a junior financial analyst who has now been transferred to another department. Her workings are correct but incomplete.

Cost driver charge out rates	
Waste emissions kg	$350 per kg
Waste water output m³	$2.2 per m³
Kg of general waste	$840 per kg
Kg of recycled waste	$2,300 per kg
Internal audit hours	$250 per hour
Training time (hours)	$1,670 per hour
R&D hours	$53 per hour

	Product A			Product B		
	Activity	Cost	Cost/Unit	Activity	Cost	Cost/Unit
	'000	$'000	$	'000	$'000	$
Air pollution	6.3	2,205	26.9	0.7	245	30.6
Water pollution	1,120	2,464	30.0			
General waste	2.7	2,268	27.7	0.3	252	31.5
Hazardous waste	0.8	1,840	22.4			
Monitoring	0.6	150	1.8	0.5	125	15.6
Training	0.3	501	6.1	0.2		
R&D	90	4,770	58.2	50		
Total			**173.1**			

Required

Complete the ABC analysis and comment on its implications for performance management.

(8 marks)

Solution

7.2 Life cycle costing

Life cycle costing estimates and records a product or project's costs over its whole life rather than for a single year, or a specific phase of the product life (ie the production phase).

Applying this concept to environmental issues can usefully highlight environmental costs incurred **prior** to production (eg compliance with environmental legislation) and costs incurred **after** production (eg cleaning up the site after production).

This can help to ensure that investment appraisal captures all the costs that are relevant to a project.

Activity 3: Filin Co

Filin Co is considering a new product which is expected to have a limited market life of three years. The accounting team have forecast the following data associated with this product and calculated Filin's traditional performance measure of product profit for the new product.

	20X2	20X3	20X4
	$m	$m	$m
Revenue	45.0	47.5	55.1
Costs			
Production costs	26.8	26.1	28.6
Marketing costs	8.0	6.0	5.0
Development costs	5.6	3.0	0.0
Product profit	4.6	12.4	21.5

Subsequently, the following environmental costs have been identified from Filin Co's general overheads as associated with the production of the new product.

	20X2	20X3	20X4
	$m	$m	$m
Waste filtration	2.7	2.7	2.7
Carbon dioxide exhaust extraction	1.7	1.8	1.8

Additionally, other costs associated with closing down and recycling the equipment involved in production and clearing up the site used for production are estimated at $18 million in 20X4.

Required

Evaluate the costing approach used for performance measurement compared to a life cycle costing approach, performing appropriate calculations. **(7 marks)**

Solution

7.3 Non-financial measures

The general importance of non-financial performance measures, which can include social, environmental and sustainability measures, is covered in Chapter 6 where we look at integrated reporting and also in more general terms in Chapter 10.

A specific example of the application of non-financial performance measurement to environmental management is **input/output analysis**.

Input/output analysis records physical material flows (eg materials/energy/water) and balances them with outflows (products/ waste/emissions) on the basis that what comes in must go out or be stored.

This provides **environmental information** to a business on:

- **Inputs,** eg type of energy being used and whether it is renewable or non-renewable
- **Outputs,** eg the amount of waste, and how much of this is being recycled.

This information may lead to **changes in working practices** that reduce the impact on the environment arising from the inputs acquired by a business, and the processes used to turn these inputs into outputs.

In order to use this approach, information systems would need to be capable of monitoring physical volumes of a variety of inputs and outputs.

Real life example

Crisps firm Walkers has analysed that potato waste, a **waste output** arising from the crisp-making process, can be used to produce methane gas which is burned to make electricity in the crisp-making process – saving on burning fossil fuel gas.

In 2020, Walkers also announced plans to work with a brewery to extract CO_2 from their beer making process and add this to potato waste to make a fertiliser for use in growing potatoes and thereby saving on the CO_2 emissions associated with fertilizer manufacture.

PER alert

Performance objective 3 – Strategy and innovation – highlights that you should be able to contribute to your organisation by identifying innovative business solutions to improve performance by making or recommending business process changes and improvements. Although these improvements may not be as dramatic as the changes generated by business process re-engineering (which we cover in Section 4 of this chapter), models such as the value chain (covered in Section 3) might identify ways of improving business processes.

A number of the elements in Performance objective 12 (PO 12) – Evaluate management accounting systems – also link to the topics in this chapter:

PO 12(a): 'Determine the appropriateness and adequacy of management accounting techniques and approaches in an organisation'

PO 12(d): 'Contribute to development and improvements of management accounting systems and internal reporting'

PO 12(e): 'Monitor new developments in management accounting and consider their potential impact on performance and to management accounting systems'

Chapter summary

Organisational change, environmental and ethical issues

Performance management in different business structures

Functional
- Advantages
  - Specialism
  - Economy of scale
- Disadvantages
  - Co-ordination
  - Communication
  - Centralised planning and control
  - Focus on operational efficiency

Divisional
- Advantages
  - Decision making
  - Motivation
- Disadvantages
  - Loss of economy
  - Head office control
  - Need for goal congruence
  - Need divisional performance measures

Network structures
- Key issues:
  - Flow of information between network partners
  - Managing relationships with partners
  - Service level agreements?

Performance management in service businesses
- Simultaneous
- Heterogeneous
- Intangible
- Perishable
- Importance of non-financial measures:
  - Customer satisfaction
  - Employee morale

Business integration

Need to link people, operations, strategy & technology

Value chain
- Activities and processes need to be linked and aligned to create value
- Nature of processes needs to be consistent with generic strategy (cost leadership; differentiation)
- Can be used to improve performance by:
  - (a) Inventing better ways to perform activities
  - (b) Combining activities in better ways
  - (c) Managing the linkages in the value chain

McKinsey's 7S
- Strategy
- Structure
- Systems
- Style
- Staff
- Skills
- Shared values
- All elements must be aligned in order to be effective

Business process re-engineering (BPR)
- Fundamental rethinking and radical redesign of business processes to achieve dramatic improvements in areas of performance such as cost, quality, service and speed
- Work units change from functional departments to process teams
- Performance measures focus on processes
- Processes need to be customer-focused, not just doing 'tasks'

Influence of structure, culture and strategy

- Structure: Measures in divisional vs functional structure
- Flexibility, adaptability (network; virtual structures)
- Culture:
  - Recognition
  - Influence
- Importance of alignment and consistency
- Recognition of non-financial aspects of performance (quality; innovation)
- Influence of Japanese management techniques (JIT; TQM)
- Strategy:
  - Performance measures need to support strategy (eg cost leadership; differentiation)
  - Need to compete in increasingly competitive, global environment

Stakeholders

- Internal
- Connected
- External
- Important to consider stakeholder interests/objectives when designing performance measurement systems
- Link to HRM (managing/ motivating employees)

Social and ethical issues

- Social responsibility
- Sustainability
- Need performance measures for these?

		Interest	
		Low	High
Power	Low	Minimal effort	Keep informed
	High	Keep satisfied	Key players

Environmental management accounting (EMA)

- Builds on ideas of social responsibility and sustainability
- EMA: Generation and analysis of financial and non-financial information
- In order to support internal environmental management processes
  - Life cycle costing
  - Activity-based costing
  - Importance of non-financial measures

Knowledge diagnostic

1. Performance management in different business structures

The way an organisation is structured (eg on a functional, divisional or network basis) can influence the way performance is managed and controlled. Performance information in functional structures may need to focus more on cost control and efficiency, whereas it could be more appropriate to treat divisions as profit centres or investment centres.

2. Business management in service businesses

Services are characterised by:

- Simultaneity
- Heterogeneity
- Intangibility
- Perishability

In addition to financial performance information, information about non-financial factors (customer satisfaction; employee motivation) can be particularly important in service businesses.

3. Business integration

All the aspects of an organisation need to be aligned to ensure the most efficient use of its resources, and so that it can achieve its objectives effectively. An organisation's structure, culture and strategy can all influence the performance measurement methods and techniques which are most appropriate for an organisation.

Two frameworks which can be used to analyse business integration are: **Porter's value chain**, and **McKinsey's 7S**.

The value chain enables organisation to understand how activities link together in order to create value (for the customer). The nature of activities (and therefore the aspects of performance which are most important) depends on an organisation's strategy (eg cost leadership or differentiation).

4. Business process re-engineering (BPR)

'The fundamental rethinking and radical redesign of business processes to achieve dramatic improvements in... critical measures of performance, such as cost, quality, service and speed.'

Can often lead to restructuring of work teams (eg to a greater focus on processes, rather than functions), and performance measures may also need to be redesigned to look at processes rather than departments or functions.

5. Stakeholders

Stakeholders have an interest in the strategies and actions of organisations, but the levels of **power** and **interest** of different stakeholder groups varies. Organisations need to ensure their strategies and actions are acceptable to key stakeholder groups and need to ensure they monitor performance in any areas which are particularly important for these stakeholder groups.

Social and ethical dilemmas can arise when there are conflicts between the objectives and interests of different groups.

6. Environmental management accounting (EMA)

The increased public focus on issues of social responsibility and sustainability means organisations need to pay greater attention to the environmental impact of their operations.

EMA includes the generation and analysis of financial and non-financial information in order to support internal environmental management processes.

Activity-based costing and **life cycle costing** are techniques which can be applied here.

Further study guidance

Question practice

Now try the following from the Further question practice bank (available in the digital edition of the Workbook):

Q5 FCI Co

Q19 FGH Telecom

Further reading

There is a Technical Article available on ACCA's website, called *Management control – a pre-requisite for survival*, which looks at the importance of management information in enabling organisations to satisfy the needs of different stakeholders, and to respond effectively to the changing environments in which they operate.

You are encouraged to read this article in full as part of your preparation for the APM exam.

There is also an article called *Environmental Management Accounting* in the Technical Articles section on ACCA's website which looks at the increasing importance of environmental management accounting. You are strongly advised to read this article in full.

In the section on social and ethical issues in this chapter, we alluded to the important issue of sustainability. There is a section on ACCA's website called 'ACCA and sustainability' which discusses a number of current issues in this area, and which could be a useful source of further reading in this area.

Activity answers

Activity 1: Service business

You may have thought of other answers for this activity, but some possible solutions are as follows:

Simultaneous: Manufactured foods need to be produced before they are consumed, but services are created at the same time as they are consumed. A dentist can only check a patient's teeth, or carry out any necessary treatment, when the patient is at the dental surgery. Similarly, a patient's experience of the dental service is formed during their time at the surgery.

Heterogeneous: One of the key issues that service businesses face is ensuring consistency in the standard of the service they provide. For example, different dentists within a dental practice could treat patients in different ways. However, the dentist's manner and behaviour could have a significant impact on the patient's perception of the service they are receiving.

Equally, the nature of the dental work required will vary according to the individual needs of a patient, and this also illustrates the characteristic of heterogeneity.

Intangible: In contrast to manufactured goods, which are physical products, services do not have any substantial tangible aspects. When a patient has a check-up or a filling at the dentist's surgery, they are not primarily buying a physical product; rather than are buying the dentist's expertise in addressing any problems they have with their teeth.

Perishable: Services only last for a period of time. For example, when a patient books an appointment it is for a certain time. If the patient doesn't attend the dental surgery at that time, they miss their appointment. This is also linked to the characteristic that services do not result in any **transfer of ownership**. When a patient books a dental appointment, this allows them to benefit from the dentist's expertise for a limited period of time. However, they do not 'own' the dentist or the dentist's surgery (as, for example, customers do when buying a manufactured product, such as a car).

Activity 2: Fantasia Co

Cost driver charge out rates	
Waste emissions kg	$350 per kg
Waste water output m^3	$2.2 per m^3
Kg of general waste	$840 per kg
Kg of recycled waste	$2,300 per kg
Internal audit hours	$250 per hour
Training time (hours)	$1,670 per hour
R&D hours	$53 per hour

	Product A			*Product B*		
	Activity	*Cost*	*Cost/Unit*	*Activity*	*Cost*	*Cost/Unit*
	'000	$'000	$	'000	$'000	$
Air pollution	6.3	2,205	26.9	0.7	245	30.6
Water pollution	1,120	2,464	30.0	**480**	1,056	**132.0**
General waste	2.7	2,268	27.7	0.3	252	31.5
Hazardous waste	0.8	1,840	22.4	**0.8**		**230.0**

	Product A			Product B		
	Activity	Cost	Cost/Unit	Activity	Cost	Cost/Unit
	'000	$'000	$	'000	$'000	$
Monitoring	0.6	150	1.8	0.5	125	15.6
Training	0.3	501	6.1	0.2	334	
R&D	90	4,770	58.2	50	2,650	
Total			173.1			812.8

Implications for performance management:

Under the existing costing system the environmental cost per unit is $20,700,000/90,000 = $230 per unit.

Under the revised costing, Product B will see a significant cost increase and as a result will be correctly seen as a less profitable product.

This may affect the R&D spending being targeted at Product B.

It may also affect B's pricing – which may need to increase.

Finally it provides clear visibility to the environmental impact of Product B which can be used to control the activities that are driving these costs. For example, it may be sensible from an environmental and a costing viewpoint to amend the formulation of Product B to reduce its use of hazardous chemicals.

Activity 3: Filin Co

Filin Co's traditional performance measure of product profit suggests it will generate a profit of $41.5 million over five years. However, this ignores the environmental costs (of waste filtration, and carbon dioxide exhaust extraction) as well as the cost of decommissioning at the end of the project.

By contrast, a life cycle analysis would include all of these costs:

Product profit	$m
Traditional view:	
Revenue:	147.6
Production, marketing and development costs	109.1
Product profit (over three years)	38.5
Profit margin	26.1%
Adjusted for environmental costs:	
Revenue	147.6
Production, marketing and development costs	109.1
Waste filtration	8.1
Carbon dioxide exhaust extraction	5.3
Decommissioning costs	18.0
	140.5
Revised product profit	7.1
Profit margin	4.8%

When the environmental costs are all included, the forecast profit margin is reduced from 26.1% to 4.8%, which makes it a much less attractive investment. Moreover, if the actual costs of decommissioning in three years' time are higher than the forecast ($18.0m) – for example, due to changes in environmental legislation in the next five years – then the profit margin will be reduced even further.

Importantly, also, life cycle costing makes the post-production costs visible at the start of the project and in the design stage of the product. This should help Filin Co appreciate early in the project the need to minimise the costs of decommissioning.

Impact of risk and uncertainty

Learning objectives

On completion of this chapter, you should be able to:

	Syllabus reference no.
Assess the impact of the different risk appetites of stakeholders on performance management.	B1(a)
Evaluate how risk and uncertainty play an important role in long-term strategic planning and decision making that relies upon forecasts of exogenous variables.	B1(b)
Apply different risk analysis techniques in assessing business performance such as maximin, maximax, minimax regret and expected values.	B1(c)

Exam context

The exam often tests your understanding of how the attitude of stakeholders, especially managers, to risk affects planning and decision making. Linked to this, you may need to use the clues in a question scenario to assess what different stakeholders' attitude to risk seem to be.

Exam questions could also look at the techniques which can be used to assess performance in the context of risk and uncertainty. These techniques, and how they may be used to reflect the attitude of stakeholders to risk, have been tested regularly.

ACCA's Study Guide identifies that the 50-mark Section A question in the exam will focus mainly on syllabus Sections A, C and D. This chapter covers **Section B** of the syllabus (Impact of Risk and Uncertainty on Organisational Performance) so the topics in this chapter are more likely to be tested in a 25-mark Section B question in the APM exam.

You should already be familiar with the techniques covered here from your earlier studies (of the *Performance Management* syllabus). However, it is important to revise them here and to make sure that you can apply them, as necessary, to the scenario-based questions that you will face in the APM exam.

Chapter overview

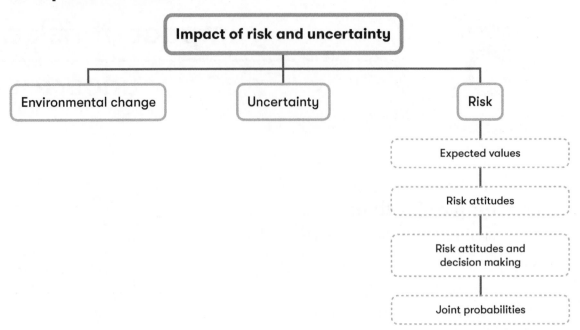

BPP
LEARNING
MEDIA

1 Environmental change

In Chapter 1 you have covered a variety of models (eg PEST, Porter's five forces) that can be used to analyse the external environment in which an organisation operates, because that environment can have a significant impact on an organisation's performance. This can be particularly noticeable when there are adverse changes in the environment (eg due to new competitors entering a market). The possibility of such changes occurring is a major source of **risk** and **uncertainty**.

Performance management needs to consider the possibility (or probability) of changes in elements of its environment. These are sometimes referred to as **exogenous variables**, which means that they are outside the control of the organisation.

> **Exogenous variables:** Variables that are determined externally, for example the cost of a raw material imposed by the supplier.

2 Uncertainty

> **Uncertainty:** When the future is unknown and the decision maker has no past experience on which to base predictions of change so that **outcomes cannot be predicted, or assigned probabilities**.

Sensitivity analysis is a method used to **describe** uncertainty to decision makers. It quantifies the maximum amount by which any variable would have to change before the objective (of a project) is not attained.

The smaller the percentage change required, the more sensitive the project is to this variable, and the greater the uncertainty surrounding the project; such variables need to be **carefully managed** if a project is implemented.

Activity 1: Sensitivity

A grocery retailer is considering whether to make, in store, a new type of bread loaf that claims to reduce cholesterol levels. The following information is available:

(1) The number of loaves sold per year in the retailer's country of operation is 425 million. The retailer expects this loaf to have a market share of 1%.

(2) The average selling price of all loaves sold is $1.50. The retailer expects 85% of all loaves to be sold, with the rest needing to be thrown away at the end of the day.

(3) The average cost of ingredients per loaf is $0.60, of which $0.17 is caused by the special ingredient that renders the loaf able to reduce cholesterol. There is only one supplier in the market for this ingredient.

(4) Packaging and labelling costs will be $0.12 per loaf.

(5) Distribution costs are expected to be 4% of revenue.

(6) Fixed overheads have been estimated to amount to $270,000 per annum to include all wages and salaries costs as all employees are subject to fixed-term employment contracts.

The retailer has a target profit margin of 35%, and the finance director has stated that she believes the new type of loaf can achieve this, although she is concerned about the effect that an increase in the cost of the special ingredient will have on the forecast profits.

Required

Using only the above information, show how the finance director has reached her conclusion regarding the expected sales margin and also state whether she is correct to be concerned about an increase in the price of ingredients (assuming that all other revenue/cost data remains unchanged). **(6 marks)**

Solution

Essential reading

See Chapter 5 Section 1.1 of the Essential reading for more detail about other simple techniques for dealing with uncertainty including a recap on breakeven analysis and margin of safety.

The Essential reading is available as an Appendix of the digital edition of the Workbook.

3 Risk

KEY TERM

Risk: Where a decision maker has knowledge that several different future outcomes are possible, the probabilities of which are known, or can be estimated, usually due to past experience.

Where there is **risk**, a range of possible future outcomes can be quantified (best, worst and most likely) and probabilities assigned to them and an expected value or weighted average of these outcomes calculated.

It is important to note the distinction between risk and uncertainty. In a risk situation, the probability of an event occurring can be estimated. However, uncertainty implies that the probability of an event occurring cannot be predicted.

In the absence of any information about a particular risk attitude (see section 3.2) it can be assumed that a decision maker will be concerned with making a decision that is 'most likely' to create the best expected outcome (or value). So, when faced with a number of alternative decisions, the one with the best expected value (EV) will be chosen.

3.1 Expected values

An expected value is a weighted average that is calculated using probabilities. It is likely that you have used this technique before, but if not you will need to learn the formula and approach outlined below:

Formula to learn

$$EV = \sum px$$

Where p is the probability of the outcome occurring and x is the value of that outcome.

Activity 2: Expected values

John must decide how best to use a monthly factory **capacity of 1,200 units**. His demand from regular customers is risky and as follows:

Monthly demand (units)	Probability
400	0.2
500	0.3
700	0.4
900	0.1

Regular customers generate contribution of $5 per unit. John has the opportunity to enter a special contract which will generate contribution of only $3 per unit. For the special contract John must enter a binding agreement now at a level of 800, 700, 500 or 300 units.

John has partially calculated the following contributions (in $) at various contract and demand levels.

Demand (units)	p	Special contract (units) 800	700	500	300
400	0.2	4,400	4,100	To be completed	2,900
500	0.3	4,400	4,600	To be completed	3,400
700	0.4	4,400	4,600	To be completed	4,400
900	0.1	4,400	4,600	To be completed	5,400

Required

Advise John as to the optimal level of special contract to commit to every month, assuming his aim is to maximise profits. **(2 marks)**

Solution

3.1.1 Limitations of EV

(a) Ignores attitudes to risk (see next section)

(b) Heavily dependent on probability estimates which may not be reliable

(c) It is a long run average and may not be appropriate if a decision is a one-off

3.2 Risk attitudes

Risk attitude is the amount of risk an organisation is willing to take on, or is prepared to accept, in pursuing its strategic objectives. Organisations may be **risk seekers**, **risk neutral** or **risk averse**.

> **Risk seeker:** A decision maker who is interested in trying to secure the best outcomes, no matter how small the chance that they may occur.
>
> **Risk neutral:** A decision maker is risk neutral if they are concerned with what will be the most likely outcome.
>
> **Risk averse:** A risk-averse decision maker acts on the assumption that the worst outcome might occur.

It is also important to recognise that **different stakeholders have different risk appetites** or different perspectives on risk.

For example, equity investors are likely to want to see a return on their investments and may be prepared to support relatively high-risk strategies if these strategies offer the prospect of high returns. By contrast, managers may prefer to implement a lower risk strategy because they may feel it offers them greater security.

3.3 Risk attitudes and decision making

An understanding of risk appetite can be a useful tool for managing risk and enhancing overall business performance, by making sure that business decisions are aligned with risk appetite of shareholders. This has implications for the reward and remuneration systems in organisations (which we will look at in more detail in Chapter 12). One of the key characteristics of reward systems is that they should help to align the risk preferences of directors and managers with those of the organisation and its owners.

Risk attitude	Decision-making technique
Risk seeker	For this risk appetite **maximax** may be appropriate. This involves making decisions that are based on making the maximum possible return (regardless of the probability of this).
Risk averse	For this risk appetite **maximin** may be appropriate. This involves selecting decisions that minimise downside risk by selecting the option that gives the best of the worst outcomes (regardless of the probability of the worst outcomes occurring). **Minimax regret** may also be appropriate here; this is where a

Risk attitude	Decision-making technique
	decision is chosen that minimises the impact of it turning out to be the wrong decision.
Risk neutral	Only a risk-neutral decision maker will be concerned with the most likely outcome, using **expected values** (EVs).

Maximax: Looks at the best possible results from each decision option and selects the option that gives the best possible result.

Maximin: Suggests that a decision maker should select the alternative that offers the least unattractive worst outcome.

Minimax regret: Aims to minimise the regret from making the wrong decision.

Activity 3: Attitudes to risk

1 Following on from the previous example, advise John as to the optimal level of special contract to commit to every month:

- Assuming John is a risk seeker
- Assuming John is risk-averse

(2 marks)

2 Consider what factors may affect John's risk appetite. (2 marks)

(Total = 4 marks)

Solution

Essential reading

See Chapter 5 Section 1.2 of the Essential reading for more detail about another simple application of the concept of expected value.

The Essential reading is available as an Appendix of the digital edition of the Workbook.

3.4 Joint probabilities

Where probabilities are provided for **two variables,** the range of possible outcomes can be recorded in a **joint probability** table.

KEY TERM

> **Joint probability:** The probability of two events occurring at the same time and is calculated by multiplying together the probability of each individual variable occurring.

Example

For example, if you withdraw a single card from a pack of 40 cards containing four different types of colours (black, red, green and blue) with each colour consisting of ten cards numbered 1–10, then the probability of selecting a red number 8 is:

Probability of the occurrence of the first variable (a number 8) × Probability of the second (red card)

Here this gives:

$4/40 \times 10/40 = 40/ (40 \times 40) = 1/40$

This makes sense because there is only one red number 8 in the pack of 40.

Joint probability tables **allow the risks to be assessed.**

Activity 4: Joint probability

Brown Ltd makes and sells a single product for which current profits are $25,000 per annum.

The company is confident that the product can be manufactured for a variable cost of $19, but is considering a change in marketing and distribution which could have an effect on both sales demand and sales price. Brown Ltd believes that the following circumstances could occur:

Price $	Prob	Demand '000 units	Prob
28	0.2	30	0.4
29	0.35	35	0.5
30	0.45	40	0.1

Brown Ltd has fixed costs of $320,000.

Manager A has suggested that the changes should be made only if they will generate an expected profit of at least the current level of $25,000.

Required

Complete the following analysis (which has been partially completed) and discuss the impact of the possible changes in marketing and distribution on the profits of Brown Ltd.

Contribution generated ($'000)

	Demand ('000 units)		
Price ($)	30	35	40
28	270	315	☐
29	300	350	☐
30	330	385	☐

Joint probability table

	Demand ('000 units)		
Price ($)	30	35	40
28	0.08	0.1	☐
29	0.14	0.175	☐
30	0.18	0.225	☐

EV of contribution ($)

	Demand ('000 units)		
Price ($)	30	35	40
28	21,600	31,500	☐
29	42,000	61,250	☐
30	59,400	86,625	☐

(4 marks)

Solution

Chapter summary

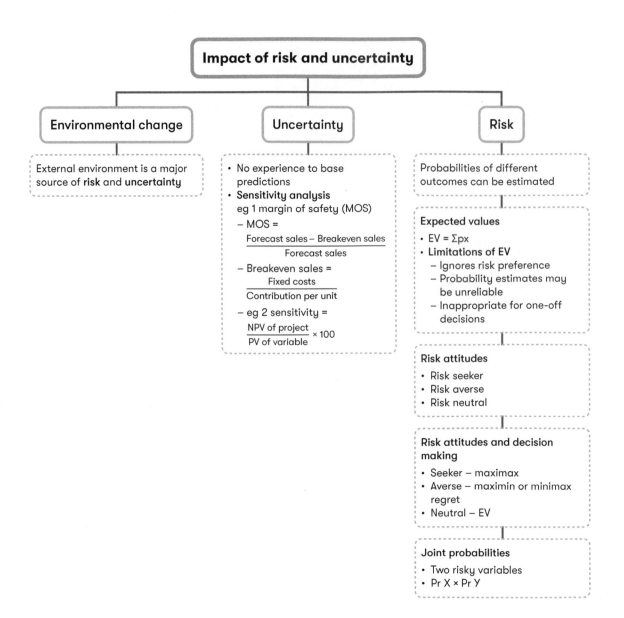

Impact of risk and uncertainty

Environmental change

External environment is a major source of **risk** and **uncertainty**

Uncertainty

- No experience to base predictions
- **Sensitivity analysis**
  eg 1 margin of safety (MOS)
  - MOS =

  $$\frac{\text{Forecast sales} - \text{Breakeven sales}}{\text{Forecast sales}}$$

  - Breakeven sales =

  $$\frac{\text{Fixed costs}}{\text{Contribution per unit}}$$

  - eg 2 sensitivity =

  $$\frac{\text{NPV of project}}{\text{PV of variable}} \times 100$$

Risk

Probabilities of different outcomes can be estimated

Expected values
- EV = Σpx
- **Limitations of EV**
  - Ignores risk preference
  - Probability estimates may be unreliable
  - Inappropriate for one-off decisions

Risk attitudes
- Risk seeker
- Risk averse
- Risk neutral

Risk attitudes and decision making
- Seeker – maximax
- Averse – maximin or minimax regret
- Neutral – EV

Joint probabilities
- Two risky variables
- Pr X × Pr Y

Knowledge diagnostic

1. Uncertainty

Uncertainty occurs when the outcome of a situation (eg environmental change) cannot be predicted, and neither can probabilities be assigned to different outcomes. Where this is the case, sensitivity analysis is a useful way of describing the degree of uncertainty being faced.

2. Risk

Although the outcomes of different situations are not known, their probabilities can be estimated.

3. Expected values

Where probabilities are given, expected values may be calculated by multiplying each outcome by the probability of the outcome.

4. Risk attitude

Decision makers may have a number of different attitudes to risk:

Risk seekers look to choose the decision with the best up-side result.

Risk-averse decision makers look to choose the decision with best 'worst case' scenario.

Risk neutral decision makers have balanced attitude to risk and make decision based on the most likely outcome.

5. Risk attitude and decision making

Different decision-making techniques will be more appropriate given the risk attitude of the decision maker:

Risk seeker: maximax decision criterion.

Risk averse: maximin, or minimax regret decision criteria.

Risk neutral: expected values.

Further study guidance

Question practice

Now try the following from the Further question practice bank (available in the digital edition of the Workbook):

Q6 *Unique Components*

Further reading

There are two Technical Articles available on ACCA's website, called *The risks of uncertainty* (parts 1 and 2).

The first article looks at the use of probability in decision making, and revises expected values, dispersion (standard deviation), decision rules and decision trees.

The second looks at the value of perfect information compared with the value of imperfect information; it also covers the concept of value-at-risk which is not formally mentioned in the APM syllabus but is interesting background information.

We recommend you read these articles as part of your preparation for the APM exam.

Activity answers

Activity 1: Sensitivity

Forecast income statement for the bread loaves

		$'000
Turnover	425m × 1% × $1.50	6,375
Materials – special	5m × $0.17	850
Materials – other	5m × $0.43	2,150
Packaging	5m × $0.12	600
Distribution	4% × $6,375	255
Fixed costs		270
Profit		2,250
Profit/sales (%)	2,250/6,375	35.3%
Target rate of return (%)		35%
Target return ($'000)	35% × 6,375	2,231

Working

Production volume

Sales level	425m × 1%
Gross up for wastage	0.85
Production volume	5 million

The special ingredient can increase by the excess profit over target (2,250,000 – 2,231,000) = $19,000; in percentage terms this is:

$$\frac{19,000}{850,000} \times 100 = 2.2\%$$

The finance director is correct to be concerned with an increase in the cost of the special ingredient as the success of the product depends primarily on this ingredient and the percentage return is very sensitive to an increase in the cost of an ingredient with only one supplier.

Any opportunities to manage this risk, such as fixing the price of this ingredient with the supplier, should be investigated if this project proceeds.

Activity 2: Expected values

A pay-off table is a useful way of analysing expected values, which could be profits, costs or project Net Present Values. This table shows the outcome (in each column) of each decision (top row).

Here, the pay-off table has been partly completed, with only the decision on the special contract for 500 units and the expected values for each decision in the final row left to be completed.

Demand (units)	p	Special contract (units)			
		800	700	500	300
400	0.2	4,400	4,100		2,900

		Special contract (units)			
500	0.3	4,400	4,600		3,400
700	0.4	4,400	4,600		4,400
900	0.1	4,400	4,600		5,400
EV					

Outcome of special contract of 500 units:

Demand (units)	Decision 500 units	Workings
400	3,500	(400 × 5) + (500 × 3)
500	4,000	(500 × 5) + (500 × 3)
700	5,000	(700 × 5) + (500 × 3)
900	5,000	(700 × 5) + (500 × 3) Note: full capacity means that the extra demand from regular customers cannot be met

Expected values:

	Special contract (units)			
	800	700	500	300
	1 × 4,400	0.2 × 4,100	0.2 × 3,500	0.2 × 2,900
		0.8 × 4,600	0.3 × 4,000	0.3 × 3,400
			0.5 × 5,000	0.4 × 4,400
				0.1 × 5,400
EV	4,400	4,500	4,400	3,900

John should commit to a special contract of 700 units, based on expected value.

Activity 3: Attitudes to risk

1   Different risk attitudes require the application of different techniques.

(1)   Using maximax – the possibility of the best of the best options (5,400) is created by choosing 300 units for the special contract.

(2)   Using maximin – the best of the worst outcomes (4,400) is created by choosing 800 units for the special contract.

Alternatively using **minimax** regret:

Demand Units	Regret table	800	Special contract Units 700	500	300
400	Best option = 800 unit special contract	0	300 (4,400-4,100)	900	1,500

Demand Units	Regret table	Special contract Units			
		800	700	500	300
500	Best option = 700 unit special contract	200 (4,600 −4,400)	0	600	1,200
700	Best option = 500 unit special contract	600 (5,000 −4,400)	400	0	600
900	Best option = 300 unit special contract	1,000 (5,400 −4,400)	800	400	0
	Maximum regret	**1,000**	**800**	**900**	**1,500**

The decision with lowest maximum regret is 700 units for the special contract.

2   A risk-averse attitude may result from a business being under cash flow pressure, so that it cannot afford an unexpected drop in cash flow. One reason for this may be that the business has high financial gearing and has interest payments that need to be made.

A risk-seeking attitude may reflect the values of the decision maker and may also be affected by any incentives that are based on ambitious performance targets being hit. Venture capitalists often encourage a risk-seeking attitude because they are often highly ambitious in their growth targets.

Activity 4: Joint probability

	$
EV contribution = $\sum px$	343,375
Fixed costs	320,000
EV profit	23,375

An expected profit of only $23,375 will be achieved so manager A will reject this opportunity.

However, there is a 50% chance of achieving the desired profit (which requires contribution to be $345,000; so it depends on the manager's attitude to risk).

Performance
measurement systems and reports

Learning objectives

On completion of this chapter, you should be able to:

	Syllabus reference no.
Discuss, with reference to performance management, ways in which the information requirements of a management structure are affected by the features of the structure.	C1(a)
Evaluate the compatibility of management accounting objectives and the management accounting information systems.	C1(b)
Discuss the integration of management accounting information within an overall information system, for example the use of enterprise resource planning systems.	C1(c)
Evaluate whether management information systems are lean and the value of the information that they provide (eg using the 5 Ss).	C1(d)
Evaluate the external and internal factors (eg anticipated human behaviour) which will influence the design and use of a management accounting system.	C1(e)
Discuss the principal internal and external sources of management accounting information, their costs and limitations.	C2(a)
Demonstrate how the information might be used in planning and controlling activities eg benchmarking against similar activities.	C2(b)
Demonstrate how the type of business entity will influence the recording and processing methods.	C3(a)
Discuss how IT developments (eg unified corporate databases, process automation, the internet of things, RFIDs, cloud and network technology) may influence management accounting systems.	C3(b)
Explain how information systems provide instant access to previously unavailable data that can be used for benchmarking and control purposes and help improve business performance (for example, through the use of artificial intelligence, ERP, knowledge management, CRM systems and data warehouses).	C3(c)
Discuss the difficulties associated with recording and processing data of a qualitative nature.	C3(d)

	Syllabus reference no.
Discuss the development of big data and its impact on performance measurement and management, including the risk and challenges it presents.	C4(a)
Discuss impact of big data and data analytics on the role of the management accountant.	C4(b)
Evaluate the output reports of an information system in the light of: (i) Best practice in presentation (ii) The objectives of the report/organisation (iii) The needs of the readers of the report (iv) Avoiding the problem of information overload (v) The use of presentation techniques such as data visualisation	C5(a)
Advise on common mistakes and misconceptions in the use of numerical data for performance measurement.	C5(b)
Explore the role of the management accountant in providing key performance information for integrated reporting to stakeholders.	C5(c)

Exam context

Management accounting and information systems play a vital role in performance management, because they provide the information which managers use as the basis for planning and control, and which enables performance measurement to take place.

However, note the number of the Learning outcomes in this chapter where the verb requirement is either 'discuss' or 'evaluate'. As such, in an exam question you may need to consider the extent to which an organisation's information systems provide managers with the information they need for planning, control and decision making within the organisation, and perhaps also how those systems could be improved.

The Study Guide identifies that candidates should expect the 50-mark Section A question in the exam to focus on a range of issues from across syllabus sections A, C and D. So you should be prepared for issues around an organisation's performance measurement systems (Section C of the syllabus) to be included as a part of the 50-mark case study question.

Remember, however, that APM is an accountancy exam, not an IT exam. You will not be expected to explain the technical details of different systems. Instead, your focus should be on how effective the systems are in providing the information needed to manage an organisation's performance.

Another important topic covered in this chapter is performance reports. Questions in the APM exam frequently ask candidates to evaluate performance reports. Again, as with information systems, if performance reports do not provide managers with the information they need to control the business, or to assess how well it is performing in key areas, this will significantly reduce the manager's ability to manage performance effectively.

Chapter overview

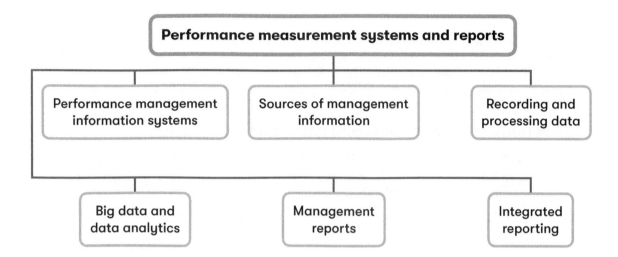

1 Performance management information systems

In this chapter we will discuss the characteristics of different systems, but let's begin by identifying the underlying characteristics and purpose of a (performance) management information system:

Management information system: A system to convert data from internal and external sources into information and to communicate that information, in an appropriate form, to managers at all levels in all functions to enable them to make timely and effective decisions for planning, directing and controlling the activities for which they are responsible (*Lucey, 2005*).

1.1 Information requirements and management structure

Many types of performance information will be required by a business.

In Chapter 1 we identified that information could be required at different levels in an organisation: strategic, operational and tactical.

In Chapter 4, we noted that the information requirements in different organisational structures (functional, divisional, network) are influenced by the design of that structure. For example, in a functional structure, information is needed about the operational efficiency of each of the functions. But in a divisional structure, information is needed about profitability and ROI of the division.

Also, in a divisional structure, it may be necessary to identify controllable and non-controllable costs, in order to distinguish between a divisional manager's performance and the division's performance.

Note. Responsibility centres are discussed in more detail in Chapter 8.

1.2 Objectives of management accounting information

Management accounting information can be used by managers for a variety of purposes:

- To **measure performance** (of whole organisation; or of individual divisions/functions within the business)
- To **control** the business (set targets/budgets; then compare actual performance against target)
- To **make decisions** (strategic; tactical; operational)

The quality of management accounting information in an organisation depends on how well it allows managers to fulfil these purposes.

Essential reading

See Chapter 6 Section 1 of the Essential reading for more detail about the factors to consider when evaluating the management accounting information produced in an organisation.

The Essential reading is available as an Appendix of the digital edition of the Workbook.

1.3 Integration of management accounting information

It is also important that management accounting information does not exist in isolation, but is also part of the wider information system in an organisation.

An **enterprise resource planning system** (ERPS) is a database management system designed to integrate and automate business processes in medium-sized and large organisations. ERPSs help to identify and plan the resources need to make, account for, and fulfil customer orders, by improving the flow of information between business functions within an organisation.

An ERPS can incorporate many aspects of operations including **manufacturing, distribution, inventory, invoicing** and **accounting**. It can also cover support functions, such as **human resource management** and **marketing**.

Supply chain management software can provide links with **suppliers,** and **customer relationship management** software can provide links with **customers**.

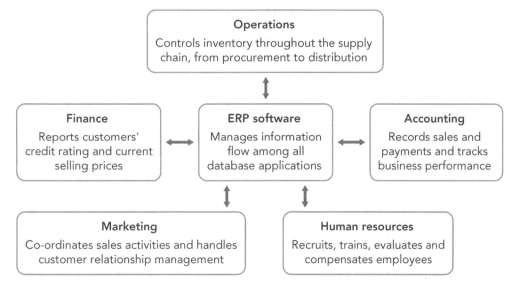

An ERPS can also be used to produce customised reports and can **support performance measures** such as the **balanced scorecard** (see Chapter 13), and can also provide data on all aspects of operations in a **real-time** environment. An ERPS can result in **lower costs** and increased **flexibility** and **efficiency of production** (because sales, production and purchasing are closely integrated).

However, an ERPS can often be expensive and time-consuming to implement. In addition, a **problem** with one function can affect all the other functions.

An ERPS will also require a **data warehouse**. Organisations may build a single central data warehouse to serve the entire organisation or may create a series of smaller **data marts**.

1.4 Lean information and information systems

Lean information aims to get the **right information** to the **right people** at the **right time** with the **minimum of waste**.

The key characteristics of lean systems and lean information are that they are developed in a **collaborative manner,** focused on the needs of the **end user,** avoid waste (ie unnecessary detail, or unnecessary reports), and are easy for the user to access and understand.

1.4.1 5S model

The 5S model (based on *Imai, 2012*) can be used to **help implement lean systems** or **evaluate** existing systems. The five Ss are:

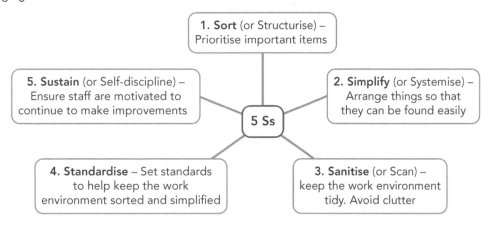

The 5S model can be applied to operational processes and systems in an organisation, as well as to information systems, to help make them lean.

Essential reading

See Chapter 6 Section 2 of the Essential reading for more detail about 'lean' and lean information systems.

The Essential reading is available as an Appendix of the digital edition of the Workbook.

Activity 1: Yellow Co

Yellow Co (Yellow) operates a warehouse and distribution centre, storing and distributing products for a national retail company. The warehouse's performance has deteriorated recently, and a number of deliveries have either been late or have had items missing, as staff have had problems locating products in the warehouse.

A new warehouse manager has now been appointed, and she believes the process for storing goods in the warehouse has been responsible for many of Yellow's problems.

When deliveries are received, the goods are stored in the nearest available space. In some instances, where there have been shortages of shelf space, goods have been left on the floor at the entrance of the unloading area.

Every product Yellow stores and distributes has a six-digit product code. The new manager has proposed that the warehouse should be reorganised so that goods are stored in number order, based on their product code.

She has also instructed staff that all items must be stored on shelves, with none remaining on the warehouse floor. The manager carries out daily inspections to ensure this policy is being adhered to.

Required

With reference to 5S model, evaluate the extent to which the new manager's proposals will make the systems in Yellow Co's warehouse 'leaner'. **(8 marks)**

Solution

1.5 Design and use of management accounting systems

The design of management accounting systems is influenced by the following:

*   The **environment** in which an organisation operates:

    -   The faster the pace of change in the environment changes, the quicker and more frequently reports might be needed

    -   The greater the level of competition an organisation faces, the more complex the accounting system is likely to be to incorporate information about competitive forces

*   **Human behaviour**, and the way people interpret information they are given (eg whether users of information want detail or a 'broad-brush' approach.

Essential reading

See Chapter 6 Section 3 of the Essential reading for more detail about the way anticipated human behaviour can influence the design of management accounting systems.

The Essential reading is available as an Appendix of the digital edition of the Workbook.

2 Sources of management information

An exam question may require you to briefly comment on potential **internal** and **external** sources of information (for example to support performance measures, or as part of a benchmarking exercise).

When evaluating possible sources of information it is important to consider the **costs** of different types of information and their practical benefits/limitations.

Essential reading

See Chapter 6 Section 4 of the Essential reading for discussion of the sources of management information.

The Essential reading is available as an Appendix of the digital edition of the Workbook.

3 Recording and processing data

3.1 The importance of context

It is important to recognise that the methods of recording and processing data may vary between organisations, and may depend on:

- The **volume and complexity of data** being processed (eg batch processing may be appropriate for a small furniture shop to update its inventory records at the end of a day, but a large supermarket may need to update its sales and inventory records in real time)
- **Level of accuracy** required (eg a bank processes large numbers of customer transactions, but recording each of them correctly is vital)
- **Speed** with which information is required (eg use of EPoS devices in supermarkets to update inventory and enable re-ordering)
- **Size and structure of the organisation** – the information requirements of a large, multinational corporation, with managers in different countries, are likely to very different to those of an owner-managed business, based at a single site

The nature of an organisation's business could also affect the information required.

We have already noted the different information requirements of services businesses (in Chapter 4), and will see later (in Chapter 9) the different information requirements of not-for-profit companies.

3.2 Developments in recording and processing systems

Developments in IT systems have made it far easier for the management accounting system to share data with other information systems, and for users to access it.

3.2.1 Unified corporate databases

ERPSs have already been introduced. An ERPS is built on a single **unified corporate database**. Unified corporate databases allow users to access the same information across an organisation.

Potential benefits of unified corporate databases

(a) Unified corporate database **integrates data from different functions** across an organisation (eg production and sales). This should help to improve planning and decision making (eg helping to match production with forecast demand).

(b) All departments **share the same information** (reducing the risk of departments looking at inconsistencies between departments from each using 'local' figures).

(c) Information is available in **real time,** or near time (rather than, for example, individual departments preparing their own data and then consolidating them at period end).

3.2.2 Radio frequency identification (RFID)

RFID allows organisations to keep track of assets by tagging them with small radio transmitters (typically referred to as an RFID tag) applied to or incorporated into an asset, product, animal or person.

RFID is becoming increasingly widely used in **supply chain management**. RFID tags attached to materials or inventory enable an entity to track the movement of that inventory between locations, and to get an exact, **real-time** count of items coming into storage and items held in storage.

Real life example

RFID systems are being used in hospitals to track a patient's location, and to provide real-time tracking of the location of doctors and nurses. In addition, the system can be used to track the whereabouts of expensive and critical equipment, and even to control access to drugs, paediatrics and other areas of the hospital that are considered 'restricted access' areas.

RFID in retail stores offers real-time inventory tracking that allows companies to monitor and control inventory supply at all times. RFID could also be used in the downstream supply chain: tracking the delivery of a product from a retail store to the consumer's home.

3.2.3 Network technology

Network technology (eg virtual public networks (VPNs)) allow remote workers to connect to an organisation's systems as if they were physically in the organisation. This has played an important role in the increasing **flexibility of the workforce** (eg enabling employees to work from home).

3.2.4 Cloud technology

> **Cloud computing:** A model for enabling ubiquitous, convenient, on-demand network access to a shared pool of configurable computing resources (eg networks, servers, storage, applications and services) that can be rapidly provisioned and released with minimal management effort or service provider interaction (*National Institute of Standards and Technology, 2011*).

Cloud computing technologies have changed the ways in which organisations store and manage their data. An increasing amount of organisational data is now held in servers operated by cloud-based service providers.

One of the key benefits cloud computing can provide an organisation is **improved access** to data because it is accessible from anywhere around the world where there is internet connectivity.

Cloud-based services can also be very useful for **increased collaboration** between teams working in different locations. Instead of having to send files as email attachments to be worked on by colleagues (with the associated risk of conflicting versions, formats etc) the cloud enables all files to be stored centrally, so that everyone can see the same version of a file.

However, before adopting cloud computing technologies, an organisation should consider any potential data privacy, risk and security issues. If information is critical to the business, or the organisation cannot be assured that information will be adequately protected, then it should probably not be moved to the cloud.

3.2.5 Process automation

> **Process automation:** The use of digital technology to automate business processes.

The aim of process automation is to reduce human intervention and to enable smooth and sequential transition from one task to the next.

Many **repetitive business processes** can be automated, from production and supply chain management through to sales and marketing.

Process automation can improve business efficiency, reduce costs and minimise errors. Employees have time to focus on more value-adding activities which can lead to greater motivation.

Real-time data from the process gives managers the ability to resolve problems more quickly.

Example

Process automation is being used to simplify new employee recruitment and induction.

Automated recruitment tools, which look for key words in applications, can be used to quickly sort through applications and create a candidate shortlist.

Once interviews have been completed by HR personnel, an automated process can send out the employment contract and key forms for new recruits to complete. Such digital forms are simpler to complete but also store information that can be useful in conducting workforce data analytics.

A workflow system can automatically notify the appropriate teams when they need to act on the next task.

Payroll can be notified to set up a new employee and IT will know when to set up the employee workstation and grant users access to key software.

3.2.6 Internet of things

Internet of things: Refers to any physical object connected to and sharing data over the internet. This extends beyond wireless 'smart' devices, such as smartphones and computers, to any device containing sensors with the ability to track and upload data.

The internet of things provides data that allows companies to better understand their own needs as well as those of their customers.

For example, the **use of sensors** in computer printers enables printer manufacturers to monitor the ink used by customers. The manufacturers can respond better to individual customer needs by automatically issuing new cartridges when ink levels are low.

However, the increasing use of sensors does heighten the risk of hackers stealing the data they capture.

3.3 Instant access to data

Developments in technology have also increased the speed with which data is processed and distributed, making it instantly available to those who require it.

To help managers make effective decisions, it is important that data is accessible in order that it can be analysed to provide improve understanding about processes and performance.

It is also important that knowledge and insights are shared within organisations, and **knowledge management systems** (eg groupware, intranet, data warehousing) help to achieve this.

3.3.1 Customer relationship management (CRM) systems

Customer relationship management (CRM) relates to the process of analysing a customer's interactions with an organisation throughout the customer life cycle, with the aim of improving the organisation's relationship with the customer, helping customer retention, and driving sales growth.

CRM software supports this by capturing customers' interactions with an organisation, so that this can be used to improve the organisation's understanding of the customer (eg by tailoring future marketing communications more precisely to the customer's interests or requirements).

Essential reading

See Chapter 6 Section 5 of the Essential reading for more detail about knowledge management systems.

The Essential reading is available as an Appendix of the digital edition of the Workbook.

3.4 Qualitative data

As well as discussing issues around processing quantitative data, an exam question may also require you to discuss the difficulties with recording and processing qualitative data. These are often related to the unstructured and subjective nature of qualitative data, and we will look at these points in more detail in Chapter 10.

4 Big data and data analytics

Big data is a term given to extremely large collections of data ('data sets') that are available to organisations to analyse.

The internet, smartphones, social media, sensors and other digital technologies are all helping to fuel a data revolution.

In the so-called 'internet of things', **sensors** embedded in physical objects, such as mobile phones, motor vehicles, smart energy meters, RFID tags, tracking devices and traffic flow monitors, all **create and communicate data** which is shared across wired and wireless networks that function in a similar way to the internet.

A frequently used definition of big data is that given by the technology research firm, Gartner:

> **Big data:** High-volume, high-velocity and/or high-variety information assets that demand cost-effective, innovative forms of information processing that enable enhanced insight, decision making, and process automation' (*Gartner, 2018*).

The definition **highlights three key characteristics of big data:**

- **Volume:** Very large amounts of data to analyse

  The bigger the data the more potential insights it can provide in terms of identifying trends and patterns; for example, enabling organisations to get a deeper understanding of customer behaviour and requirements.

- **Velocity:** The speed with which data is generated, captured and analysed

  Data is continuously arriving and needs to be processed quickly within an organisation (eg online retailers who can use information about customer 'clicks' and interactions on a website could use this to recommend additional purchases while the customer is still on the site).

- **Variety:** The number of different types of data to analyse

  Data comes from a wide variety of sources, with much of it being **unstructured** (ie not in a database). For example, key words from conversations people have on social media about a product or service could be a source of unstructured data.

4.1 Big data analytics

The process of collecting, organising and analysing large data sets is known as big data **analytics**.

This involves **data mining** (analysing data to identify patterns and establish relationships, for example where and among which age groups is a product selling well) and **predictive analytics** (a type of data mining which aims to predict future events; for example, having bought one product, what other products might a consumer be interested in buying?).

> **Data analytics:** The process of collecting and examining data in order to extract meaningful business insights, which can be used to inform decision making and improve performance.

Big data analytics could result in performance improvements in the following areas:

(a) **Better understanding of customer behaviour**

For example, identifying what customers are saying on social media about an organisation's products or its customer service could help the organisation identify how well it is meeting customers' needs.

Customers' conversations could help the organisation identify potential changes which are needed to its products, or the way they are delivered, in order to meet customers' needs more effectively, and thereby to increase sales.

(b) **Targeted marketing messages**

Big data could facilitate targeted promotions and advertising – for example, by sending a tailored recommendation to customers' mobile devices while they are in the right area to take advantage of the offers.

(c) **Decision making**

For example, trends identified by a retailer in in-store and online sales – in real time – could be used to manage inventories and pricing.

(d) **New products and services**

More generally, big data could also provide new business opportunities in their own right.

For example, the online retailer Amazon makes recommendations for customers linked to the purchases made by other customers with similar interests.

Essential reading

See Chapter 6 Section 6 of the Essential reading for more detail about knowledge management systems.

The Essential reading is available as an Appendix of the digital edition of the Workbook.

4.1.1 Potential risks and challenges of big data

Critics have argued that although data sets may be big, they are not necessarily representative of the entire data population as a whole; eg if a firm uses tweets from the social networking site Twitter to provide insight into public opinion on a certain issue, there is no guarantee the tweets will be representative.

Quality of data

There can be a misconception that increasing the amount of data available automatically provides managers with better information for decision making. However, in order to be useful, data has to be relevant and reliable.

Veracity

In order to be valuable, data also needs to be reliable. A fourth V – veracity – is often added to the other 'V' characteristics of big data (volume, velocity and variety).

Using big data requires organisations to maintain strong governance on data quality. For example, the validity of any analysis of that data is likely to be compromised unless there are effective cleansing procedures to remove incomplete, obsolete or duplicated data records.

Cost

It is expensive to establish the hardware and analytical software needed and to comply with data protection regulations which vary from country to country.

IT teams or business analysts may become burdened with increasing requests for data, ad hoc analysis and one-off reports. Equally, this will mean that the information and analysis will not be available to decision makers as quickly as the 'velocity' may initially imply.

Skills

Do organisations have staff with the necessary analytical skills to process and interpret the data? The scale and complexity of data sets may require a **data scientist's** level of analytical skills for data mining, deriving algorithms and predictive analytics.

Loss and theft of data

Companies could face legal action if data was stolen. More generally, when collecting and storing data they need to consider data protection and privacy issues, and ensure they comply with current legislation in these areas (eg having appropriate controls in place to prevent breaches of data security).

4.2 Big data and the role of the management accountant

Big data can lead to improved decision making and performance in organisations. But the characteristics of volume, velocity and variety could have important implications for management accountants:

- **Velocity** – managers could expect to receive information more quickly, in order to help them make timely decisions
- **Volume and variety** – accountants may need to work with an increased volume of data – including unstructured data

Processing this data could mean that accountants will **need to work more closely with IT professionals and data analysts**.

4.2.1 Data visualisation

> **Data visualisation:** The presentation of data in a pictorial or graphical format which is easier for recipients to process than detailed written data.

One of the challenges of big data is the sheer volume of structured and unstructured data that is created. Managers may find it difficult to interpret the data and to draw meaningful conclusions.

When preparing reports, presenting data in graphs and charts can overcome the problem of data overload by improving clarity.

Data visualisation can also be an interactive experience. Instead of users being the passive recipients of a standard report, they can create their own bespoke dashboard of data, with the ability to drill down into areas of particular interest to them.

Example

The diagram below uses data visualisation to track the progress of a project. The graphs and charts make information easier to interpret. For example, a pie chart shows the task completion status whilst a bar chart highlights the variance between budgeted and actual expenditure.

Sample dashboard

Project Name: Project Alpha
Report Date   3/15/2016
Project Status **On track**
Completed   27%

Tasks	Assigned To	Priority	Status
Set kick-off meeting	Alex B.		Complete
Agree on objectives	Frank C.	★	Complete
Detailed Reqs.	Jacob S.		Complete
Hardware Reqs.	Jacob S.	★	Overdue
Final Resource Plan	Jacob S.		In progress
Staffing	Alex B.	★	In progress
Technical Reqs.	Frank C.		Not started
Testing	Kennedy K.	★	Not started
Dev. Complete	Jacob S.	★	Not started
Hardware Config.	Alex B.		Not started
System Testing	Kennedy K.	★	Not started
Launch			

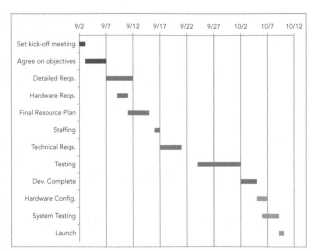

Overall Task Status

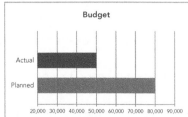

Budget

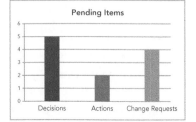

Pending Items

Essential reading

See Chapter 6 Section 7 of the Essential reading for more detail about the potential implications of big data for accountants.

The Essential reading is available as an Appendix of the digital edition of the Workbook.

4.3 Artificial intelligence (AI) and machine learning

KEY
TERM

Artificial intelligence: Systems that sense, comprehend, act and learn.

AI systems are increasingly capable of **analysing Big Data to solve problems for themselves.**

4.3.1 Applications of AI

Product development	Using **data collected from sensors** attached to existing equipment to test **digital prototypes** under different operating conditions.
Manufacturing	**Robotic arms,** working on an assembly line, can be given a picture of a successful outcome and develop their own approach to assembling a product. **Self-adapting assembly lines.** Allowing manufacturers to customise products (eg cars).

Delivery	Using **robots to transport goods within a warehouse to delivery points** to allow rapid delivery to customers and minimising the space needed to store in-bound deliveries from suppliers.
Quality management	AI data can help to **build models able to predict when machines will require maintenance** and to identify conditions under which parts may fail. AI can **process customer data** from a variety of sources (email, social media, fax) to read and sort complaints and to deal with routine complaints.
Data security	Developing **systems that detect malicious software** by detecting unusual network traffic behaviour and **learning from each issue that is identified.**
Customer interactions	AI can allow **direct interaction with the customer** (eg Siri) allowing a better understanding of customer behaviour. **Analysis of transactional data** can generate predictions of what customers want to purchase in the future. This analysis can then be refined on the basis of actual customer behaviour.
Reporting	AI is capable of presenting and reporting business performance **objectively**, without the problem of human bias.

(Daugherty & Wilson, 2018)

4.3.2 Drawbacks of AI

- **Distrust**
  - Customers may **react adversely** to interactions with technology (there may be a preference for human interaction).
  - Staff may feel their jobs are threatened. This will not always be true, as AI will sometimes move the nature of human input to more creative areas. Opportunities for **collaboration** between machines and humans should be explored.
- **System malfunctions**
  - AI systems may operate in a way that is not predicted (eg use of inappropriate language), so some **controls over AI behaviour** (eg content filters) may be useful.
- **Misuse**
  - AI systems (eg route mapping) may be ignored or misused by human operators. Ideally **AI systems should explain their course of action** to encourage buy-in from operators.
- **Data problems**
  - AI systems will be less effective at learning if they only use data generated within a business. As we have seen, Big Data should be sourced from a **wide variety of media**.

5 Management reports

Past exam questions have often asked candidates to evaluate the suitability of management reports.

When evaluating the **design of a performance report** there are a number of issues to look for:

(a) **Strategic relevance**

Does the report provide information which is relevant to the organisation's performance against its mission or objectives? Does the report include key performance indicators that are consistent with the organisation's mission and objectives, and help to identify whether these are being achieved?

Performance should be judged with reference to the key areas which drive success (ie CSFs, and KPIs associated to them).

This will often require **non-financial information**, eg in the form of the balanced scorecard or a similar model (see Chapter 13).

(b) **Audience**

Who is the report being read by?

You may need to think about whether the audience will be sophisticated enough to understand the information presented. Has the report provided the appropriate level of detail, layout and terminology?

Information will need to be supported by adequate **narrative explanations**, eg simply reporting a variance without attempting to explain how it might have been caused adds little value for the information user.

(c) **Information**

What information is needed – financial and/or non-financial? (The importance of non-financial information is discussed in Chapter 10.)

Does the report provide all the information needed? Chapter 13 provides a number of frameworks, such as the Balanced Scorecard, that could be useful in spotting that some important information is not being provided.

Non-financial qualitative information (eg staff morale) is often turned into something quantifiable as part of a report on performance assessment. You may need to consider whether, in doing this, distortions to the information have been introduced.

For example, measuring staff morale by the level of staff turnover may be more of an indication of the difficulties of finding a job in the local area!

Other potential issues with quantifying non-financial information include:

(i) **Ranking systems**: Rankings (eg of customer satisfaction) don't give any indication of the extent of performance differences.

(ii) **Percentages**: Give no visibility to absolute values, eg is a 5% adverse variance significant?

(iii) **Graphical reports**: These can be manipulated to exaggerate trends (eg by the choice of scale on the axis).

(d) **Layout**

Does the report make it clear for readers to identify the most important information, or does it present too much information ('information overload') so that valuable information (and assumptions made) is hard to find and interpret?

To deal with this, you could recommend:

(i) Using **graphs and summary tables**

(ii) Leaving detailed information in **appendices** to the main report

Essential reading

See Chapter 6 Section 8 of the Essential reading for more detail about potential issues with numerical data.

The Essential reading is available as an Appendix of the digital edition of the Workbook.

Activity 2: Hydra Co

An example of the sales information that Hydra Co (a bicycle retailer) currently produces for the board is shown below. This report is produced quarterly for each retail outlet; cost information is also provided but this is not shown below.

Hydra's stated mission is to become "the leading bicycle retailer in its country, by providing quality bicycles at a competitive price".

	Sales (£)				
	Actuals last year	**Budget for current year**	**Forecast for current year**	**Latest quarter**	**Previous quarter**
Men's bikes	x	x	x	x	x
Ladies' bikes	x	x	x	x	x
Children's bikes	x	x	x	x	x
Parts	x	x	x	x	x
Clothing	x	x	x	x	x
Servicing	x	x	x	x	x
Total	**x**	**x**	**x**	**x**	**x**

Required

Critically assess the existing performance report and suggest improvements. **(10 marks)**

Solution

It is vital to distinguish questions asking you to evaluate performance management **reports** from question about the organisation's **performance**.

In past exams, the examining team have commented that when candidates have been asked to evaluate a performance report, they have chosen instead to evaluate the performance of the organisation – meaning they haven't answered the question actually asked.

Essential reading

See Chapter 6 Section 9 of the Essential reading for more detail about avoiding information overload.

The Essential reading is available as an Appendix of the digital edition of the Workbook.

6 Integrated reporting

KEY
TERM

> **Integrated report (IR):** 'A concise communication about how an organisation's strategy, governance, performance and prospects, in its commercial, social and environmental context, leads to the creation and enhancement of value over the short, medium and long term' (*IIRC, 2013*).

Integrated reporting (IR) aims to explain an organisation's ability to **create** and **sustain value**. In doing so, it also highlights the importance of long-term **business sustainability** within an organisation.

IR should help stakeholders make a meaningful assessment of the long-term viability of an organisation's business model and its strategy. It is a practical application of strategic management accounting (Chapter 1) and links to many of the themes in the APM syllabus.

Rather than focusing on narrow financial performance objectives, IR should encourage management to focus on creating and sustaining value over the longer term. This is the ethos of strategic management accounting.

6.1 Six capitals

The International Integrated Reporting Council's (IIRC's) International Integrated Reporting Framework (*IIRC, 2013*) encourages organisations to report on six categories of capital:

Category of capital	Characteristic elements of the category of capital
Financial	Funds available, obtained through financing or generated from operations
Manufactured	Manufactured physical objects used in production or service provision including buildings, equipment, and infrastructure
Human	Alignment and support for an organisation's governance framework and ethical values. Ability to understand and implement organisation's strategies Loyalties and motivations for improvements and innovation
Intellectual	Intangible assets, providing competitive advantage (patents, brands etc)
Natural	Areas where an organisation's activities have an impact on the natural environment: including water, land, minerals and forests
Social	Key stakeholder relationships, willingness to engage with stakeholders

Impact of integrated reporting on information requirements

Integrated reports describe an organisation's performance in relation to the six different capitals – in contrast to 'traditional' annual reporting which focuses primarily on financial performance.

This means an organisation needs information about its performance in relation to each of the different capitals, which means that organisations will need to record non-financial (eg social; environmental) performance in a way which provides it with suitable information to include in an integrated report.

Essential reading

See Chapter 6 Section 10 of the Essential reading for more detail about the potential implications of integrated reporting for management accountants.

The Essential reading is available as an Appendix of the digital edition of the Workbook.

PER alert

Performance objective 12 (PO 12) of the PER requires you to evaluate management accounting systems.

Two elements of the objective are particularly relevant to the issues we will discuss in this chapter in the Workbook:

PO 12(c): 'Assess and advise on the impact of the output of an organisation's management accounting and information systems'

PO 12(d): 'Contribute to development and improvements of management accounting systems and internal reporting'

A key point to note in this context is that the quality of an organisation's management information systems are likely to have a significant impact on the accountant's ability to provide managers with the information they require. This could be an issue which you face in the workplace, just as much as it could be an issue with the information systems being described in a case study scenario in an exam question in the APM exam.

Chapter summary

Performance measurement systems and reports

Performance management information systems

- Information requirements depend on:
  - Organisation structure
  - Context
- Integration of systems
  - eg **ERPS**: integrate and automate business processes
- Lean systems
  - Avoiding waste
  - Right information; right people; right time
  - Focus on user requirements
  - **5S model** can be used to help evaluate/implement lean systems

Sources of management information

Sources of information:
- Internal vs external
- Cost vs benefit of different sources

Recording and processing data

- Issues:
  - Volume of data to process
  - Speed required
  - Complexity of data
  - Accuracy
- Development in recording and processing systems
  - ERPS
  - **RFID**: asset tracking; applications in supply chain?
  - **Network technology**: VPN; facilitates flexible working
  - **Cloud**: enables global access to data; increased collaboration
  - **Knowledge management systems**: intranet; extranet; data warehouses –> data mining
  - **CRM systems**: improve understanding of customers; customer retention

Big data and data analytics

- Characteristics of big data:
  - Volume
  - Velocity
  - Variety
- Data analytics: extract meaningful insights from data to inform decision making and improve performance
- Potential issues with big data:
  - Veracity
  - Infrastructure to capture/store
  - Skills required to analyse (data scientists?)
  - Security and control over data (especially personal data)
- Implications of big data for management accountants
  - Speed required in reporting
  - Volume and variety of data to process
- Artificial intelligence
  - Use of Big Data to automatically learn

Management reports

- Evaluating design of reports:
  - Strategic relevance (eg link to objectives; CSFs)
  - Audience
  - Information: appropriate mix: financial/non-financial; qualitative/quantitative
  - Layout: clarity for readers; avoid information overload
- Beware of unreliable or misleading information

Integrated reporting

- Integrated report (IR)
  - How strategy, governance, performance and prospects creates and sustains value
  - Considers short, medium and long term
  - Considers commercial, social and environmental context
- Six capitals:
  - Financial
  - Manufactured
  - Human
  - Intellectual
  - Natural
  - Social
- Implications of IR for management accountants
  - Can information systems provide information required for IR?

Knowledge diagnostic

1. Performance management information systems

Management accounting information is used by managers for a variety of purposes: control, planning and decision making. The effectiveness of an organisation's management accounting systems can be assessed in relation to how well they provide managers with the information they need.

Management accounting information does not exist in isolation but is part of the wider information system within an organisation, as illustrated by enterprise resource planning systems (ERPS).

ERPS can be a useful way of integrating business processes.

Lean information systems aim to provide the right information to the right people at the right time with the minimum of waste. The characteristics of lean systems can be assessed using the 5S model (sort; simplify; sanitise; standardise; sustain).

2. Recording and processing data

Developments in IT systems have made it easier for users to get instant access to data via:

(a) ERPS

(b) RFID system (and asset tracking)

(c) Network technology

(d) Cloud technologies

(e) Knowledge management systems (intranets; extranets; data warehouses)

(f) Customer relationship management systems

3. Big data and data analytics

'Big data' describes the proliferation of data generated by digital interactions, and is characterised by high volume, velocity and variety.

'Big data analytics' describes the process of collecting, organising and analysing big data to discover patterns, trends and other useful information which an organisation can use to inform decision making and improve performance.

The ability to analyse large and unstructured data sets could help organisations gain a competitive advantage. However, as a prerequisite for this, organisations need to have the capacity to store and the capability to analyse the data sets.

4. Management reports

When designing or evaluating a performance report, key aspects to consider are:

(a) Strategic relevance – does the report help understand an organisation's performance in relation to its mission, objectives or critical success factors

(b) Audience – is the report suitable for its intended audience

(c) Information – is there an appropriate mix of information (financial/non-financial; quantitative/qualitative)? Is the information credible and reliable, and does it accurately represent how well an organisation has performed?

(d) Layout – is the information presented in a way which makes it clear for users to understand?

5. Integrated reporting

The aim of integrated reporting is to communicate how an organisation's strategy, governance, performance and prospects, in the context of its external environment, create value for its stakeholders – in the short, medium and long term.

An integrated report should help to explain how an organisation is developing and implementing its strategies for sustainable value creation.

Further study guidance

Question practice

Now try the following from the Further question practice bank (available in the digital edition of the Workbook):

Q8 *Cobra Golf Club*

Q21 *Mackerel* (this is a wide ranging 50 mark question that also contains elements relating to the previous chapter, and a small element in part e that has not yet been covered)

Further reading

- There is a Technical Article available on ACCA's website, called *Lean enterprises and lean information systems* which looks at key characteristics of 'lean' production, and the way 'lean' principles can be applied to information systems.

  You are strongly advised to read this article in full as part of your preparation for the APM exam.

- There are a number of technical articles on Big Data; the most useful is the article called *Data analytics and the Management Accountant an enterprises and lean information systems* which provides a number of practical examples and insights.

  You are strongly advised to read this article in full as part of your preparation for the APM exam.

- There is also a useful two-part Technical Article that reviews the impact of IT systems on performance management called *Developments in IT and the impact on performance management*.

- Another important Technical Article, available via ACCA's website is *Performance Reports*. This article discusses the factors which should influence the design of a performance report, and which can be used to evaluate how good, or useful, a performance report is for an organisation.

  Again, you are strongly advised to read this article in full as part of your preparation for your APM exam.

  In addition, the two-part Technical Article – *Improving Your Advanced Performance Management Answers* (Parts 1 and 2) – highlights some of the errors which students made in a question which asked them to evaluate an organisation's performance report. The article then goes on to demonstrate the sorts of points candidates were expected to make to score well in the question.

  Linked to this theme is another important Technical Article, written by a member of the APM examining team, which uses themes from recent exam questions to discuss the general considerations in designing effective performance reports.

- The Technical Article *Common mistakes and misconceptions in the use of numerical data for performance measurement* highlights the importance of considering whether the way data is collected, processed or presented can make an organisation's performance appear better or worse than it actually is.

  This is another article you are encouraged to read as part of your preparation for the APM exam.

- Finally, there is a Technical Article called *Integrated Reporting* available on ACCA's website which explores how the elements of integrated reporting could relate to APM.

  Again, you are encouraged to read this article in conjunction with the material on Integrated Reporting covered in this Workbook.

Activity answers

Activity 1: Yellow Co

Simplify – The proposal to store products in a structured way should help staff locate them more quickly and easily, and should therefore reduce the current problems of staff not being able to find products. This demonstrates the 'simplify' element of the 5Ss.

Sort – However, the way products are being arranged (ie by product number) is essentially arbitrary. For example, it doesn't take account of how frequently products are used, nor any of the characteristics of the products themselves.

In a 'lean' system, the products should be arranged in the way makes collecting them for distribution as efficient as possible. As such, it may be advantageous for high volume, or bulky items, to be stored close to the loading area; or for similar types of products to be grouped together.

However, in this case, the manager doesn't appear to have considered the 'sort' (structurise) aspect of lean systems, but has focused primarily on the 'simplify' aspect.

> **Tutorial note.** We don't know any details about the products Yellow stores and distributes for the retailer, and therefore how much variation in frequency of order, size etc there is. It is possible that sorting by product number order might be the most efficient way of storing the products. However, when implementing lean systems it is important that both the 'simplify' and 'sort' elements are considered, not just one or the other.

Sanitise – The instruction that all items must be stored on shelves rather than on the floor specifically addresses the issue of keeping the warehouse clean and tidy. Leaving goods on the floor at the entrance of the unloading area (as they previously were) not only clutters up the floor, but also potentially creates an obstacle to staff who are trying to move other goods out of the unloading area.

Sustain – The manager's daily inspections are part of a routine to ensure that staff continually keep the warehouse tidy (and maintain the benefits from the 'sanitise' principle of the 5Ss).

However, an important element of the principle of 'sustaining' is also motivating employees to maintain (and improve) performance. None of the manager's proposals directly focus on motivating employees. One possible way to do this would be to introduce performance reports – for example, reporting the number of products which couldn't be found, or the number of goods left on the floor rather than being properly stored on shelves. The manager doesn't appear to have introduced any performance reports like this, though.

'Leaner' – Overall, the proposals should help to make the systems in the warehouse leaner, because they demonstrate some of the 5Ss. However, they do not fully demonstrate all of the 5Ss, and therefore there is still scope for further improvement to make them even more lean.

> **Tutorial note.** The routine of inspecting the floor at the end of each day could potentially also be considered under 'Standardise' – because it is a routine aimed at keeping the workplace sorted and tidy.

Activity 2: Hydra Co

The existing performance report has some good elements and many weaknesses.

- The current report shows clearly the calculation of revenue from the main product lines of the business and how this has changed over the past year along with a forecast of the full year. There is also a breakdown of the performance in the last two quarters, which gives a snapshot of more immediate performance.

- The report does not seem over-detailed. This information is being produced for the board, so they will primarily be interested in high level, summary figures, rather than lots of detailed figures.

However, there are a number of weaknesses with the existing report.

- The style of presentation could easily be confusing to a non-accountant as it shows a large table of numbers with few clear highlights. The use of more percentage figures rather than absolute numbers may help (eg change on comparative period percentages). Also, the heading shows that sales are reported in pounds, where it would probably be sufficient to work in thousands of pounds.

- The current report does not give any benchmark data to allow comparisons of performance. It would be helpful to include variance figures; against budget or against prior year.

- Only financial sales data is reported. Retail outlets are customer-facing and so a measure of customer satisfaction based on number of complaints received or changes over time in average scores in customer surveys would be helpful.

- The timescales reported in the current format are possibly not helpful for board meetings. There is likely to be a high level of seasonality in this business which may make quarterly comparisons meaningless and the figures for last year may not be particularly relevant to current market conditions and will not reflect recent management initiatives. It may be useful to consider reporting the last quarter's monthly performance giving comparative figures from the previous year and possibly reporting more frequently since the board would not want to continue ordering sales lines that were not selling well.

- The current report only includes internal information. Therefore it doesn't provide the board with any insight into how well Hydra is performing against its mission to become 'the leading bicycle retailer'. It would be helpful to show market sales figures, to monitor Hydra's market share. Similarly, the report doesn't provide any indication whether Hydra is offering 'quality bicycles at a competitive price'. One potential indicator here could be the level of refunds given (which could indicate customers have not been satisfied with the quality of the bicycles they have bought).

Skills checkpoint 3

Evaluating performance management reports

Overview

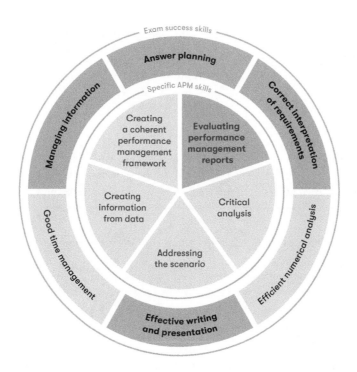

Introduction

An important element of a coherent performance management framework (discussed in Skills Checkpoint 2) are performance reports that show how well an organisation is performing in the areas which are strategically significant for it. Critically evaluating existing performance reports has already been mentioned in Skills Checkpoint 1 (creating information from data) but we focus on it in more detail here.

Exam questions, often in Section A of the exam, may require you to evaluate a performance report. This is an important skill, and will require you to assess an existing report (normally looking at positive as well as negative factors) to see if it provides appropriate information about strategically important areas of performance, in a way that is easy for the audience to understand, and which enables them to take effective control action.

The skill of evaluating performance management reports is part of syllabus Section C, Performance Measurement Systems and Design. This syllabus area, along with Section A (Strategic Planning & Control), and Section D (Strategic Performance Management), will typically form the basis for the 50-mark Section A question in the exam.

Where an exam question requires you to analyse the structure of a performance management report, it is important to complete this analysis in a practical way, making points that you feel matter in the given scenario. Avoid the temptation to simply repeat 'rote-learned', generic points.

APM Skill: Evaluating performance management reports

The key steps in applying this skill are outlined below. They will be explained in more detail in the following sections, and illustrated by answering a requirement from a past exam question.

STEP 1:
Where a question includes a significant table of data, read the requirements carefully to make sure that you understand clearly whether a question requires the analysis of the performance of an organisation, or of the performance report.

STEP 2:
Where a question requires analysis of the performance **report**, make sure that you clearly understand the mission, strategy and key objectives of a company (from the main body of the scenario) and carefully consider the degree to which the performance report gives visibility to these strategic factors.

STEP 3:
Also consider other practical factors such as the structure, clarity and level of detail of the report, and whether it distorts the meaning of data.
Look for positive as well as negative factors (where relevant given the requirement).

STEP 4:
Complete your answer plan and write up your answer.

Exam success skills

The following illustration is based on an extract from a past exam question, about a restaurant business called 'Metis'. This extract was worth 16 marks.

For this question, we will also focus on the following **exam success skills**:

- **Managing information**. It is easy for the amount of information contained in scenario-based questions to feel overwhelming. In the APM exam, each question will be scenario-based. It is therefore essential to develop a clear understanding of the scenario. It is especially important to have a clear understanding of a company's strategy and mission.

- **Correct interpretation of requirements**. The requirement clearly asks for the performance **report** to be evaluated, not the performance. Whenever this type of requirement is set in the real exam, some candidates make the mistake of evaluating the company's performance, instead of the company's performance report.

- **Answer planning**. Everyone will have a preferred style for an answer plan. For example, it may be a mind map, bullet-pointed lists, or simply annotating the question scenario. Choose the approach that you feel most comfortable with or, if you are not sure, try out different approaches for different questions until you have found your preferred style.

- **Effective writing and presentation**. In Question 1 of the exam (which this question was) there will be 4 professional marks available for the presentation and structure of your answer. The markers are looking for suitable report headings, an introduction, a logical structure, signposted by the good use of subheadings in the answer, written in a clear, concise style.

Skills activity

STEP 1 Where a question includes a significant table of data, read the requirements carefully to make sure that you understand clearly whether a question requires the analysis of the performance of an organisation, or of the performance report.

Required

Prepare a report to Mr John Sum addressing the following issues:

Critically assess the existing performance report[32], and suggest[33] improvements to its content and presentation.

(12 marks)

Professional marks[34] will be available for the format, style, structure and clarity of your report.

(4 marks)

(Total = 16 marks)

[32] This is about the performance report, not the company's performance itself.

[33] This is a two-part question; make sure that you answer both parts.

[34] This wording is standard in all Section A questions.

The key action verb is 'assess'. This is defined by the ACCA as 'judge the worth or importance' and will involve examining the strengths/weaknesses/importance/significance of an issue. Here there will be a greater emphasis on making critical points as you are asked to 'critically' assess.

Now that you can see that the question is looking at the performance report, not the company's performance itself, your reading and planning time will be spent more effectively.

STEP 2 Where a question requires analysis of the performance report, make sure that you clearly understand the mission, strategy and objectives of a company (from the main body of the scenario) and carefully consider the degree to which the performance report gives visibility to these strategic factors.

Question – Metis (16-mark extract from a 50-mark question)

You should assume it is now June 20X2.

Company information and business model

Metis is a restaurant business in the city of Urbanton. Metis was started three years ago by three friends who met at university while doing courses in business and catering management. Initially, their aim was simply to 'make money' although they had talked about building a chain of restaurants if the first site was successful.

The three friends pooled their own capital and took out a loan from the Grand Bank in order to fit out a rented site in the city. They designed the restaurant to be light and open, with a menu that reflected the most popular dishes in Urbanton regardless of any particular culinary style. The dishes were designed to be priced in the middle of the range[35] that was common for restaurants in the city. The choice of food and drinks to offer to customers is still a group decision amongst the owners.

[35] Although this is a small, young company and does not have a formal mission statement, there are clues here about its strategy, challenges, objectives and its sense of purpose.

Other **key elements** of the business were allocated according to each owner's qualifications and preferences. Bert Fish takes charge of all aspects of the **kitchen operations** while another, Sheila Plate, **manages the activities in the public area such as taking reservations, serving tables and maintaining the appearance of the restaurant.** The third founder, John Sum, deals with the **overall business issues** such as procurement, accounting and legal matters.

Market environment

Competition in the restaurant business is fierce[36] as it is easy to open a restaurant in Urbanton and there are many competitors in the city, both small, single-site operations and large national chains. The current national economic environment is one of steady but unspectacular growth.

[36] Competitive factors are flagged as a key issue. How might this be significant for the performance report?

Metis's current position

The restaurant has been running for three years and the founders have reached the point where the business seems to be profitable and self-sustaining. The restaurant is now in need of refurbishment in order to maintain its atmosphere, and this has prompted the founders to consider the future of their business. John has come to you as its accountant looking for advice on aspects of performance management in the business. He has supplied you with figures outlining the **recent performance of the business and the forecasts for the next year (Appendix 1).**

John has explained that the report he has given you **(Appendix 1) represents the quantitative data that is available to the founders when they meet each quarter to plan any short-term projects or initiatives and also to consider the longer-term future.**[37] Bert and Sheila have often indicated to John that they find the information daunting and difficult to understand fully.

[37] The purpose of the existing performance report is for decision making and strategic planning.

Performance measures

John has come to you to advise him on the performance reporting at Metis and how it could be improved. He feels that the current report is, in some ways, too complex and, in other ways, too simple[38].

[38] Clues as to what changes may be needed?

Appendix 1[39]

PERFORMANCE REPORT – METIS RESTAURANT

[39] First impressions: how user friendly is a report like this?

Year to 31 March

	Actual 20X0	Actual 20X1	Actual 20X2	Forecast 20X3	Latest quarter to 31 March 20X2 (Q4 20X2)	Previous quarter (Q3 20X2)
	$	$	$	$	$	$
Revenue						
Food	617,198	878,220	974,610	1,062,180	185,176	321,621
Wine	127,358	181,220	201,110	219,180	38,211	66,366
Spirits	83,273	118,490	131,495	143,310	24,984	43,394
Beer	117,562	167,280	185,640	202,320	35,272	61,261
Other beverages	24,492	34,850	38,675	42,150	7,348	12,763
Outside catering	9,797	13,940	15,470	16,860	2,939	5,105
Total	979,680	1,394,000	1,547,000	1,686,000	293,930	510,510
Cost of sales						
Food	200,589	285,422	316,748	345,209	60,182	104,527
Wine	58,585	83,361	92,511	100,821	17,577	30,528
Spirits	21,651	30,807	34,189	37,261	6,496	11,283
Beer	44,673	63,566	70,543	76,882	13,403	23,279
Other beverages	3,674	5,228	5,801	6,323	1,102	1,914
Outside catering	3,135	4,461	4,950	5,395	941	1,634
Total	332,307	472,845	524,742	571,891	99,701	173,165

Year to 31 March

	Actual 20X0	Actual 20X1	Actual 20X2	Forecast 20X3	Latest quarter to 31 March 20X2 (Q4 20X2)	Previous quarter (Q3 20X2)
	$	$	$	$	$	$
Gross profit	647,373	921,155	1,022,258	1,114,109	194,229	337,345
Staff costs	220,428	313,650	348,075	379,350	66,134	114,865
Other operating costs						
Marketing	25,000	10,000	12,000	20,000	3,000	3,000
Rent/mortgage	150,800	175,800	175,800	193,400	43,950	43,950
Local property tax	37,500	37,500	37,500	37,500	9,375	9,375
Insurance	5,345	5,585	5,837	6,100	1,459	1,459
Utilities	12,600	12,978	13,043	13,173	3,261	3,261
Waste removal	6,000	6,180	6,365	6,556	1,591	1,591
Equipment repairs	3,500	3,658	3,822	3,994	956	956
Depreciation	120,000	120,000	120,000	120,000	30,000	30,000
Building upgrades				150,000		
Total	360,745	371,701	374,367	550,723	93,592	93,592
Manager salary	35,000	36,225	37,494	38,806	9,373	9,373
and corporate taxes	31,200	199,579	262,322	145,230	25,130	119,515
Net margin	3.2%	14.3%	17.0%	8.6%	8.5%	23.4

STEP 3   Also consider other practical factors such as the structure, clarity and level of detail of the report, and whether it distorts the meaning of data.

Look for positive as well as negative factors (where relevant given the requirement).

Refer back to Appendix 1 of the question (see earlier)

The practical points noted below could be added to the margin of the question or shown as part of an answer plan (see Step 4).

For decision making

Profitability of different product groups is not clear

Absence of budget makes performance harder to assess

For strategic planning

Current overall profitability is clear

Only forecasting one year ahead, is that enough?

Too many numbers – need to work to the nearest $?

Too much information – are so many cost categories needed? Are three years of actual figures necessary?

STEP 4   Complete your answer plan and write up your answer.

Answer plan

Issue	Points addressing the issue
Critical analysis of report as a mechanism for decision making	Profitability of different product groups is not clear Absence of budget makes performance harder to assess Absence of non-financial information Absence of competitive data Only forecasting one year ahead, is that enough? Too many numbers – need to work to the nearest $? Too much information – are so many cost categories needed? Are three years of actual figures necessary? Quarterly information needed?
Suggested improvements	Simplify/less precision Add non-financial information Include competitive (or market) information if possible Longer-term focus

Complete your answer. (One possible solution is shown below.)

REPORT

To   J. Sum

From   Accountant

Date   [Today's date]

Subject   Performance management at Metis

Introduction[40]

This report assesses the existing performance reporting pack and suggests improvements which could be made to it.

The existing report does provide some useful performance information. However, there are also a number of areas where it could be improved in order to assist in decision making and strategic planning.

Strategically relevant performance measures

The report does not currently provide any information about how the different functional areas of the business are performing in a number of key areas that will have a bearing on the long-term success of Metis.

[40] To score professional marks, set this up as a report and include a short introduction.

For example, there are no measures which indicate how well the service staff are performing[41]. This issue could be addressed by identifying key objectives and establishing KPIs which will support those objectives. For example, Metis could use a customer survey to find out how satisfied its customers are with the service they have received, and average scores from these surveys could be used as an indicator of the quality of service being offered.

Similarly, there don't currently appear to be any indicators which relate to the performance of the **kitchen operations**. For example, it might be useful to monitor how long it takes for meals to be delivered from the kitchen, or how much food is wasted (for example, if the chef is not happy that a plate of food is up to standard and so it has to be thrown away).

Both of these points also highlight that the current report only looks at financial performance. However, the owners should also be monitoring how well Metis is performing in relation to its non-financial performance indicators.[42] These are likely to be crucial in attracting and retaining customers, and hence to the longer-term success of the business.

It is likely that **procurement** is another important functional area, because Metis will need sufficient food to satisfy customer demand, but it will need to avoid over-ordering perishable items. Equally, it will be important that Metis buys food and drink of high enough quality to satisfy its customers, yet secures it for the best price possible. The gross margins obtained for different product categories could be used as an indicator for this area, which again highlights the need for gross margin percentages to be provided rather than just an absolute figure.

[41] Apply your points to the scenario. We'll look at this skill again in Skills Checkpoint 5.

[42] Remember you are asked to 'suggest improvements' as well as critically assessing the current report.

External information

The existing report only looks at internal aspects of performance. For example, it does not give any indication of how Metis's margins or product mix compare against those of other similar restaurants. Such comparisons or benchmarking could be useful, although it may be difficult to obtain the necessary data. There may be a local restaurant association, or similar trade association, which Metis could join, which has a database of such information.

Profit information[43]

Highlights profit – The existing report shows clearly how profitable the business is, both in terms of gross profit and net profit. Showing the net profit margin (%) is also useful because, for example, it shows that not only has Metis been able to increase its revenue over the last three years, but also it has been able to control its costs sufficiently well so that the net margin (%) has increased. This is an indicator that the current strategy seems to be working, which will be important to consider in strategic planning (for example, further restaurant opening may be sensible).

Absolute figures only – However, although the figures show that revenues and profits have increased over the three years under review, the figures would be more useful if they showed the percentage increases each year, rather than just showing each year's figures. This would allow the relative growth of the different business areas to be more visible.

Product information

Revenue streams – It is also useful that the report shows revenues and costs for different product categories (eg desserts/starters/main courses), because this could help identify if the revenues or costs for certain products are increasing more than for other products[44]. This may assist in decision making to address favourable or adverse trends.

[43] Use sub-headings to score professional marks.

[44] Ensure that you explain why your point matters (this is addressed further in Skills Checkpoint 5).

Again, however, this information could be more useful if it showed the percentage increases each year.

Margins by product – Equally, although the report shows revenues and cost of sales for different product categories, it doesn't show the gross profit or gross profit percentage for each product category. However, such information would be useful for decision making. For example, in 20X2, the gross margin Metis earned on food was 68% ($657k/$974k) and the margin on beer was 62% ($115k/$186k) but on wine it was only 54% ($109k/$201k).

Performance comparison

The report only shows the actual results; it doesn't show any budget or forecast figures as a comparison. It would be useful if these were included, in order to gauge whether Metis is performing better or worse than had been anticipated, and therefore whether any corrective action (decision making) is required to bring actual performance back in line with forecast.

Quantity of information

While it would be useful to have some additional information (percentage changes; performance against budget) it is important to avoid showing too much information in the report.

Given that the report is a quarterly summary, there is a danger that it already contains too much detailed information[45]; for example, instead of showing the detail of all the operating costs, this could be shown as a single line for 'Operating costs'. If this total line showed any unusual results, these could then be investigated separately by drilling down into the total.

[45] Your assessment of the report should relate to both its content and its presentation.

Equally, it is debatable how much value is added by showing three years' worth of historical information. It could be useful to show the current year and the prior year, but any more than this seems to be superfluous. As Metis was only started three years ago, there is likely to be little value in comparing performance in 20X2 with 20X0 as the business will have developed and become much more established over the intervening period. Equally, market conditions could have changed over this period.

The comparison between the latest quarter and the previous quarter also appears to have little value. There is a fall in revenue of 42% between Q4 and Q3, which suggests Metis's business is seasonal. Therefore, it might be more useful to compare performance in the current quarter with the equivalent quarter in the previous year. Also a longer-term forecast may be needed in order to feed into strategic decision making. For example, the impact of new competition may mean that strategic decisions are needed now to address medium-term performance issues.

Presentation

The overall presentation of the report could also be improved. It might not be clear to a non-accountant what the most important figures are, so the key figures (eg gross profit, net margin) could usefully be highlighted in bold. Similarly, the report might look less crowded if the figures were shown in thousands of dollars rather than to the last dollar.

Exam success skills diagnostic

Every time you complete a question, use the diagnostic below to assess how effectively you demonstrated the exam success skills in answering the question. The table has been completed below for the Metis activity to give you an idea of how to complete the diagnostic.

Exam success skills	Your reflections/observations
Managing information	Did you spend sufficient time reading the scenario and planning your approach?
Correct interpretation of requirements	Did you realise that the performance report needed to be analysed – not Metis's performance? Did you both 'critically assess' the existing report **and** recommend improvements?
Answer planning	Did you produce a plan to ensure that both aspects of the requirement were addressed in your answer?
Effective writing and presentation	Did you use a report format, and include an introduction and sub-headings?
Most important action points to apply to your next question	

Summary

The 50-mark Section A question in the APM exam often features a significant amount of data. This data will sometimes require further analysis, to provide information about an organisation's performance – as covered earlier in Skills Checkpoint 1. However, on other occasions, you will not be required to analyse the data, but the performance report itself.

Where an exam question requires the **evaluation of a performance report**, you will need to consider the format of the report, and the nature of the information provided.

Most importantly you will be trying to assess the extent to which the report allows visibility of areas that matter strategically and therefore will be crucial in allowing a company to achieve its mission and objectives. For example, do the performance measures shown in the report help managers assess how well a company is performing in relation to its objectives or its CSFs?

In this sense, a well-designed performance report is a key part of a coherent performance management framework.

7

Strategic performance measures in the private sector

Learning objectives

On completion of this chapter, you should be able to:

	Syllabus reference no.
Demonstrate why the primary objective of financial performance should be primarily concerned with benefits to shareholders.	D1(a)
Discuss the appropriateness of, and apply different measures of, performance, including: • Gross profit and operating profit • Return on Capital Employed (ROCE) • Return on Investment (ROI) [*Also covered in Chapter 8*] • Earnings per Share (EPS) • Earnings before Interest, Tax, Depreciation and Amortisation (EBITDA) • Residual Income (RI) [*Also covered in Chapter 8*] • Net Present Value • Internal rate of return and modified internal rate of return (IRR, MIRR) • Economic Value Added (EVA™) [*This is covered in Chapter 8*]	D1(b)
Discuss why indicators of liquidity and gearing need to be considered in conjunction with profitability	D1(c)
Compare and contrast short and long-run financial performance and the resulting management issues	D1(d)
Assess the appropriate benchmarks to use in assessing performance	D1(e)

Exam context

This chapter starts to cover syllabus Section D, strategic performance measurement. As we have mentioned before, the 50-mark Section A question in the APM exam will focus on syllabus sections A, C and D, so you should be prepared to discuss issues around financial performance measures in the context of the 50-mark question.

Here we start to look at some of the key financial performance measures used to assess company performance. You may already be familiar with most of these measures from previous studies, but at the Strategic Professional level you will be expected not only to be able to calculate the measures but also to apply them in the context of a scenario-based question.

The examining team have highlighted that the increased use of technology by accountants (eg spreadsheets and databases) means there should be less need to perform calculations manually, particularly at strategic level. Equally, qualified accountants might reasonably expect to have more junior members of staff supporting them, who can perform some of the more routine calculations.

Consequently, you should not expect there to be significant amounts of purely computational work in the APM exam. Instead, the focus is more likely to be on analysing calculations which have already been carried out (and what they indicate about an organisation's performance), or on evaluating the choice of different performance metrics which an organisation is using to measure and control its performance.

Chapter overview

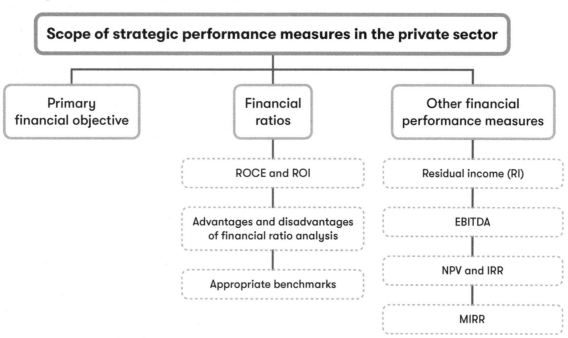

1 Primary financial objective

Although there is increasingly a recognition that the needs of a broad range of stakeholders are important, performance reports in profit-making organisations often tend to focus on financial performance in general, and on the interests of shareholders in particular.

The logic for this is that shareholders are the legal owners; the company belongs to them, and so their interests are paramount. Consequently, the underlying financial objective of commercial organisations should be to **maximise the shareholders' wealth**.

Although the dividends they receive provide one source of wealth for shareholders, the main source of shareholder wealth – particularly in the **longer term** – comes through increases in the value of the shares. As a firm's share price increases, the value of the firm increases, and therefore the wealth of the shareholders who hold shares in the firm also increases.

An overall measure of whether shareholder wealth has increased is given by **total shareholder return (TSR)**.

Formula to learn

Total shareholder return = dividend yield + capital gain/(loss)

Dividend yield = dividend per share/share price at start of the year

Capital gain/loss = gain or loss/share price at the start of the year

Exercise: Robertson Co

Summary financial information for Robertson Co is given below, covering the last two years.

	Previous year	Current year
Dividends payable on ordinary shares ($'000)	2,000	2,200
Number of shares in issue ('000)	9,000	9,000
End-year share price ($)	9.63	11.40

Here we can estimate Robertson Co's total shareholder return in the current year as follows:

- The end-year share price of $9.63 for the previous year is the same as the opening share price for the current year.
- Current dividend per share = 2,200/9,000 = $0.244
- Capital gain is $11.40 – $9.63 = $1.77

So the total shareholder return = 0.244/ 9.63 + 1.77 / 9.63 = 0.025 + 0.184 = 0.209 or **20.9%**.

Changes in the value of a company's shares are influenced by a company's current and forecast financial position. This can be assessed using **financial ratio analysis**.

PER alert

The topics covered in Section D of the APM syllabus as a whole could all help you fulfil Performance objective 14: Monitor performance. The objective requires you to 'measure and assess department and business performance'.

The topics we cover in this chapter are particularly relevant to element (c) of the objective: 'Identify and use appropriate performance measurement techniques to assess aspects of performance within the organisation'.

However, element (e) also reiterates the importance of performance management, rather than just measurement: 'Advise on appropriate ways to maintain and improve performance'.

2 Financial ratios

2.1 Profit, liquidity, gearing and investor ratios

Shareholders are interested in a number of aspects of a company's financial performance, including:

(a) **Profitability** – how well a company performs, given its asset base

(b) **Liquidity** – short-term financial position

(c) **Gearing** – measure of financial risk

(d) **Investor performance** – share value and dividends

2.1.1 Discussion of liquidity and gearing ratios

Key profitability ratios are covered in the next section, however it is worth noting that it is not uncommon for profitable companies to **fail** because of liquidity issues. It is therefore important to include an analysis of **liquidity and gearing ratios** in an assessment of company performance. This analysis is covered later in the Workbook in the context of corporate failure (Chapter 15).

Essential reading

Please refer to Chapter 7 Section 1 of the Essential reading for a review of brought forward knowledge relating to ratio analysis, including a reminder of how the main ratios are calculated.

The Essential reading is available as an Appendix of the digital edition of the Workbook.

2.2 Return on capital employed (also return on investment)

KEY
TERM

> **Return on capital employed (ROCE):** A ratio which indicates the productivity of capital employed. It is calculated as:
>
> $$\frac{\text{Profit before interest and tax (PBIT)} \times 100}{\text{Average capital employed}}$$

Capital employed is shareholders' capital **plus** long-term debt finance (this is the same as total assets less current liabilities). The underlying principle is that we must compare like with like, and so if capital means share capital and reserves **plus** long-term debt capital, profit must mean the profit earned by all this capital together, which is measured as profits **before interest** (and tax).

Capital employed is normally calculated as the **average** of the capital employed at the beginning and end of the year.

If a company's (or a division's) performance is being assessed on the basis of ROCE, this may discourage capital investment, because an increase in capital will lead to a fall in ROCE if PBIT remains the same.

However, such a failure to invest is likely to have an adverse effect on a business's performance in the longer term. One of the main criticisms of ROCE as a performance measure is that it can encourage **short-term decision making**.

Return on investment (ROI) is calculated in the same way as ROCE, and tends to be used when evaluating divisional performance (see next chapter).

Activity 1: Basil Co

EXTRACT FROM STATEMENT OF FINANCIAL POSITION FOR BASIL CO AS AT 31.12.X8

	$m
End of year	
Total assets	202.0
Current liabilities	(112.0)
Beginning of year	
Total assets	189.0
Current liabilities	(69.0)

INCOME STATEMENT EXTRACT FOR BASIL CO AS AT 31.12.X8

	$m
Revenue	275.1
Cost of sales	(210.1)
Gross profit	65.0
Administrative expenses	(15.0)
Write off of goodwill	(35.0)
Operating profit	15.0
Interest payable	(3.0)
Profit before tax	12.0
Tax	(2.4)
Net profit	9.6

Notes.

1 Basil Co's cost of capital is 8%.

2 Operating profit is after charging depreciation of non-current assets of $24 million.

Required

Calculate the ROCE for Basil Co.   **(1 mark)**

Solution

2.2.1 Comparisons of ROCE

ROCE can be compared to the performance of similar companies, or evaluated over time.

2.3 Advantages and disadvantages of financial ratio analysis

Advantages	Disadvantages
Puts performance into context by relating one number to another Eg comparing profit to the capital employed to generate that profit	Focusses only on variables which can be expressed in monetary terms
Enables performance to be compared between organisations of different size	Tendency to focus on short-term performance, and ignores future potential
Easier to look at changes over time	

2.4 Appropriate benchmarks for ratio analysis

2.4.1 Over time

Ratio analysis often involves benchmarking the performance of a company **against an earlier time period**, or periods, to identify if performance is improving or getting worse. However, interpreting performance in this way ignores the impact of changes in the environment on the performance potential of a company. For example, is the economy in recession this year and wasn't in the previous year(s)?

2.4.2 Other companies

Alternatively, ratio analysis may involve benchmarking the performance of a company **against other companies**. Different forms of benchmarking have already been discussed (in Chapter 1), but when benchmarking performance of different companies a key issue is likely to be whether the companies are truly comparable; ie are they involved in exactly the same business operations, and in the same markets? Are they pursuing the same strategies?

2.4.3 Internal target

Finally, if ratio analysis is being used to evaluate management performance then the benchmark may be **an internally set target**. However, care will need to be taken to ensure the target is not unreasonable and that it reflects items that are under the control of management. (The issue of controllability is covered in the next chapter).

3 Other financial performance measures

3.1 Residual income (RI)

> **Residual Income (RI):** A measure of a company's profit after deducting an imputed cost of capital. It is calculated as:
>
> PBIT – (imputed cost of capital × capital employed)

Moving away from ratio analysis, RI is a similar profitability measure to ROCE. The key difference is that RI uses an **imputed cost of capital** to measure the expected return on the capital base. This will typically be the organisation's **weighted average cost of capital**. Alternatively, if RI is being used for a specific division (see Chapter 8), it will be **adjusted to allow for the risk characteristics of that division**, with a higher interest rate being applied to **higher risk divisions.**

The fact that different costs of capital can be applied to units with different risk characteristics makes RI a more flexible performance measure than ROCE.

However, the fact that RI produces an absolute value (rather than a %) means it does not enable comparison between organisations of different size.

Activity 2: Basil Co (continued)

Using the information from Activity 1, calculate the RI for Basil Co.   (1 mark)

Solution

3.1.1 Comparator for RI

RI embeds the cost of capital into the performance measure. Note that an RI of zero means that performance is satisfactory since PBIT covers the return expected on the capital employed. Positive RI therefore indicates good performance, and negative RI indicates poor performance.

3.2 EBITDA

> **EBITDA:** Earnings before interest, tax, depreciation and amortisation.

EBITDA is measure of financial performance that has grown in popularity in recent years. EBITDA can be seen as a useful performance measure for a number of reasons:

- Useful for evaluating companies with **low levels of tangible assets** (eg service companies), compared to ROCE (ROCE will be artificially high if the asset base is low).
- **Removes tax and interest, as these are unrelated to business performance**
- EBITDA is argued to be a good proxy for **cash flow from operations** and therefore is a measure of underlying performance. It can be seen as the proportion of operating profits converted to cash.
- EBITDA can be used to **assess the performance of a manager who has no control over investment and financing policy**, as it excludes costs associated with assets (depreciation) and debt (interest).
- Depreciation and amortisation also relate to historical decisions – for example, depreciation charges could relate to an asset acquired a relatively long time ago. By **stripping out costs relating to historical decisions**, EBITDA can help get a better understanding of an organisation's current performance.
- **Easier to assess the performance of different companies (compared to earnings per share (EPS))** with different capital structures (if taken as a percentage of capital employed). Also, EBITDA removes the subjective judgement that can go into calculating depreciation and amortisation, such as useful lives and residual values, and therefore makes it easier to compare the financial performance of different companies.

3.2.1 Drawbacks of EBITDA

- Critics of EBITDA point out that it allows a company to make its financial picture more attractive by removing these costs (eg interest; depreciation) from the measures of its performance. It can be used as window dressing to excuse poor performance in a loss-making company.

- Although EBITDA can be a good proxy for cash flow from operations, critics of EBITDA argue that it doesn't take account of the cash required to fund working capital or to replace or acquire assets (as well as to pay tax and interest).

Activity 3: Basil Co (continued)

Using the information from Activity 1, calculate the EBITDA for Basil Co.   **(2 marks)**

Solution

3.3 Net present value (NPV) and internal rate of return (IRR)

Net present value (NPV) and internal rate of return (IRR) can also be used as measures of performance. These calculations are typically used when planning future projects, but can be used as performance measures by retrospectively comparing actual results to those planned. These techniques are useful because they focus on future cash flows and risk, and encourage a longer-term perspective on performance.

A **positive net present value** indicates that **shareholder wealth** is being created. According to one model of share valuations, the market value of the shares is based on the expected future cash flows.

In a **computer-based exam**, net present value can be calculated using a spreadsheet formula. For example, if the future cash flows from a project arise over five years and are in cells B10 to F10, and need to be discounted at 10%, then the formula would be =NPV(0.1, B10:F10).

This would give the present value of cash flows from time period 1-5. The cash outflow in time 0 would then need to be deducted to calculate the net present value.

A project's IRR is the required rate of return (or cost of capital) which leads to the project having an NPV of zero when that rate of return is used to discount the project's cash flows. Good performance is indicated by the IRR exceeding the organisation's cost of capital.

In a **computer-based exam**, internal rate of return can also be calculated using a spreadsheet formula. For example, to identify the internal rate of return of a project arising over five years (involving time periods 0-5) the formula could be =IRR(A10:F10).

Exam focus point

When using the =NPV and =IRR functions remember that the =NPV function **should not** include the time 0 cash flow, but the =IRR function **should** include the time 0 cash flow.

Activity 4: Project evaluation

Fame Ltd is considering expanding its range of dance facilities by investing in 30 new studios.

The following estimates have been made relating to the cash outflows and inflows:

(1) Initial investment of $12 million

(2) Capital development/improvement costs of $2 million per year at the end of each of Years 2 and 3

(3) Projected income from 30 studios of $400,000 per studio per year

(4) Variable costs are estimated at $120,000 per studio per year

(5) Total directly attributable fixed costs of $1.2 million per year in each of Years 1 to 6

(6) Corporation tax at the rate of 30%, payable in the year in which cash flows occur. Tax allowances are not available

(7) All cash flows are stated in current prices and with the exception of the initial investment will occur at the end of each year

(8) The cost of capital is 11%

Required

Calculate the net present value (NPV) and internal rate of return (IRR) of the project and recommend whether it should be undertaken. Evaluate the project over six years. **(10 marks)**

Solution

NPV of the proposal

Time	0	1	2	3	4	5	6
	$'000	$'000	$'000	$'000	$'000	$'000	$'000
Net cash flows (W1)	–	7,200	☐	☐	7,200	7,200	7,200
Taxation at 30%	–	(2,160)	☐	☐	(2,160)	(2,160)	(2,160)
Net cash flow		5,040	☐	☐	5,040	5,040	5,040
Capital costs	(12,000)	–	☐	☐			
Net cash flow	**(12,000)**	**5,040**	☐	☐	**5,040**	**5,040**	**5,040**
Discount factors 11%	1.0	0.901	☐	☐	0.659	0.593	0.535
Present value	**(12,000)**	**4,541**	☐	☐	**3,321**	**2,989**	**2,696**

3.4 Modified IRR (MIRR)

IRR assumes that the cash flows after the investment phase (time 0 in Activity 4 above) are **reinvested at the project's IRR** over the life of a project. This is known as the **reinvestment assumption**, and is a weakness of IRR.

A better assumption is that the funds **are reinvested at the investor's minimum required return (weighted average cost of capital)**, which is 11% in Activity 4.

This can be addressed by using the modified internal rate of return (MIRR), which distinguishes between the **investment phase** of a project and the **return phase**.

In the formula below, the **return phase** is the phase of the project from when cash inflows have commenced. The investment phase is the phase with the cash outflows.

Formula to learn
$$\left(\frac{\text{PV return phase}}{\text{PV investment phase}}\right)^{1/n} \times (1 + i) - 1$$
i = cost of capital; n = the life of the project (in years)

In a **computer-based exam**, modified internal rate of return can be calculated using a spreadsheet formula. Like the formula for IRR, this should highlight the undiscounted cash flows for all years of the project, including time 0. The formula is =MIRR (values, finance rate, reinvestment rate).

The finance rate is the cost of raising finance for a company can borrow at and the reinvestment rate is the rate of return a company can obtain when reinvesting project inflows; the two rates will normally be the same.

For example, to identify the MIRR of the future cash flows from a project arising over five years (involving time periods 0-5) where the cost of capital to be applied to cash outflows (the finance rate) and cash inflows (reinvestment rate) is 10%, then the formula could be as follows:

=MIRR(A10:F10, 0.1, 0.1)

Activity 5: Technique demonstration

Using the formula, calculate the modified IRR of the proposed investment described in Activity 4.

Solution

3.5 Advantages of MIRR

Using the formula, MIRR is **quicker** to calculate than IRR, it makes a **more realistic assumption about the reinvestment rate**, and **does not give the multiple answers** that can sometimes arise with the conventional IRR.

Essential reading

Please refer to Chapter 7 Section 2 of the Essential reading for further discussion of MIRR, including an illustration of how to deal with different reinvestment and finance rates.

The Essential reading is available as an Appendix of the digital edition of the Workbook.

Chapter summary

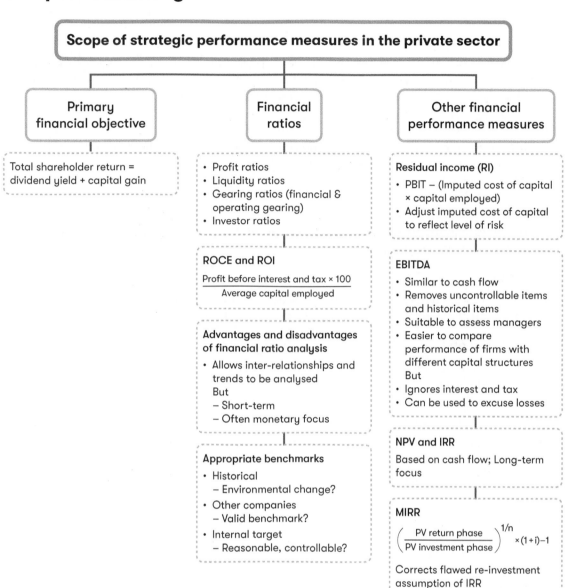

Scope of strategic performance measures in the private sector

Primary financial objective

Total shareholder return = dividend yield + capital gain

Financial ratios

- Profit ratios
- Liquidity ratios
- Gearing ratios (financial & operating gearing)
- Investor ratios

ROCE and ROI

$$\frac{\text{Profit before interest and tax} \times 100}{\text{Average capital employed}}$$

Advantages and disadvantages of financial ratio analysis

- Allows inter-relationships and trends to be analysed
  But
  – Short-term
  – Often monetary focus

Appropriate benchmarks

- Historical
  – Environmental change?
- Other companies
  – Valid benchmark?
- Internal target
  – Reasonable, controllable?

Other financial performance measures

Residual income (RI)

- PBIT – (Imputed cost of capital × capital employed)
- Adjust imputed cost of capital to reflect level of risk

EBITDA

- Similar to cash flow
- Removes uncontrollable items and historical items
- Suitable to assess managers
- Easier to compare performance of firms with different capital structures
  But
- Ignores interest and tax
- Can be used to excuse losses

NPV and IRR

Based on cash flow; Long-term focus

MIRR

$$\left(\frac{\text{PV return phase}}{\text{PV investment phase}} \right)^{1/n} \times (1+i) - 1$$

Corrects flawed re-investment assumption of IRR

Knowledge diagnostic

1. Total shareholder return

Maximising benefits to shareholders is generally agreed to be a company's primary financial objective. TSR measures the dividend yield plus capital gain over a period of time. Generating capital gain (increases in the share price) depends on expectations of long-term performance.

2. Return on capital employed (ROCE)

This compares operating profit to average long-term capital (shareholders and long-term debt). However, there is a danger ROCE can discourage capital investment, and encourage short-term decision making.

3. Residual income

This also compares operating profit to average long-term capital but includes a charge for using capital which can be adjusted to reflect risk.

4. EBITDA

This attempts to measure underlying business performance, focussing on areas that are under management control. Criticised for allowing window-dressing of poor performance.

5. NPV/IRR/MIRR

These techniques attempt to monitor long-term performance, which is essential to create shareholder value.

Further study guidance

Question practice

Now try the following from the Further question practice bank (available in the digital edition of the Workbook):

Q9 *Metis*

Activity answers

Activity 1: Basil Co

Opening capital employed (Total assets – current liabilities)	$120.0m	(189.0 – 69.0)
Closing capital employed	$90.0m	(202.0 – 112.0)
Average capital employed	$105.0m	((120.0 + 90.0)/2)
ROCE (Operating profit / average capital employed)	14.3%	(15.0/105.0)

Activity 2: Basil Co (continued)

PBIT = $15.0m

Average capital employed = $105.0m (from Activity 1)

Cost of capital (given in Activity 1) = 8%

RI = $15.0m – (0.08 × $105.0m) = $6.6m

Activity 3: Basil Co (continued)

EBITDA	$m
Operating profit	15.0
Add back:	
Depreciation on non-current assets	24.0
Write off of goodwill	35.0
EBITDA	74.0

Activity 4: Project evaluation
NPV of the proposal

Time	0	1	2	3	4	5	6
	$'000	$'000	$'000	$'000	$'000	$'000	$'000
Net cash flows (W1)	–	7,200	7,200	7,200	7,200	7,200	7,200
Taxation at 30%	–	(2,160)	(2,160)	(2,160)	(2,160)	(2,160)	(2,160)
Net cash flow		5,040	5,040	5,040	5,040	5,040	5,040
Capital costs	(12,000)	–	(2,000)	(2,000)			
Net cash flow	**(12,000)**	**5,040**	**3,040**	**3,040**	**5,040**	**5,040**	**5,040**
Discount factors 11%	1.0	0.901	0.812	0.731	0.659	0.593	0.535
Present value	**(12,000)**	**4,541**	**2,468**	**2,222**	**3,321**	**2,989**	**2,696**

Net present value ($'000) 6,237

The NPV of the proposal is positive so the proposal should go ahead on this basis.

Using the spreadsheet NPV function, the answer is as follows:

C9		× ✓ fx	=NPV(0.11,D8:I8)					
▲	A	B	C	D	E	F	G	H	I
6									
7		Time	0	1	2	3	4	5	6
8		Net cash flow		5040	3040	3040	5040	5040	5040
9		NPV	18,236						
10		outlay	- 12,000						
11			6,236						
12									

Working

Annual cash flows

	$'000
Revenues 30 × $400,000	12,000
Variable costs 30 × $120,000	(3,600)
Fixed costs	(1,200)
Net cash flow	7,200

IRR of the proposal

Now try any other cost of capital, eg 15%

Time	0	1	2	3	4	5	6
	$'000	$'000	$'000	$'000	$'000	$'000	$'000
Net cash flow	(12,000)	5,040	3,040	3,040	5,040	5,040	5,040
Discount factors	1.0	0.870	0.756	0.658	0.572	0.497	0.432
Present value	(12,000)	4,385	2,298	2,000	2,883	2,505	2,177

Net present value ($'000) 4,248

The proposal is also giving a return above 15%. Now we can estimate the IRR using the formula:

$$IRR = a + \frac{NPVa}{NPVa - NPVb}(b - a)$$

Where a is the lower discount rate (11%) giving NPVa, b is the higher rate (15%) giving NPVb

$$IRR = 11 + \frac{6,237}{6,237 - 4,248}(15 - 11) = 11 + (3.136 \times 4) = \mathbf{23.5\%}$$

The IRR > cost of capital so accept

Alternatively, using the spreadsheet IRR function gives the answer more accurately as follows:

C5		× ✓ fx	=IRR(C3:I3)					
▲	A	B	C	D	E	F	G	H	I
1									
2		Time	0	1	2	3	4	5	6
3		Net cash flow	-12,000	5040	3040	3040	5040	5040	5040
4									
5		IRR	27%						
6									

Activity 5: Technique demonstration

$$\left(\frac{\text{PV return phase}}{\text{PV investment phase}}\right)^{1/n} \times (1 + i) - 1$$

i = cost of capital

Investment phase = 12,000

so PV of return phase = project NPV (at 11%) + 12,000 = 6,237 + 12,000 = 18,237

$$\left(\frac{18,237}{12,000}\right)^{1/6} \times (1 + 0.11) - 1 = 0.19 \text{ or } \mathbf{19\%}$$

The proposal is still acceptable because the MIRR is above the cost of capital.

Alternatively, using the MIRR spreadsheet formula the answer is:

C5		fx	=MIRR(C3:I3, 0.11,0.11)						
	A	B	C	D	E	F	G	H	I
1									
2		Time	0	1	2	3	4	5	6
3		Net cash flow	- 12,000	5040	3040	3040	5040	5040	5040
4									
5		MIRR	19%						
6									

8

Divisional performance and transfer pricing issues

Learning objectives

On completion of this chapter, you should be able to:

	Syllabus reference no.
Describe, compute and evaluate performance measures relevant in a divisionalised organisation structure including ROI, RI and economic value added (EVA™).	D2(a)
Discuss the need for separate measures in respect of managerial and divisional performance.	D2(b)
Discuss the circumstances in which a transfer pricing policy may be needed and discuss the necessary criteria for its design.	D2(c)
Demonstrate and evaluate the use of alternative bases for transfer pricing.	D2(d)
Explain and demonstrate issues that require consideration when setting transfer prices in multinational companies.	D2(e)

Exam context

This chapter continues to cover Section D of the syllabus: Strategic Performance Measurement.

Following from Chapter 7, which looked at some of the key financial performance measures used to assess **company** performance, this chapter moves on to look at **divisional** performance measurement, and the associated area of transfer pricing. The topics in this chapter provide plenty of material for an exam question, and will often be examined along with the topics covered in the previous chapter.

You may already be familiar with most of these measures from your previous studies, but at the Strategic Professional level you will be expected not only to be able to calculate the measures correctly but also to discuss and apply them in the context of a scenario-based question. For example, the primary focus of a transfer pricing question in an APM exam is unlikely to be detailed transfer pricing calculations in their own right. Instead, you are more likely to be asked to comment on the transfer pricing system being used in an organisation – for example, how useful is it in allowing managers to measure and evaluate divisional performance; or how well does it ensure that decisions taken by individual divisions (with a view to maximising their own divisional profits) also help to maximise group profit as a whole.

Chapter overview

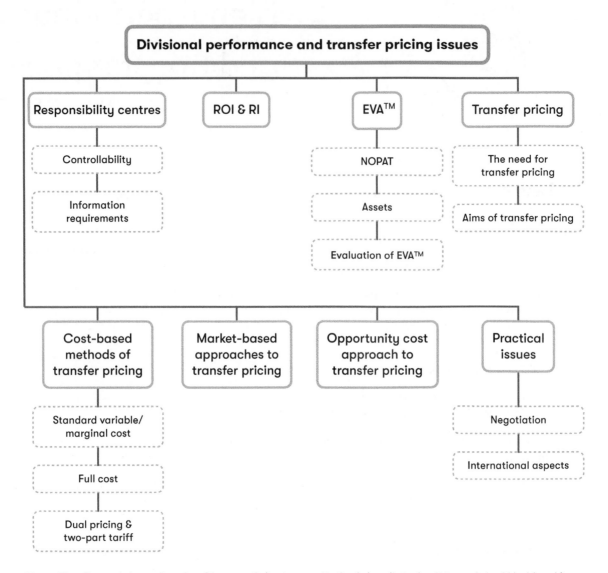

Note. The Essential reading for Chapter 8 (in Appendix 2 of the digital edition of the Workbook) covers the potential significance of negotiation in transfer pricing, and the issues relating to transfer pricing in the context of multinational organisations.

1 Responsibility centres

KEY
TERM

> **Responsibility accounting:** A system of accounting that segregates revenues and costs into areas of management responsibility in order to control performance.
>
> **Responsibility centre:** Any part of an organisation which is headed by a manager who has direct responsibility for its performance and is accountable for it.

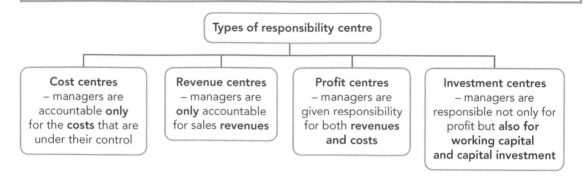

1.1 Controllability

The **appropriate type of responsibility centre** will depend on the areas that are under a manager's control.

The design of **managerial performance reports** (in any type of responsibility centre) should also be based on **controllable items**. Managers should only be accountable for aspects of performance which are under their control. This means that there may be a **difference** between the reporting of **divisional performance** and the reporting of **managerial performance**.

1.1.1 Divisional performance

Divisional performance should be evaluated on all the items which are directly **traceable** to the division. Divisional results may need to be **adjusted** for items that are not traceable in order to reflect **divisional performance**.

For example, **allocated** head office costs that **do not directly reflect the activity of the division** should be excluded when calculating traceable profit.

1.1.2 Managerial performance

However, **managerial performance** should only be based on items that are under **managerial control**.

This means that **to assess managerial performance,** divisional results first have to be adjusted to reflect **traceable items** and then may need to be **further adjusted** to reflect areas that are **controllable** by divisional management, by **stripping out** items over which divisional managers have **no control.**

For example, a division's results may need to be adjusted for the purpose of assessing **managerial performance,** by stripping out the effects of environmental changes that impact on divisional performance (these are traceable, but are **not controlled** by divisional managers).

The impact of **controllable costs** and **traceable costs** on divisional profit could be viewed as follows:

Revenue	X
Controllable divisional costs	(X)
Controllable divisional profit	X
Traceable divisional costs	(X)
Traceable divisional profit	X

	(X)
Net profit	X

You may be expected to adjust a division's results to reflect the issues of **traceability and controllability** in the exam, so that they can be used to assess managerial performance.

Activity 1: Controllability

Division X is part of Control Co; both are based in Xland where the currency is the X$.

Division X is a profit centre and exports all its products to Yland where the currency is the Y£. Division X's costs are all incurred in X$s.

Division X's customers are invoiced in Y£s, at prices fixed at the start of the year.

During 20X8, the head office at Control Co invested in a new e-commerce platform which significantly increased the efficiency of the division.

At the beginning of the final quarter of 20X8 the value of the X$ fell by 8%, and remained at this level for the rest of the year.

The manager of Division X is currently appraised on the net profit margin of the division, and is awarded a large bonus if this exceeds 7% for the year.

The manager of Division X has complained that the net margin target is not suitable for appraising her performance.

Appendix – Extracts from Division X management accounts for year ended 20X8

	X$'000
Revenue **(Note)**	2,000
Cost of sales	(1,200)
Gross profit	800
Depreciation	(100)
Allocated head office costs	(90)
Other overheads	(500)
Net profit	110
Net profit margin on revenue	5.5%

Note. Revenue accrued evenly over the financial year.

Required

Recommend, using appropriate calculations, whether it is appropriate for the manager of Division X to receive a bonus for 20X8. **(8 marks)**

Solution

1.2 Information requirements

The type of responsibility centre a division is will also have an impact on its information requirements.

Clearly, the focus of management information in **cost centres** should be on costs, but there may also be a requirement for non-financial information that can indicate the cause of cost overruns (eg defect levels).

The focus of management information in **revenue centres** should be on the revenues generated, but again there may also be a requirement for non-financial information that can indicate the cause of a fall in revenue (eg customer satisfaction; customer loyalty), and also for cost information for any costs that are directly related to selling (for example salesperson salaries).

However, we will now turn our attention to the information requirements of **investment centres** by looking at potential financial performance measures. (Again, non-financial performance measures may also be important, but these are discussed in later chapters). In an investment centre, because managers have a degree of control over both profits and the asset base, performance measures need to cover both of these areas. This can be achieved using ROI, residual income, or economic value added (EVA™).

2 ROI and RI

These techniques were introduced in the previous chapter in the context of assessing the performance of a company. They can also be employed in assessing the performance of an investment centre.

2.1 Return on investment (ROI)

ROI is similar to the return on capital employed (ROCE) figure used in corporate analysis.

> **Formula to learn**
>
> $$ROI = \frac{\text{Controllable divisional profit}}{\text{Divisional investment}}$$

2.1.1 Comparisons of ROI

Return on investment (ROI) will be normally be compared against an ROI target, or against last year's ROI. (Often the target will be based on historical performance.)

2.1.2 Dysfunctional behaviour

If ROI is used as the principal performance measure then it is likely that a manager will only take decisions that will increase divisional ROI, which may be at the expense of growth in corporate profits. This may occur because:

(a) New projects have an immediate impact on the division's asset base but may only increase profits over time.

(b) The current ROI may be artificially high because the division has been under-investing in recent years. (As with ROCE, one of the problems of ROI is that it can encourage short-term decision making.)

2.2 Residual income (RI)

Residual income (RI) gives a hurdle figure for profit based on the minimum return required from a division.

	$
Controllable divisional profit	X
Less imputed interest (investment × cost of capital)	(X)
RI	X

2.2.1 Dysfunctional behaviour

RI is less likely than ROI to encourage dysfunctional behaviour, because it encourages any investments earning above the cost of capital. However, dysfunctional behaviour may still occur if new projects have an immediate impact on the division's asset base but may only increase profits over time.

Activity 2: Divisional performance

Chi Ltd has two divisions in different parts of town and wants to monitor their performance.

Results for the last year were:

	Div A	Div B
	$'000	$'000
Profits	90	135
Net assets	500	750
Turnover	300	540

Division A is considering developing a new product at a cost of $8,000. This should add $1,200 to profits from next year onwards. Division B is reliant on several long-term product lines and sees little value in R&D expenditure.

Chi Ltd has a target ROCE of 12%, based on its WACC.

Required

Evaluate the performance of the two divisions and explain how these evaluations may lead to dysfunctional behaviour. **(10 marks)**

Solution

2.3 ROI vs RI

In practice, ROI is used more frequently than RI. RI is, however, technically superior.

2.3.1 Advantages of RI

(a) RI increases in the following circumstances:

    (i)   Investments earning above the cost of capital are undertaken.

    (ii)   Investments earning below the cost of capital are eliminated.

(b) RI is more **flexible** since a different cost of capital can be applied to evaluate different divisions with different risk characteristics.

2.3.2 Weaknesses of RI

(a) It **does not facilitate comparisons** between companies or divisions of different sizes because it does not relate the size of a centre's income to the size of the investment.

(b) It can be **difficult to decide on an appropriate and accurate measure of the capital employed** on which to base the imputed interest charge (especially when applied to divisions).

2.4 Reasons for using ROI

In practice, ROI may be used more frequently than RI because:

(a) ROI is **consistent with corporate assessment** (ROCE).

(b) **Ratios** are more easily understood compared with, say, costs of capital and are **more appropriate for comparing divisions of different sizes**.

(c) Calculation of cost of capital in RI is **subjective and time consuming**.

(d) A company may feel that the dysfunctional behaviour associated with ROI, such as underinvestment, is unlikely to occur. For example, if a company is using ROI as a part of a balanced scorecard then customer, internal business and innovation measures should all highlight the impact of underinvestment.

2.5 Problems common to ROI and RI

The calculation of **'profit'**:

(a) May need to be adjusted to reflect **controllable and traceable items** only.

(b) Transfer prices or quantities may be imposed or set at non-commercial rates.

(c) Both **ignore tax**.

The calculation of **'investment'**:

(a) Historical, net book or replacement value. Using net book value (NBV) **discourages replacement**. Replacement value is complex to obtain and update.

(b) Cash may be controlled by the company's treasury department (ie not at divisional level).

(c) Intangible assets may have no accounting value or may be complex to update. **Hard to apply to service divisions** (create more value from intangible assets).

3 Economic value added (EVA™)

KEY TERM

> **EVA™:** Calculated as net operating profit after tax (NOPAT) less a capital charge
>
> (where the capital charge = weighted average cost of capital × net assets at the start of the period)

The logic behind EVA™ is that if the primary objective of commercial organisations is to **maximise the wealth of their shareholders**, then performance measures should evaluate how well they are doing this. It is argued that profit-based measures, which many organisations use as their primary measure of financial performance, do not do this because:

(a) Profit ignores the cost of equity capital.

(b) Profits calculated in accordance with accounting standards do not truly reflect the wealth that has been created.

EVA™ is a variation of RI, but differs from RI in the figures it considers as profits and assets.

3.1 NOPAT

There are **differences in the way that NOPAT is calculated**, compared with the profit figure that is used for RI (and ROCE).

(a) Costs which would normally be treated as expenses in the financial statements, but which are considered within an EVATM calculation as **investments building for the future**, are added back to derive a figure for **'economic profit'**. These costs are included instead as assets in the figure for net assets employed; in other words, they are deemed to be investments for the future. Costs treated in this way include such items as **research and development expenditure**, and **advertising costs**.

(b) **Cash accounting versus accruals.** Investors are primarily interested in cash flows, so accounting adjustments for non-cash items, such as provisions, or allowances for doubtful debts, are eliminated.

(c) The charge for accounting depreciation in the income statement should be added back to profit, and a charge for **economic depreciation** made instead. The value of non-current assets (and therefore capital employed) should also be adjusted to reflect the revised charge.

Economic depreciation reflects the true change in value of assets during the period. If no detail is given about economic depreciation in a question scenario, then you should assume that accounting depreciation is a reasonable approximation for it, and therefore you should not make any change to the depreciation figure.

(d) **Tax paid** (in cash terms) is **deducted** from the profit figure. (Remember, 'NOPAT' stands for net operating profit **after** tax.)

Also note that interest is excluded from NOPAT because interest costs are taken into account in the capital charge (this is the same as the calculation of the profit figure for RI).

Two alternative ways of laying out your NOPAT calculations are shown in the following table.

BPP LEARNING MEDIA

Approach 1	Approach 2
PAT (profit after tax)	**PBIT** less (cash) taxes paid on operating profit
Add back	Add back
Goodwill amortised	Goodwill amortised
R&D and advertising	R&D and advertising
Non-cash items (eg provisions)	Non-cash items (eg provisions)
Depreciation (charge economic depreciation)	Depreciation (charge economic depreciation)
Interest (net of tax)	

3.2 Assets

There are **differences in the way that the asset base is calculated**, compared with the approach that is used for RI (and ROCE).

(a) Assets are usually valued at their opening year value and at replacement cost (if given).

(b) The asset base is also increased by any costs that have been capitalised.

Where accounting adjustments are made to NOPAT (eg to add back R&D expenditure and advertising, or non-cash items) a similar adjustment needs to be made to capital employed in the relevant year.

Activity 3: Economic value added

B Division of Z Ltd has operating profits and assets for the year ended 31 December 20X5 as below:

	$'000
Operating profit	156.0
Less: Non-cash expenses	8.0
Amortisation of goodwill	5.0
Interest @ 10%	15.0
Profit before tax	128.0
Tax @ 30%	38.4
Profits after tax	89.6
Total equity	350.0
Long-term debt	150.0
	500.0

Z Ltd has a target capital structure of 25% debt/75% equity. The cost of equity is estimated at 15%. The capital employed at the start of the year amounted to $470,000. Goodwill previously written off against reserves on acquisitions in previous years amounted to $40,000.

Required

Calculate EVA™ and residual income for B Division for the year ended 31 December 20X5, and comment on your results. **(6 marks)**

Solution

3.3 Evaluation of EVA™

Advantages	Disadvantages
Calculates return in line with shareholder expectations, therefore aligns to the objective of maximising shareholder wealth	Complex due to adjustments required
Replaces multiple goals with one financial measure that can be used at all levels of decision making	Based on historical data (ie accounts) so may have limited use as a guide to future performance
Encourages expenditure in areas that create benefits for the long term (eg advertising & research and development)	Absolute measure making interdivisional comparisons difficult (where divisions are different sizes)
Removes distortion from accounting policies (eg the impact of provisions is removed)	Inconsistent with published financial information
Consistent with NPV (both show the return on investments in relation to the cost of financing them)	

4 Transfer pricing

The decision to create divisions often creates the need for a transfer price to be agreed between divisions for goods and services that are provided to each other.

KEY TERM

Transfer price: The price at which goods or services are transferred from one division to another, or from one member of a group to another.

4.1 The need for transfer pricing

Where there are transfers of goods or services between divisions, these **transfers could be made 'free' or 'as a favour'** to the division receiving the benefit.

Example

A car dealership has two divisions, one for car repairs and servicing, the other for car sales. The servicing division is also required to service cars before they are sold and delivered to customers.

In the absence of a transfer pricing system, the servicing division could do its work for the car sales division **without making any record** of the work done.

4.1.1 Control information

It is necessary for **control purposes** that some **record** of the inter-divisional services should be kept, and one way of doing this is **through the accounting system**. Inter-divisional work can be given a cost or charge: a transfer price.

Returning to the illustration of the sales division and a repairs/servicing division in the car dealership, unless the cost or value of service work performed for the sales division is recorded, management cannot keep a proper check on the amount of resources (like labour time) being used on servicing cars for the sales division.

4.1.2 Performance measurement

The illustration also demonstrates the need for transfer pricing to help **evaluate the performance of divisions** fairly. If the service division does not receive any credit for the work it does for the sales division, then its revenue and profitability are effectively understated. Conversely, the performance of the sales division is effectively overstated.

Therefore, transfer prices are required to prevent the performance of the two divisions being distorted.

4.1.3 Motivation of managers

Preventing distortion of performance in this way should also help maintain the **motivation** of the divisional managers. For example, if the selling division (in our example, the service division) doesn't get any credit for the work it does, this could demotivate the manager and staff of that division.

It may also motivate the repair and services division to do a poor job (as they don't get any credit for the work performed). In turn, this could **damage the interests of the company as a whole** (if the cars subsequently sold on to customers have problems which should have been fixed by the service division, but weren't).

4.2 The aims of transfer pricing

Aim	Achieved by
Preserve **goal congruence** ie aligning divisional behaviour with the best interests of the group as a whole	Decisions that managers take to improve the profit of their division will also improve the profit of the company as a whole (*Drury, 2004*); achieved by setting a transfer price which reflects the **true cost to the company** of products or services being transferred between divisions
Allow managers to retain **autonomy**	Not forcing internal transfers on to a division; instead, allowing divisions to decide where they buy from, or who they supply, and in what quantities
Permit **performance evaluation** of divisions	Preventing unfair impact on performance measures of either division

The diagram below illustrates the process of an internal transfer by a selling division that is supplying a product to a buying/receiving division.

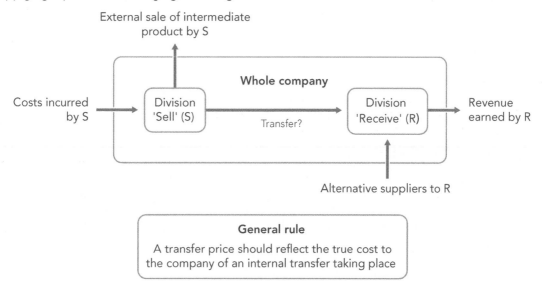

Transfer prices are most commonly negotiated between divisions based on either cost or market price.

5 Cost-based methods of transfer pricing

The supplying division has its costs of manufacturing refunded and may also be allowed a mark-up to encourage the transfer. Cost-based approaches may be necessary if there is **no external market** for the product that is being transferred.

5.1 Actual cost vs standard cost

Actual costs:

(a) All inefficiencies passed on to buying division, as there is no encouragement for cost control in the selling division

(b) Buying division does not know in advance what price it will be paying

Using standard costs overcomes all of these problems.

5.2 Standard variable/marginal cost

The selling division (S) should transfer goods to the buying division at the marginal cost of production if:

(a) S has **spare capacity** as the marginal costs reflects the true cost to the company of the transfer taking place;

(b) S has no external market so could operate as a cost centre. If S is a profit centre, it will be demotivated as fixed costs will not be covered.

5.3 Full cost

Full cost (variable costs plus fixed overheads) – sometimes this also includes a mark-up.

(a) May lead to high transfer price, and therefore the receiving division may look to use an external supplier instead.

(b) This may lead to the wrong decision being made, because fixed costs are not a relevant cost.

Using variable costs overcomes these problems, but does mean that the selling division will not cover its fixed costs.

Activity 4: Cost + transfer pricing

	$
Division S	
Direct cost	20.00
Fixed overhead absorbed	8.00
	28.00
Standard profit @ 10%	2.80
Transfer price	30.80

Division S has proposed a transfer price of $30.80 per unit, for goods which it supplies to Division R (based on the calculations in the table above).

Division R, the receiving division, can buy externally at $26.

Required

Discuss the likely outcome of setting the transfer price at $30.80. **(5 marks)**

Solution

5.4 Dual pricing and two-part tariff systems

Fixed costs can be considered in a **marginal cost-based transfer pricing system** in the following ways:

(a) **Dual pricing**

Where an external market exists, credit the selling division with the market price of the transfers made but debit the buying division with the variable cost.

(b) **Two-part tariff**

Transfer prices are set at variable cost and once a year there is a **transfer of a fixed fee to the supplying division** representing an allowance for its fixed costs. This should allow the supplying division to cover its fixed costs and make a profit.

6 Market-based approaches to transfer pricing

Where a market price exists it can be used as the basis for a transfer.

If the supplying division is at full capacity then the revenue it loses as a result of an internal transfer shows the true cost (revenue foregone) to the division of an internal transfer.

If a division would have to incur marketing costs to sell externally then the market price should be **adjusted** to reflect the fact that an internal transfer would not incur this cost. So the transfer price becomes lower, ie market price less marketing costs.

Activity 5: Creative division

The creative division (CD) of Unique Components Ltd produces wooden components that it sells to external customers and transfers to other divisions within its own group of companies.

Production involves the preparation of timber, cutting the timber into shapes and the assembly of the shapes into components. The total component cost for Component A has been estimated as $41.21 per unit (variable costs account for 45% of this).

Selling costs incurred in selling to external customers are $5 per unit.

The selling price is $55.63.

Required

Discuss the application and acceptability of the following transfer price bases at which Component A may be offered by CD to other divisions within the same group of companies:

- Market price
- Marginal cost

(8 marks)

Solution

---

7 Opportunity cost approach to transfer pricing

The optimal transfer price (TP) should be calculated using opportunity costs.

> **Formula to learn**
>
> Minimum TP = marginal cost to selling division + opportunity cost of resources used

(a) If external market exists for the intermediate product: opportunity cost is contribution lost from the external sale forgone.

(b) If no external market for the intermediate product exists, the opportunity cost (or shadow price) is:

(i) Nil; or

(ii) Opportunity lost by not using resources on alternative products.

Note. If this price is above the external market price or the receiving division's net revenue then the internal transfer will not and should not happen.

Activity 6: Synfib

Company C is engaged in synthetic fibre production. It is situated in Country A where it operates two production plants.

Plant 1 manufactures a single product, which is a special grade of polymer.

The polymer is then transferred to Plant 2 which produces a synthetic fibre, 'Synfib'.

The polymer produced by Plant 1 is of a special grade and manufactured specifically for the production of Synfib, so there is no intermediate market for it.

Demand for Synfib

There is strong worldwide demand for Synfib and Company C is the only producer, although substitute products are available.

The following schedule shows the monthly demand for Synfib.

Litres (millions)	$ per litre
75	200
100	175
125	150

The manager of Plant 2 has autonomy to choose the level of output of Synfib, and always selects the level of output which maximises Plant 2's contribution.

Output of Synfib is produced in batches of 25 million litres. The minimum monthly quantity produced is 75 million litres, and the maximum monthly demand is 125 million litres (which is the maximum quantity that can be produced each month).

Costs

The marginal costs incurred in the production of Synfib are as follows:

	Synfib
	$ per litre
Costs incurred within Plant 1	12
Costs incurred within Plant 2	24

Disagreement over transfer prices

The transfer price for the polymer has been set at $40 per litre.

Recently the divisional manager of Plant 2 has argued that the transfer price of $40 per litre is too high. She believes that a transfer price set at Plant 1's marginal cost of $12 per litre would result in increased contribution for C as a whole.

Required

Evaluate whether C's contribution could be increased by changing the transfer price as suggested. **(10 marks)**

Solution

Essential reading

Please refer to Chapter 8 Section 1 of the Essential reading for a discussion of other practical transfer pricing issues including issues relating to transfer prices in multinational companies.

The Essential reading is available as an Appendix of the digital edition of the Workbook.

Chapter summary

Divisional performance and transfer pricing issues

Responsibility centres

Cost, revenue, profit and investment centres

Controllability
- Divisional performance based on **traceable** costs
- Managerial performance based on controllable factors

Information requirements
- Should reflect type of responsibility centre
- A mix of financial and non-financial information

ROI & RI

- Dysfunctional behaviour?
  – ROI: Can discourage investment because this can decrease divisional ROI in the short term
  – RI: Less likely because encourages investments to take place if the return exceeds the cost of capital, but can still discourage investment and makes inter-divisional comparisons harder
- ROI more popular than RI
  – ROI is consistent with corporate assessment (ROCE)
  – More appropriate for comparing divisions of different sizes
  – Easier to understand and calculate
- Problems common to ROI and RI
  – Identification of controllable profit
  – Distorted by transfer prices
  – Ignore tax
  – Use of NBV discourages replacement
  – Hard to apply to service divisions

EVA™

Focuses on maximising shareholder wealth

NOPAT
- Add back 'value building' expenses (eg R&D; marketing)
- Eliminate non-cash items
- Economic depreciation (if given)
- Cash taxes
- Interest is excluded

Assets
- The calculation of 'investment':
  – Opening values
  – Replacement cost
- Adjustments to profit (to give NOPAT) also need to be reflected in capital employed

Evaluation of EVA™
- Focus on shareholder value
- Encourages investment
- Removes distortion from accounting policies
- Consistent with NPV
But
- Complex
- Inter-divisional comparisons harder than with ROI
- Inconsistent with published financial information

Transfer pricing

The need for transfer pricing
- Generates control information
- Performance measurement
- Motivation

Aims of transfer pricing
- Goal congruence
- Autonomy
- Performance evaluation

Cost-based methods of transfer pricing

Standard variable/ marginal cost
- If supplying division has spare capacity
- Demotivational if a profit centre

Full cost

May lead to incorrect decision making

Dual pricing & two-part tariff

To credit the supplying division with an element of profit

Market-based approaches to transfer pricing

- Needs an external market for transferred goods
- If supplying division is at full capacity
- Adjusted for cost savings from internal sales (eg advertising)

Opportunity cost approach to transfer pricing

Marginal cost + lost profit

Practical issues*

Negotiation
- Negotiation
- Head office intervention

International aspects
- Tariffs
- Exchange controls
- Other factors
- Competitive pressures
- Tax on profits
- Arm's length price

*The Essential reading for Chapter 8 (in Appendix 2 of the digital edition of the Workbook) covers the potential significance of negotiation in transfer pricing, and the issues relating to transfer pricing in the context of multinational organisations.

Knowledge diagnostic

1. Cost centre

Managers are responsible for controllable costs only.

2. Revenue centre

Managers are responsible for controllable revenue only.

3. Profit centre

Managers are responsible for controllable costs and revenue.

4. Investment centre

Managers are responsible for controllable costs, revenue and asset base.

5. Performance measurement

One of the key problems of measuring managerial performance is in distinguishing managerial performance from the overall performance of a division. The issue of control is crucial here; managers should only be assessed on the aspects of performance they can control.

6. EVA™

$$EVA™ = NOPAT - \text{net assets at start of year} \times WACC$$

EVA is similar to RI, in that both are calculated by subtracting an imputed interest charge from the profit earned by a division or company. However, there are key differences in the way 'profit' figure is calculated in EVA™, with NOPAT being derived by making a series of adjustments to accounting profit. The replacement cost of net assets also needs to be used when calculating the capital charge.

7. Transfer prices

The aims of transfer pricing should be to: preserve goal congruence; to allow divisions to retain autonomy; and to enable performance evaluation of divisions.

8. Bases of transfer pricing

Transfer prices may be based on **market price** (or adjusted market price) where there is an external market for the good or service being transferred. If no external market exists, a **cost-based** approach to transfer prices may need to be used, but this should be based on standard costs, not actual costs. In practice, transfer prices are often **negotiated** between divisions.

Further study guidance

Question practice

Now try the following from the Further question practice bank (available in the digital edition of the Workbook):

Q10 *Transfer pricing*

Q11 *Creative Division*

Further reading

There are two articles in the Technical Articles section for APM on ACCA's website, *Economic value added versus profit-based measures of performance* (Part 1 and 2). You are strongly advised to read these as part of your preparation for the exam.

The first of the articles points out that, in practice, there could be a very large number of adjustments required to accounting profits when calculating NOPAT. The examining team will, however, only expect you to be aware of the most common adjustments.

There is also a Technical Article available on ACCA's website, called *Transfer Pricing* which summarises why transfer prices are needed, and discusses different approaches to transfer pricing. We recommend you read this article as part of your preparation for the APM exam.

Activity answers

Activity 1: Controllability

The net profit margin of the division is currently 5.5%, so under the stated basis of calculation, the manager will not receive a bonus. However, the performance measure should focus on 'controllable profit'.

The controllable net profit is arrived at after items which are not under the manager's control are added back. Division X is a profit centre (not an investment centre) so depreciation is not a controllable cost for the divisional manager. Similarly, allocated head office costs need to be added back when assessing the manager's performance (this assumes that none of the Head Office costs can be directly attributed to Division X).

The net profit margin **controllable** by the manager of Division X is 13.4%. On that basis, the manager should be awarded a bonus for the year.

It could be argued that the increase in productivity due to the corporate investment in the new e-commerce platform is not a factor that is controllable by the manager of Division X.

However, the exact increase in Division X's productivity resulting for the new e-commerce platform is unclear, so it is difficult to accurately adjust the controllable net profit margin to reflect this.

To reduce the controllable net profit margin to 7% (the threshold at which the manager is awarded their bonus) the net profit would have to fall by 6.4% of adjusted sales or approximately by X$125,632 (X$1,963 × 6.4%).

Workings

1   *Controllable net profit margin for Division X*

Controllable net profit	X$'000
Reported net profit	110
Non-controllable items	
Add back:	
Depreciation	100
Allocated head office costs	90
Deduct:	
Currency gain (W2)	(37)
Controllable net profit	263

Controllable revenue	
Reported revenue	2,000
Deduct currency gain (W2)	(37)
Controllable revenue	1,963

Controllable net profit margin (263/1,963)	13.4%

2   *Currency gain*

Three months of revenue was increased by 8% due to currency gain.

Three months revenue after currency gain = 500.0

Before the currency gain this would have been lower, ie 500/1.08 = 463.0

So the gain due to currency is 500 − 463 = 37

> **Tutorial note.** The principle matters more than mathematical precision here, so it would be also be acceptable to multiply 500 by 0.92 to reflect the currency issue, even though this produces a slightly different answer (of 460).

Activity 2: Divisional performance

Performance	Div A	Div B
Profit margin	30% (90/300) × 100	25% (135/540) × 100
Asset turnover	0.6 (300/500)	0.72 (540/750)
ROCE (ROI)	18% (90/500) × 100	18% (135/750) × 100

Both divisions have 18% ROI. However, if they communicated and shared knowledge on margins and asset turnover, ROI could become 30% × 0.72 = 21.6% (assuming the divisions sell similar products). However, there may well be a trade-off between increasing both margins and revenues simultaneously.

As both exceed the target of 12% there is little incentive to do so.

	Div A $'000	Div B $'000
RI:		
Profits	90	135
Less imputed interest		
12% × $500k	60	
12% × $750k		90
Residual income	<u>30</u>	<u>45</u>

Division B appears to be outperforming Division A, but that is only because it is larger.

ROI takes size into account so is more equitable for comparing performance.

Decision making (dysfunctional behaviour)

The NPV of the new product (assuming that profit is equivalent to cash flow over the long term) is:

Time	0	1 onwards
	($8,000)	$1,200
Discount factor	1.0	1/0.12
PV	($8,000)	$10,000
NPV	$2,000	

The new product is generating a positive NPV and therefore from the group's perspective it is value creating and should be accepted by the division.

New product – divisional analysis:

$$\text{ROI} = \frac{\$1,200}{\$8,000} = 15\%$$

	$
RI profit	1,200
Less imputed interest ($8,000 × 12%)	960
	240

Using ROI, the new product would be unlikely to be developed, as Division A's performance would appear to fall. However, under RI measurement the product would be launched as it exceeds the minimum required return.

RI is better for decision making than ROI.

Division B sees little value in R&D. Given the ways its performance is assessed this is not surprising.

(1) R&D increases either capital or expenditure and therefore decreases ROI in the short term.

(2) The short-term nature of the measures discourages long-term or risky investments.

(3) High levels of depreciation or amortisation will depress returns early in a product's life. This may also be when sales are low.

Activity 3: Economic value added

PAT	$'000	$'000
Net profit		89.6
Add back:		
Non-cash expenses	8	
Amortisation of goodwill	5	
Interest (net of 30% tax) 15 × 0.7	10.5	23.5
NOPAT		113.1
	–	

Alternative approach:	
PBIT	143.0
Less tax @ 30%	(42.9)
Add back	
Non-cash expenses	5.0
Amortisation of goodwill	8.0
NOPAT	113.1

Assets	
At start of year	470
Add back amortised goodwill	40
	510

WACC	
Equity 15% × 75%	0.1125
Debt (10% × 0.7) × 25%	0.0175

	$'000	$'000
PAT		
WACC		0.13
EVA™ NOPAT	113.1	
Capital charge (13% × $510)	66.3	
	46.8	
RI		
PBIT	143	
Capital charge (13% × $500)	65	
	78	

The business is creating value, as its return (however calculated) is greater than the group's WACC

Activity 4: Cost + transfer pricing

Transfer @ $30.80

S wishes to sell   **R declines and buys externally**

Is this goal congruent?

From the group perspective the decision is to make or to buy.

If these absorbed overheads are general:

Cost to make	$20
Cost to buy	$26
Extra cost if bought	$6

The item should be made in-house and transferred from S to R.

The transfer price needs to be amended $26 ≥ TP > $20

If these absorbed overheads are specific:

Cost to make ($20 + $8)	$28
Cost to buy	$26
Saving if bought	$2

The item should be purchased externally.

Activity 5: Creative division

(1) **$55.63 – $5 selling costs saved = $50.63**

Reflects the revenue forgone by the supplying division from the transfer as long as there is **no spare capacity.**

Since this is a fair price, reflecting the true cost of an internal transfer, this should not distort performance.

(2) **$41.21 × 0.45 = $18.54**

Reflects the 'true cost' of the supplying division from the transfer **if there is spare capacity.**

However, the supplying division is not guaranteed to cover its overheads and therefore may be loss making. This issue could be addressed by:

Dual pricing – supply division receives market price, receiving division is charged at marginal cost.

Marginal cost + lump sum – the amount of the lump sum depends on capacity (ie opportunity cost) and therefore stimulates discussion of capacity issues.

Activity 6: Synfib

Output of Synfib	(i) Transfer price of Polymer at $40 per litre		
	Total revenue	Marginal costs	Total contribution
Litres (million)	$m	$m	$m
75	15,000	4,800	10,200
100	17,500	6,400	**11,100**
125	18,750	8,000	10,750

Output of Synfib	(ii) Transfer price of Polymer at $12 per litre		
	Total revenue	Marginal costs	Total contribution
Litres (million)	$m	$m	$m
75	15,000	2,700	12,300
100	17,500	3,600	13,900
125	18,750	4,500	**14,250**

The above table shows the best contribution **made by Plant 2** from the production of Synfib (the maximum contribution is underlined). The marginal costs are made up of the transfer price plus the other Plant 2 costs ($24 per litre).

This suggests that pre-tax contribution will increase by $3,150 million if the transfer price is set at $12 and production increased from 100 million litres to 125 million litres.

However, Plant 1 will suffer a loss in contribution because the transfer price is lower and contribution will fall from $2,800 million (($40 – $12) × 100m litres) to zero.

The net impact on Company C is therefore $3,150m – $2,800m = **$350m.**

C's profits have therefore increased. This is because there is no opportunity cost from the sale of the polymer so the true cost of the transfer is $12 per litre. The inflated transfer price of $40 is causing the price of Synfib to be artificially inflated and the output to be reduced as a result. However, this conclusion assumes that this capacity is available and that C is not able to use spare capacity for any other activity which earns more contribution.

9

Strategic performance measures in not-for-profit organisations

Learning objectives

On completion of this chapter, you should be able to:

	Syllabus reference no.
Highlight and discuss the potential for diversity in objectives depending on organisational type.	D3(a)
Discuss the difficulties in measuring outputs when performance is not judged in terms of money or an easily quantifiable objective.	D3(b)
Discuss the use of benchmarking in public sector performance (league tables) and its effects on operational and strategic management and client behaviour.	D3(c)
Discuss how the combination of politics and the desire to measure public sector performance may result in undesirable service outcomes, eg the use of targets.	D3(d)
Assess 'value for money' service provision as a measure of performance in not-for-profit organisations and the public sector.	D3(e)

Exam context

So far, we have focused mainly on performance management in commercial organisations in the private sector. The primary objective of such organisations is to generate value for their shareholders. However, that is not the primary objective for all organisations, and in the APM exam you may also need to discuss performance measurement in not-for-profit organisations.

One of the key characteristics of not-for-profit organisations is the range of different objectives they may have, which in turn has implications for the way performance is measured in them.

Chapter overview

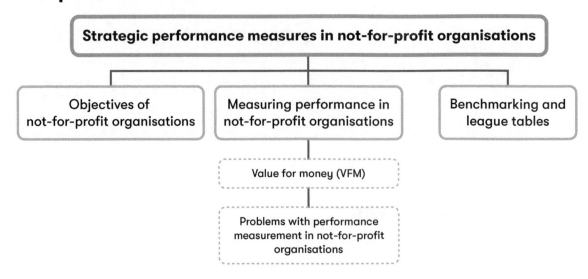

1 Objectives of not-for-profit organisations

KEY TERM

> **Not-for-profit organisation (NFPO):** An organisation whose attainment of its prime goal is not assessed by economic measures. However, in pursuit of its primary goal it may undertake profit-making activities, and then use any surplus funds to help pursue its goal.

Not-for-profit organisations (NFPOs) comprise many different types of business (eg charities, government departments, co-operatives) and exist in both the private and the public sector.

The main difference between NFPOs and the private sector is the lack of profit motive. Profits may be made, but as a means to an end, not an end in themselves. It is, however, important that costs of operations are covered or the organisation's survival is at stake.

Instead of looking to make profit for shareholders, NFPOs aim to provide value to their **stakeholders** in other ways.

1.1 Stakeholders and objectives

An important characteristic of NFPOs is the wide range of different stakeholders they have. Managers have to take account of the interests of these different stakeholders when setting objectives and making decisions.

One of the major challenges for performance management in NFPOs is that it can be **difficult to define the organisations' objectives**. NFPOs often have **multiple objectives**, and it can be very difficult to say which the organisation's **overriding objective** is. This can be a particular problem when different objectives could **conflict** with one another.

Activity 1: Hospital

Using the example of a not-for-profit hospital, consider the following:

1   Which stakeholder groups will need to be considered when setting the hospital's objectives?

(2 marks)

2   What potential areas of conflict could there be between different stakeholder groups?

(5 marks)

(Total = 7 marks)

Solution

The range of different stakeholders can also present problems when **setting targets** (particularly in the public sector), because the targets will need to reflect the objectives of different stakeholder groups.

The objectives of NFPOs will depend on the sector the NFPOs serve. However, compared to a 'for profit' organisation (with an underlying objective to maximise profit) there is likely to be:

- A wider variety of different performance measures
- Greater emphasis on **non-financial measures**

PER alert

Element (b) of Performance objective 14 – Monitor performance – identifies that you should be able to 'analyse and provide appropriate information to measure performance'.

The issue of identifying 'appropriate information' to measure can sometimes be a particular challenge in not-for-profit organisations due to the number of different objectives they can have, and therefore the number of different aspects of performance which could potentially be measured.

2 Measuring performance in not-for-profit organisations

2.1 Value for money (VFM)

As the performance of not-for-profit organisations cannot be properly assessed by using conventional accounting ratios (eg profit margins; ROCE), they are usually judged in terms of input and outputs. What is being achieved? And what is the cost of achieving this?

This approach also links in with value-for-money criteria.

Value for money: Providing a service in a way which is economical, efficient and effective.

(a) Economy
- Spending money carefully
- Achieving the appropriate quantity and quality of inputs at the lowest possible

    Note: 'Economy' doesn't simply mean spending as little as possible; to achieve value for money organisations need to obtain inputs of appropriate quantity and quality.

(b) Efficiency
- Maximising outputs relative to inputs
- Operating within a budget

(c) Effectiveness
- Achieving the organisation's objectives
- The relationship between outputs and objectives

One of the problems in achieving VFM is that there could be **conflicts** between the different elements.

For example, reducing the number of police officers in a police force might improve efficiency, but might also reduce the force's effectiveness in tackling crime.

When evaluating VFM it is important to consider **all three elements** of performance (economy, efficiency, effectiveness) together, rather than prioritising one element of performance to the detriment of others

Essential reading

See Chapter 9 Section 1 of the Essential reading for more detail about measuring VFM and the potential problems with it.

The Essential reading is available as an Appendix of the digital edition of the Workbook.

Activity 2: Performance objectives

Using the value-for-money framework, suggest some suitable aspects of performance to be included in objectives for the following NFPOs:

1   A hospital   **(4 marks)**

2   A waste management service responsible for the collection and disposal of household and commercial waste   **(4 marks)**

(Total = 8 marks)

Solution

2.2   Problems with performance measurement in not-for-profit organisations

Although value for money (VFM) can provide a framework for measuring performance, there are still a number of problems with performance measurement in NFPOs.

Problem	Implications
Multiple objectives	The range of different objectives and stakeholders means it is difficult to determine **which are most important** (eg government funding cuts may restrict hospitals' ability to buy new equipment. However, buying new equipment could save lives. Which is more important? Controlling expenditure, or saving lives?)
Measuring outputs	It can be **difficult to measure outputs** in a way that is meaningful, and where the outputs are controllable. For example, are good exam results alone an adequate measure of the quality of teaching? One solution to these issues could be to use a range of performance targets and measures, but there is then an issue of how to weight the different objectives to give an overall measure of performance.

Problem	Implications
Data collection	Data about service provisions can often be **qualitative**, which can make it harder to quantify and assess. For example, a hospital could report the number of operations carried out, but this does not measure the quality of its procedures, or patient care, nor does it take account of the complexity of the operations being performed. It may also be difficult to obtain complete data (eg unreported crimes will not be included in data used to measure the performance of a police force... but a crime still took place).
Political and social considerations	Public sector organisations may be required to offer a range of services (for political or social reasons), even if it is uneconomic to do so (eg providing public transport services in rural areas). Alternatively, the ability of public sector bodies to provide services might be dependent on the amount of funding they receive from central government.
Lack of comparisons	The diverse range of NFPOs makes it hard to find comparable businesses to act as benchmarks.
'Tunnel vision'	If a decision is made to focus only on certain areas of performance, this could lead to performance improvements in those areas, but at the expense of worsening performance in other areas. (This is a potential issue with league tables which we will look at next.)

3 Benchmarking and league tables

Benchmarking has been introduced in Chapter 1. Benchmarking can be especially relevant to NFPOs because it can help to create a discipline to encourage high standards of performance.

If, as is sometimes the case in the not-for-profit sector, organisations are prepared to collaborate with each other, then benchmarking can produce extremely useful data for performance management.

Benchmarked measures are often presented in **league tables**, which provide a readily available bank of data which users of public services can use to compare how well the providers of those services are performing.

Real world example

In the UK, university league tables are produced based on selected aspects of the universities' performance, with weightings attached to each aspect of performance. For example, *The Guardian* newspaper's university league table uses the following performance areas to determine its rankings (with 2019 weightings in brackets):

- 'Entry score' (15%)
- 'Student satisfaction with facilities' – as rated by graduates of the course (5%)
- 'Assessment and feedback' – as rated by graduates of the course (10%)
- 'Career prospects' (15%)
- 'Academic spending per student' (5%)
- 'Staff/student ratio' (15%)
- 'Teaching quality' – as rated by graduates of the course (10%)
- 'Value added' (15%)
- 'Continuation' – students progressing from 1st to 2nd year (10%)

3.1 Benefits of league tables

Different areas of performance can be summarised into a **final score**, showing how well an organisation has performed overall. This can also help to address the problems of multiple objectives by assessing performance across a number of different areas.

League tables can also inspire competition among organisations, and provide an incentive to those performing relatively poorly to improve their performance and improve their ranking in the table.

3.2 Problems with league tables

3.2.1 Choice of measures

There is an element of subjectivity around the areas of performance included. Organisations are likely to focus mainly on improving their performance in these areas of activity, **and less attention will be given to other areas**. This highlights the adage (which we will look at again in the next chapter in relation to non-financial performance indicators) that '**What gets measured, gets done**'. For example, in *The Guardian*'s measure of university performance (in the Real world example above), there is no importance attached to research output, so will this mean universities place less emphasis on the amount and quality of research they undertake?

3.2.2 Use of weightings

Another common criticism of league tables is that they apply **weightings** to different factors used in the calculation of the final performance score. These weightings are arbitrary, but the rankings in the table might be different if different weightings were used.

In addition, if an organisation feels that a performance measure included in a league table is **not controllable** (eg 'exam results' for a school may be determined by the capability of the pupils as much as the quality of the teaching) then league tables could serve to demotivate.

Essential reading

See Chapter 9 Section 2 of the Essential reading for more detail about the issue or undesirable outcomes and the use of targets in league tables, particularly in relation to the adage that 'What gets measured, gets done'.

The Essential reading is available as an Appendix of the digital edition of the Workbook.

Chapter summary

Strategic performance measures in not-for-profit organisations

Objectives of not-for-profit organisations

- Multiple objectives
- Often non-financial
- Reflect interests of multiple stakeholder groups

Measuring performance in not-for-profit organisations

Value for money (VFM)

- Economy
  - Optimising use of productive resources
  - Achieving the appropriate quantity and quality of inputs at the lowest cost possible
- Efficiency
  - The relationship between inputs and outputs
  - Maximising the output generated per unit of resource used
- Effectiveness
  - The extent to which an organisation achieves its goals and objectives

Problems with performance measurement in not-for-profit organisations

- Multiple objectives; which aspects of performance are most important to measure?
- Can outputs be measured in a way which is meaningful?
- Hard to quantify qualitative data
- Political and social influences
- 'Tunnel vision'?

Benchmarking and league tables

- +ve:
  - Comparing performance can be an incentive to improve
  - Can summarise how well an organisation has performed
- -ve:
  - 'What gets measured gets done'
  - May be demotivational; is performance controllable?
  - Subjective: Measures chosen/weightings used can influence the ranking

Knowledge diagnostic

1. Objectives

Unlike commercial companies, not-for-profit organisations (NFPOs) do not exist primarily to generate profit and value for their shareholders. NFPOs typically have **multiple objectives**, reflecting the interest of different **key stakeholder groups**.

However, although NFPOs don't have a primary goal to generate profit, they must cover their costs to guarantee long-term survival.

2. Performance measurement in NFPOs

Measuring performance in NFPOs can be problematic due to issues with:

- Deciding which aspects of performance are most important to measure
- Measuring outputs in a way that is meaningful
- Quantifying non-financial (and potentially qualitative) aspects of performance
- Assessing the impact of external political and social considerations

3. Value for money (VFM)

The performance of NFPOs can be assessed using value for money:

- **Economy**: the extent to which an organisation achieves the appropriate quantity and quality of inputs at the lowest cost possible.
- **Efficiency**: the extent to which an organisation maximises the 'output' it generates from units of resource used.
- **Effectiveness**: the extent to which an organisation achieves its objectives.

When assessing VFM, the relationship between the three elements is important, not simply looking at each element individually.

4. Benchmarking and league tables

League tables provide a way of comparing an organisation's performance with that of similar organisations. These comparisons could help to stimulate performance improvements (in organisations which perform less well in the tables).

However, potential issues with league tables include: deciding which aspects of performance to measure, and what weighting to give to different measures. These decisions can affect the rankings in the tables.

Another potential consequence of league tables is that they can influence behaviour in organisations: 'What gets measured, gets done'.

Further study guidance

Question practice

Now try the following from the Further question practice bank (available in the digital edition of the Workbook):

Q12 *Seatown*

Q20 *Ganymede*

Further reading

There are two Technical Articles about not-for-profit organisations we have selected from ACCA's website. The first article – *Not-for-profit organisations – Part 1* – explains what not-for-profit organisations are, while Part 2 looks in more detail at charities as a specific type of not-for-profit organisation. You should read these articles to develop your knowledge of not-for-profit organisations if you are not familiar with them.

There is also a Technical Article available on ACCA's website called *Performance management in public sector organisations*. This looks at targets and benchmarking in the public sector. We advise you to read this article as part of your preparation for your APM exam.

Activity answers

Activity 1: Hospital

You may have thought of other answers in both parts of this activity, but some possible solutions are as follows:

1   A not-for profit hospital's stakeholders include:

- Its funding authority (eg the NHS in the UK)
- Management
- Medical staff
- Patients (and their families)
- Support staff
- Pharmaceutical companies (who supply drugs and medical equipment)

2   The following areas of conflict could emerge between different stakeholder groups:

- Conflict between funding authority and hospitals over the range of treatments which can be offered (eg whether a treatment which could be medically effective, but which is very expensive, can be offered to a patient)
- Conflict over the quality of services and waiting times, between funding authority (and/or hospital) and patients
- Conflict over pay levels between the funding authority and hospital staff
- Conflict over pricing of drugs between hospital and suppliers
- Conflict between different patient groups over range of services provided

Activity 2: Performance objectives

1   **Primary goals** are likely to relate to **effectiveness**:

Quality – death rates, readmission rates

Speed – percentage of patients waiting more than x hours

Take-up – percentage of patients attending post-operation care appointments

Secondary goals will **relate to economy and efficiency**.

Economy could be measured by monitoring the cost of inputs, eg average salary per doctor, costs of medical supplies/drugs, premises costs per square metre, electricity costs per kWh etc.

Efficiency could be measured as:

- Maximising outputs, eg patients per doctor (or operations performed per doctor), ward capacity levels
- Minimising inputs, eg agency staff costs as a percentage of total staff costs
- Operating within budget

2   **Primary goals** are likely to relate to **effectiveness**:

Quality – cleanliness of streets, percentage of completion of waste collection, number of complaints (about missed collections)

Speed – percentage of collections on time

Take-up – tonnes of waste recycled

Secondary goals will relate to economy and efficiency.

Economy could be measured by monitoring the cost of inputs, eg number of waste collectors employed, average salary cost, cost of buying and maintaining vehicles, fuel costs for vehicles.

Efficiency could be measured as:

- Maximising outputs, eg tonnes of waste collected per vehicle; or tonnes collected per member of staff

- Minimising inputs, eg cost per tonne of waste collected

- Operating within budget

Non-financial performance indicators

Learning objectives

On completion of this chapter, you should be able to:

	Syllabus reference no.
Discuss the interaction of non-financial performance indicators with financial performance indicators.	D4(a)
Identify and discuss the significance of non-financial performance indicators in relation to employees and product/service quality, eg customer satisfaction reports, repeat business ratings, customer loyalty, access and availability.	D4(b)
Discuss the difficulties in interpreting data on qualitative issues.	D4(c)
Discuss the significance of brand awareness and company profile and their potential impact on business performance.	D4(d)

Exam context

In Chapter 2 we discussed critical success factors (CSFs), and noted the need for organisations to measure how well they are performing against their CSFs. CSFs are typically non-financial in nature, which means performance needs to be measured against non-financial performance indicators.

Multi-dimensional performance measurement systems – such as the balanced scorecard (*Kaplan & Norton, 1996a*) and the performance pyramid (*Lynch & Cross, 1991*) which we will look at in Chapter 13 – also explicitly highlight the role of non-financial factors in shaping an organisation's performance.

An organisation's financial performance is likely to reflect how well it is performing its key non-financial activities. For example, its revenues will be the result of developing products or services that customers want to buy, and then attracting – and retaining – customers. Therefore, non-financial aspects (eg product innovation; quality; or customer service) could all be important elements in shaping an organisation's performance.

Note that the requirements in the Study Guide expect you to be able to 'discuss' the significance of non-financial performance indicators (NFPIs), not simply to list potential NFPIs which could be useful to an organisation. So, for example, you should be prepared to discuss **how** or **why** NFPIs could be useful to the organisation identified in a question scenario.

Chapter overview

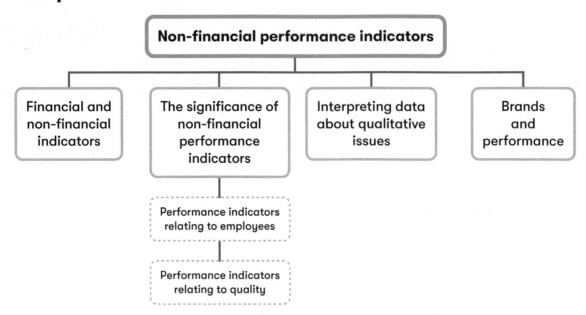

1 Financial and non-financial performance indicators

Although it is important for organisations to measure and monitor their financial performance, there may be **disadvantages to focusing solely on financial performance**.

(a) Performance measurement will concentrate only on variables which can be expressed in monetary terms, **ignoring other important variables which cannot be expressed in monetary terms** (eg productivity, quality, employee morale).

(b) Performance measurement will **not convey the full picture** of a company's performance in a modern business environment, eg quality, customer satisfaction; it will measure success but **will not measure the factors that ensure success**, ie the business's critical success factors.

(c) Measures have a **historical** perspective: financial indicators are often produced at the end of the reporting period. Non-financial information (especially operational information) can be produced in real time, providing managers with more timely insight into levels of performance.

(d) Financial measures focus on the **short term** (eg annual profit), but these may not be directly linked to longer-term organisational objectives (eg innovation and new product development).

Essential reading

See Chapter 10 Section 1 of the Essential reading for more on the importance of non-financial performance measures.

The Essential reading is available as an Appendix of the digital edition of the Workbook.

1.1 Non-financial performance indicators (NFPIs)

NFPIs are measures of performance based on non-financial information which may originate in, and be used by, operating departments to control their activities, without any accounting input.

Advantages
Better information about key areas such as quality, customer and employee satisfaction.
Information can be **provided quickly** (eg real time; per shift; daily) unlike traditional financial period end performance reports.
Easy to calculate and easier for non-financial managers **to understand and use**.
May be less likely to be manipulated than traditional profit-related measures, depending on the measure used.

Activity 1: Non-financial performance objectives

Assess, with reasons, how easily the following non-financial performance measures might be manipulated.

1 Defect levels at a factory producing shampoo   **(2 marks)**

2 Customer satisfaction levels in a financial services call centre, based on customer feedback scores at the end of calls   **(2 marks)**

                                                            (Total = 4 marks)

Solution

However, there are potential **disadvantages** to NFPIs too. These may relate to the specific non-financial measures being used, or to general problems such as:

- Data collection costs (Information systems may need to be amended to capture non-financial information.)
- Measuring too many aspects of performance could lead to information overload for managers

Essential reading

See Chapter 10 Section 2 of the Essential reading for more detail about the risk of manipulation in performance measures, including feedback from ACCA's examining team about candidates' answers in relation to this.

The Essential reading is available as an Appendix of the digital edition of the Workbook.

---

2 The significance of non-financial performance indicators

As the syllabus identifies, non-financial performance indicators could be significant in relation to managing employees and product/service quality.

2.1 Performance indicators relating to employees

For many organisations, employees are key resources ('human capital') who are vital in enabling them to implement their strategies successfully.

This can be particularly true in service businesses, due to the nature of the relationship between customers and staff (as discussed in Chapter 4).

In turn, this means performance indicators relating to employees could be particularly important in service industries. However, traditional financial performance indicators do not measure the skills, morale or training of staff.

Example

Employee-related performance measures include:

- Training time per employee (reflecting the potential importance of learning and development in an organisation)
- Staff satisfaction scores (from staff surveys)
- Staff turnover (as a potential indicator of staff satisfaction)
- Days lost through absenteeism
- Days lost through accidents/sickness (as a potential indicator of working conditions)

2.2 Performance indicators relating to quality

We will look at issues relating to quality in more detail in the **next chapter**. However, the quality of a product that a customer buys from an organisation, or the service they receive, could be critical in determining the customer's satisfaction level. In turn, this level could determine whether the customer makes any further purchases from the organisation.

Performance indicators as **customer satisfaction scores** and **repeat business ratings** (retention rates) could provide useful insight into product/service quality. If customer satisfaction scores or customer retention levels are falling, this could be a warning that the underlying quality of an organisation's product or service is also declining.

Essential reading

See Chapter 10 Section 3 of the Essential reading for more detail about performance indicators in relation to service quality and measuring customer satisfaction.

The Essential reading is available as an Appendix of the digital edition of the Workbook.

3 Interpreting data about qualitative issues

In some cases, (eg in relation to customer satisfaction) aspects of non-financial performance may need to be assessed using qualitative data, ie data based on judgements and opinion. This can make them more difficult to measure and interpret than quantitative factors; ie qualitative data is **subjective**.

If two people receive a service which is essentially the same, will they both assess it as being of the same quality? Or will their personal preferences, tastes and expectations affect their assessment of the service?

3.1 Recording qualitative data

Surveys are often used to convert qualitative data into quantitative data; eg customers are asked to rate how satisfied they are on a scale of 1 to 5, where '5' is 'Very satisfied' and '1' is 'Not at all satisfied'.

However, such scoring systems can still be subjective, because people are often reluctant to use extremes (eg they would prefer to score in the range 2 to 4, rather than using the extreme scores of 1 or 5).

One way to reduce the impact of subjectivity could be to look at **trends** in performance rather than one-off scores (eg finding the average scores from surveys, and then monitoring trends in the average will help to show if performance is improving or deteriorating over time).

4 Brands and performance

Brand strength can play an important role in creating customer loyalty, particularly where a brand conveys a sense of quality to customers.

Luxury brands use this association of quality and exclusivity to appeal to customers (so branding could be very important for a firm pursuing a differentiation strategy).

When assessing the impact a brand could have on business performance it is important to distinguish between two different aspects:

- **Brand awareness** – This relates to how widely people are aware of a product's place in the market. Brand awareness reflects a brand's potential **ability to attract new customers** (eg recall tests to assess people's awareness).
- **Brand loyalty** – This relates to the extent to which people buy a product because of its brand, and will continue to do so. Brand loyalty reflect a brand's ability to **retain existing customers**. High brand loyalty can reduce price sensitivity, which helps market-leading brands to sustain profits.

Essential reading

See Chapter 10 Section 4 of the Essential reading for more detail about branding and organisational performance.

The Essential reading is available as an Appendix of the digital edition of the Workbook.

Chapter summary

Non-financial performance indicators

Financial and non-financial indicators

- Limitations of financial indicators:
  - Focus on too few variables
  - Measure success, rather than factors which achieve success (CSFs)
  - Historical
  - Short-term
- Non-financial indicators:
  Advantages
  - Leading (rather than lagging)
  - Easy to understand
  - Provided quickly
- Disadvantages
  - Information overload?
  - Lose sight of strategy
  - Data collection costs

The significance of non-financial performance indicators

Performance indicators relating to employees

- Importance of employees in delivering strategy
- Possible indicators:
  - Employee turnover
  - Absence
  - Training

Performance indicators relating to quality

- Importance of quality in ensuring customer satisfaction and repeat business
- Possible indicators:
  - Customer satisfaction scores/ feedback
  - Complaints

Interpreting data about qualitative issues

- Problem of subjectivity
- Possible solutions:
  - Use of surveys and ratings
  - Monitor trends (averages)

Brands and performance

- Significance of brands:
  - Create loyalty
  - Reduce price comparisons
  - Increase switching costs
  - Enable new product launches
- Assess brand strength via:
  - Recognition
  - Customer surveys
  - Repeat business
  - Market research
- Two key elements:
  - Brand awareness
  - Brand loyalty

Knowledge diagnostic

1. Limitations of financial performance indicators

Financial performance indicators are not typically linked to critical success factors, so if organisations focus only on financial indicators, important aspects of performance may get overlooked.

Also, although financial indicators can be used to measure performance, they give little insight into the drivers which cause an organisation to perform.

2. Non-financial performance indicators

Non-financial performance indicators can provide greater insight into the factors shaping performance.

However, financial performance indicators also remain important, so organisations should look to monitor a balanced set of indicators – including financial and non-financial ones.

3. Indicators relating to employees

Non-financial performance indicators can be used to monitor employee satisfaction and training. Information about employees could be particularly important in a service industry where the staff providing the service can have a significant impact on a customer's impression of the service.

4. Indicators relating to quality

Indicators such as customer satisfaction scores and customer retention rates can act as useful surrogates for product/service quality. If customer satisfaction scores are falling, this could be a warning that the underlying quality of an organisation's product or service is also falling.

5. Qualitative data

Data about qualitative issues can often be unstructured and subjective, which makes it more difficult to record and analyse. Using surveys and ratings can provide a way of 'quantifying' qualitative data.

Monitoring trends in aggregate data over time can also help to reduce subjectivity and provide an indication of whether performance is improving or deteriorating.

6. Brands and performance

Brand strength can play an important role in generating customer loyalty, and – as a result – repeat business. Two aspects of brand performance which it could be important to measure are brand awareness and brand loyalty.

Further study guidance

Question practice

Now try the following from the Further question practice bank (available in the digital edition of the Workbook):

Q7 Handra

Activity answers

Activity 1: Non-financial performance objectives

These answers are suggested solutions only, and you may have come up with different answers. However, the point of this activity is to illustrate that in some cases non-financial performance measures may be relatively easy to manipulate, but in other cases they won't be. It depends on the measure and the way the data is collected.

1   Assuming that the production line is largely automated. This would be hard to manipulate. Products will be rejected if the product specification is not fit for purpose.

2   This may be easier to manipulate. Customers who have been kept waiting for a long time may simply be cut off. Customer service staff may only ask for feedback from selected customers (eg ones they think will give favourable feedback). Both of these factors could manipulate results.

11

The role of quality in performance management systems

Learning objectives

On completion of this chapter, you should be able to:

	Syllabus reference no.
Discuss and evaluate the application of Japanese business practices and management accounting techniques, including: (i) Kaizen costing (ii) Target costing (iii) Just-in-time (iv) Total quality management	D5(a)
Assess the relationship of quality management to the performance management strategy of an organisation including the costs of quality.	D5(b)
Justify the need and assess the characteristics of quality in management information systems.	D5(c)
Discuss and apply Six Sigma as a quality improvement method using tools such as DMAIC for implementation.	D5(d)

Exam context

Achieving an appropriate level of quality in its products or services is a very important aspect of an organisation implementing its strategy successfully, and maintaining its competitive success in the face of increasingly competitive markets and rising customer expectations.

As we noted in the previous chapter, product and/or service quality can have a significant impact on customer satisfaction and customer retention.

In this chapter, we will examine a range of approaches to quality management, derived from Japanese business practices – beginning with perhaps the best known of these: 'just-in-time'.

In the APM exam, you should be prepared for questions looking at quality issues and their impact on an organisation's performance, but also questions in which 'quality' issues are integrated with other topics, such as IT systems and the quality of the management information available within an organisation.

This chapter covers topics from Section D of the syllabus, so they could be included within the 50-mark case study question, as well as in one of the 25-mark questions.

Chapter overview

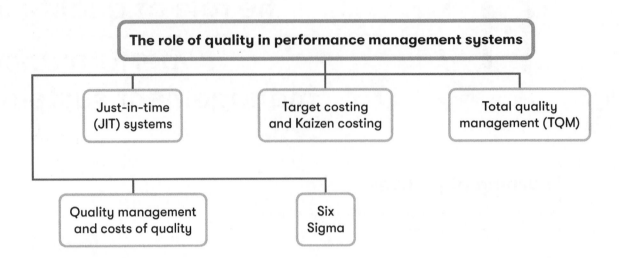

BPP
LEARNING
MEDIA

1 Just-in-time (JIT) systems

Conventional manufacturing approaches tended to involve:

(a) **Long production runs** determined by economic batch quantities;

(b) **Standardisation of product ranges** to gain efficiency;

(c) Use of **inventories** as a buffer to cope with fluctuations in levels of demand; and

(d) Focus on **improving output** per hour to gain efficiency and reduce unit cost.

KEY TERM

> **Just-in-time (JIT):** A system whose objective is to produce or to procure products or components as they are required by a customer or for use, rather than for inventory (*CIMA, 2005, p. 49*).

1.1 Overview of JIT

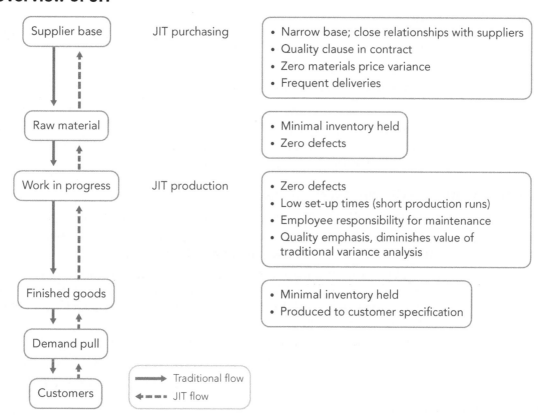

1.2 Essential elements of JIT

Element	Detail
Close relationship with suppliers	• Quality of goods is the responsibility of the supplier. • Establish a long-term commitment between supplier and customer. • Suppliers should expect to deliver material of 100% quality, on time. • Expect to purchase inputs close to the time they are needed, using small, frequent deliveries.
Small batch sizes	• Achieved by reducing set-up times. • Allows poor quality to be more easily identified.
Cellular manufacturing	• Employees should be grouped into small cells of multi-skilled workers, grouped by product, instead of the type of work performed.

Element	Detail
	• Employees are trained to operate each machine within their cell and to perform routine preventative maintenance on them.
Employee empowerment	Empowering employees to stop the production line to rectify problems.
Non-value added functions	Examples of non-value adding activities include holding inventory, supervision, and time spent setting up machinery. Non-value adding activities should all be minimised.
Simplification	Constant focus on the simplification of products and processes in order to maximise the utilisation of available resources.

Essential reading

See Chapter 11 Section 1 of the Essential reading for more detail about the key elements of JIT systems.

The Essential reading is available as an Appendix of the digital edition of the Workbook.

JIT is **more than just a production technique**. It is also an approach to management, which encompasses a **commitment to continuous improvement and the search for excellence** in the design and operation of the production management system (*Ohno, 1988*).

1.3 Implications of JIT for performance management

(a) Shift from encouraging efficiency or minimising cost to focusing on value creation.

As well as looking at cost, performance information also needs to look at quality, flexibility and speed of response; ie **extensive use of non-financial indicators**.

Note. On-time deliveries, cycle times, waste and defective items could all be important performance measures under JIT. These are very similar to the types of performance measure recommended at the operational level in the **performance pyramid** (*Lynch & Cross, 1991*), which we will look at in Chapter 13 of this Workbook.

(b) Good communication channels and effective sharing of information with suppliers are necessary to avoid production delays (in the absence of any inventories being held).

Need information about supplier performance (eg quality and reliability of suppliers).

1.3.1 Implications for costing

The desire for continuous improvement (Kaizen costing, see later) challenges the appropriateness of standard costing. Also, the absence of inventory reduces the importance of different approaches to inventory valuation (eg absorption or marginal costing).

1.4 Potential problems with JIT

(a) It is **not always easy to predict patterns of demand**, which makes operating without inventory difficult.

(b) The absence of inventories makes an organisation **vulnerable to any disruption in the supply chain.**

2 Target costing and Kaizen costing

2.1 Target costing

Competitive pressures in the modern environment mean organisations have to frequently redesign and improve their products. **Product life cycles** have also become much **shorter**.

The key implication of this is that decisions made in the **planning, design and development stages** of a product's life cycle are critical to costs (eg number of components used; using standard components; packaging). Cost reduction is therefore important at these **pre-production stages**.

Target costing involves **setting a selling price** for a product by reference to the market. From this a **desired profit margin is deducted**, leaving a **target cost**. The product's costs (including pre-production costs) are then managed to enable this target cost to be achieved.

> **Target cost:** An estimate of a product cost which is derived by subtracting a desired profit margin from a competitive market price.

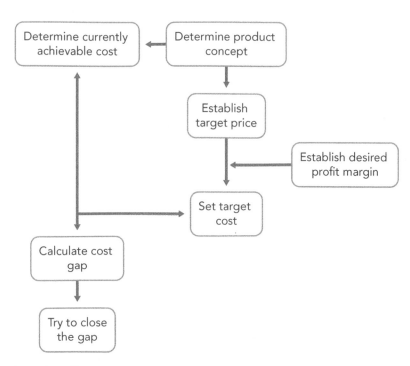

Figure 11.1: The target costing process

Essential reading

See Chapter 11 Section 2 of the Essential reading for more detail about the target costing process.

The Essential reading is available as an Appendix of the digital edition of the Workbook.

Target costing turns the traditional cost-plus approach to pricing on its head, making **price the first consideration**.

2.1.1 Attaining the target cost

Value analysis (or engineering)

This involves refining the design of a product (or service) to achieve its purpose (at the required standards of quality and reliability) at the lowest cost possible. The aim is to reduce the cost without compromising functionality; value analysis requires the use of functional analysis.

Functional analysis

A product is broken down into its various functions or attributes (eg for a laptop this might be touch screen resolution, battery life, weight, processing speed, storage space etc) and estimating (through research/surveys) the amount a customer is prepared to pay for each.

The cost of each function is compared to the value of each function. If the cost is above value, then the functions are modified to reduce cost. If this is not possible, a function may be eliminated.

Reverse engineering

This involves stripping down a competitor's product and analysing its product design to provide insights on improving quality or reducing cost.

Activity 1: Peach Co

The management accountant of Peach Co has collated the following data for a new product, the y-pad music player: the target price is $50.

Sales required = 100,000 units

ROI = 25%

	$
Investment in:	
Buildings	1,500,000
Fixtures	500,000
Machinery	1,400,000
Cost card:	
Materials	32.50
Labour	3.75
Overheads	8.00
	44.25

Required

1   Calculate the target cost and cost gap for the y-pad.   **(3 marks)**

2   Recommend how the cost gap can be closed.   **(4 marks)**

(Total = 7 marks)

Solution

2.2 Kaizen costing

Once a product goes into production, target costs will gradually be reduced. This means that cost savings must be actively sought and made **continuously.**

Kaizen costing focuses on obtaining **small, incremental cost reductions** during the **production stage** of the product life cycle.

'Kaizen' literally means 'continuous improvement' and the underlying message of a Kaizen approach is that some kind of improvement should be made somewhere in an organisation every day *(Imai, 1986)*.

2.2.1 Kaizen and continual cost reduction

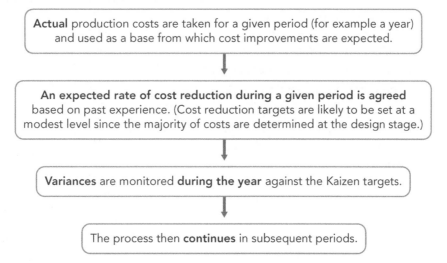

Actual production costs are taken for a given period (for example a year) and used as a base from which cost improvements are expected.

↓

An expected rate of cost reduction during a given period is agreed based on past experience. (Cost reduction targets are likely to be set at a modest level since the majority of costs are determined at the design stage.)

↓

Variances are monitored **during the year** against the Kaizen targets.

↓

The process then **continues** in subsequent periods.

Kaizen relies on **employee empowerment**; workers are given responsibility for proposing changes to achieve the Kaizen targets.

Essential reading

See Chapter 11 Section 3 of the Essential reading for more detail about Kaizen and continuous improvement.

The Essential reading is available as an Appendix of the digital edition of the Workbook.

3 Total quality management (TQM)

Quality is 'the degree to which a set of inherent characteristics fulfils requirements' *(ISO, 2005)*.

In order for an organisation to consistently deliver products and services of the level of quality expected by its customers (or other key stakeholders), it must actively manage all the factors that have an impact on quality.

Traditional views on quality management suggest that quality can be achieved by:

(a) Establishing standards;

(b) Establishing procedures to deliver the targeted quality standards (**quality assurance**);

(c) Monitoring actual quality (**quality control** simply relies on inspection); and

(d) Taking control action when standards are not achieved.

This will ensure that conformance costs are kept under control so that the costs of achieving quality do not become too great. Too high a level of quality may not be justifiable on cost grounds.

By contrast, **modern views** that follow the total quality management (TQM) philosophy believe:

(a) There is no optimal level of quality – the target should be **zero defects**.

(b) **Failure costs** are often seriously underestimated:

- Cost of scrapped items and reworking
- Management time spent sorting out problems
- Loss of confidence by customers

> **Total quality management (TQM):** The process of applying a zero defects philosophy to the management of all resources and relationships within an organisation as a means of developing and sustaining a culture of continuous improvement which focuses on meeting customers' needs and expectations.

TQM has a number of features:

(a) Customer focus (including internal customers as well as external customers)

(b) Defect prevention, not inspection

(c) Personal responsibility for quality, no 'acceptable' defect levels

(d) All departments (not just production) must be involved in getting quality right

Essential reading

See Chapter 11 Section 4 of the Essential reading for more detail about total quality management (TQM).

The Essential reading is available as an Appendix of the digital edition of the Workbook.

4 Quality management and costs of quality

The **costs of quality** represent the **actual cost** of producing, selling and supporting products or services less the **equivalent costs** if there were **no failures** during production or usage.

Cost-of-quality reports highlight the total cost to an organisation of producing products or services that do not conform to quality requirements, thereby enabling these costs to be monitored.

Costs of quality	
Prevention costs	Costs of conformance
Appraisal costs	
Internal failure costs	Costs of non-conformance
External failure costs	

4.1 Traditional view vs TQM approach

The **traditional approach** to managing costs of quality is that the amount of time and effort organisations should invest in quality management should be that at which the costs of conformance plus the costs of non-conformance are minimised (even though this may be below 100% quality conformance).

However, **TQM philosophy** is that any failures or quality issues are unacceptable. The target should be zero defects. To achieve this, organisations should invest in preventing defects, rather than detecting them. Increased spending on prevention will, in time, lead to lower total quality costs, because appraisal costs, internal failure costs and external failure costs will all be reduced.

Essential reading

See Chapter 11 Section 5 of the Essential reading for more detail about costs of quality, and the difference between the traditional approach to costs of quality and the TQM approach.

The Essential reading is available as an Appendix of the digital edition of the Workbook.

Activity 2: Kwaly Co

Kwaly Co has identified that it has incurred the following costs of quality:

	20X6	20X7
	$'000	$'000
Quality control training	40	120
Rework costs	125	60
Returns	35	15
Customer complaints department	50	20
Inspection of WIP	85	70
Scrap	60	20
	395	305

Required

Prepare a cost of quality report and analyse Kwaly Co's quality costs. **(8 marks)**

Solution

4.2 Quality in management information systems

Issues of quality relate not only to external customers, but also internal customers within an organisation. The relationship between management accountant and the users of management accounting information is an example of an internal customer relationship.

Good **quality information** will assist management's understanding or performance, and will help them control their business effectively. Good **quality information systems** will enable accountants and other system users to obtain the information they need in order to manage performance.

Essential reading

We have already discussed the characteristics of lean information in Chapter 6. Chapter 11 Section 6 of the Essential reading gives another perspective on the characteristics of good quality information.

The Essential reading is available as an Appendix of the digital edition of the Workbook.

5 Six Sigma

Six Sigma is a technique designed to improve a process so that there is only the tiniest possibility of failure. (The goal of Six Sigma is to reduce the failure rate to less than 3.4 in a million.) It is typically most appropriate for incremental improvement of fairly narrowly defined processes, rather than the fundamental rethinking or radical redesign of processes (where business process re-engineering – see Chapter 4 – is more appropriate).

Key themes in Six Sigma:

- Focus on aspects of performance and processes which are important for the **customer**
- Decisions should be based on **data and facts**, not intuition
- **Processes** are the key to success

5.1 Project phases – DMAIC

To improve an existing process, Six Sigma recommends five key steps:

Step 1 Define: **Define the scope of the project**

Identify customer requirements, clarify the problem, and set goals.

Step 2 Measure: **Measure current performance**

Select what needs to be measured within a process to help to identify the root cause of a problem, identify information sources and gather data.

Step 3 Analyse: **Analyse the existing process**

Develop and test different theories, identify the key variables and root causes.

Step 4 Improve: **Improve the process**

Generate and test solutions and put them into action, either modifying existing processes or developing new ones. Quantify costs and benefits.

Step 5 Control: **Control the new process**

Develop monitoring processes for continued high-quality performance.

Example

The following example, based on a restaurant, illustrates how a Six Sigma project could be applied in practice.

The restaurant's goal is to ensure that customers are satisfied with the quality of their meals, and of the service they receive. The restaurant is aware that there are a number of things about a dinner meal that **might** satisfy customers: quality of the food (taste, temperature); presentation of the food; variety of menu (number of items, daily specials); service (speed of food delivery, attention to customer's needs during the meal); ambience (room layout, cleanliness); and the price of the meal.

For a Six Sigma project to be effective, the restaurant will have to determine the role that each of these possible requirements actually plays in customer satisfaction (that is, the restaurant has to **define** customer requirements).

The restaurant did this by asking all their customers to complete a short questionnaire survey after their meal. The results of the survey identified the requirements which were important to customers (eg taste, speed of delivery, and attentiveness of waiting staff during the meal).

The restaurant next had to identify **measures** to see how well it performed in satisfying these requirements. One of the measures selected, in relation to speed of delivery, was the length of time between a waiter taking an order and the meal being delivered to the table.

The total time to deliver the meal is made up of the time it takes the waiter to submit the order to the kitchen, the times it takes the kitchen to cook the food and plate it up ready for service, and then for the waiter to deliver the meal.

The restaurant gathered data measuring the time it took waiters to place and deliver orders; and the time it took the kitchen to prepare and cook the food. They then analysed the data to identify what the most common causes were when meals were delayed (the **analysis** phase).

The analysis identified a number of things that take up a waiter's time and therefore interfered with the prompt placement of orders and delivery of food. These included: families with children wanting tables to be rearranged; multiple tables all requiring waiter service at the same time; and tables wanting to make frequent drink orders.

This highlighted to the project team that an important issue affecting the speed of service was the management and placement of families within the restaurant.

To deal with this, the restaurant decided that two groups of families with children should not be put in the same area if possible; or if there was no alternative to putting families together, the number of tables served by the waiter dealing with them should be reduced, and extra tables should be allocated to another waiter. (This is the **improve** stage.)

The restaurant was happy with the improvements in service following the project. However, it was agreed that customer feedback surveys would continue to be distributed to all diners eating at the restaurant. The results from these surveys should allow the restaurant manager to monitor ongoing customer satisfaction (the **control** stage).

5.2 Benefits of Six Sigma

Potential benefits claimed for Six Sigma include:

(a) Processes become more rigorous as they use hard, timely data, not opinions or intuition 'gut feeling' as the basis for decision making

(b) Reduced variation in service processes: eg the time from order to delivery in a restaurant; or offering a consistent, high-quality service experience

(c) Improved financial performance, through cost savings from projects, increased revenue from improved products and greater operating margins

(d) Increased customer loyalty as a result of delivering superior value

Essential reading

See Chapter 11 Section 7 of the Essential reading for more detail about the DMAIC phases for implementing Six Sigma project.

The Essential reading is available as an Appendix of the digital edition of the Workbook.

Chapter summary

The role of quality in performance management systems

Just-in-time (JIT) systems

- Production based on customer demand
- Minimal inventory
- Small batch sizes; make production more flexible
- Reduce or eliminate non-value-adding activities (such as inventory holding; set-up times)
- Employees carry out preventative maintenance
- Commitment to continuous improvement; aim for zero defects
- Needs close relationships with suppliers, and supplier reliability (on time; quality)

Target costing and Kaizen costing

- Target costing
  - For products being developed
  - Target cost = realistic market price less desired profit margin
- Closing a cost gap:
  - Value analysis
  - Functional analysis
  - Reverse engineering
- Kaizen costing
  - Continuous improvement
  - Cost reduction throughout production stage of product life cycle
  - Elimination of non-value-adding activities
- Employees are a source of solutions, not problems

Total quality management (TQM)

- Preventing errors is better than detecting them
- Aim to get things 'right first time'; zero defects
- Focus must be on meeting customer needs and expectations
- Everyone is responsible for quality

Quality management and costs of quality

- Prevention costs
- Appraisal costs
- Internal failure costs
- External failure costs
- TQM approach: prevention is the most effective way of minimising costs of quality

Six Sigma

- Process improvement methodology
- Focus on the aspects of performance which are important to the customer
- Decisions based on facts, not intuition
- 5 steps:
  - Define
  - Measure
  - Analyse
  - Improve
  - Control

Knowledge diagnostic

1. Just-in-time (JIT)

JIT aims to restructure production processes to improve flexibility, speed and costs. JIT systems are 'demand pull' systems. Products should be produced, and components procured, as they are required by customers, rather than to build up inventory.

Preventative maintenance is important to ensure reliability of machinery, and JIT relies on close co-operation with suppliers, because the absence of inventory holding means organisations could be vulnerable to disruption in the supply chain.

Like other Japanese approaches, one of the key characteristics of JIT is a desire for continuous improvement ('Kaizen').

2. Target costing

Target costing is a market-led approach in which the target cost is derived by subtracting a desired profit margin from a competitive market price for a product. Target costing is used when developing new products.

The difference between the 'actual' price and the target price is the 'costs gap'. This needs to be closed – eg by changing the product design or removing non-value-adding activities from the production process.

3. Kaizen costing

The aim of Kaizen costing is to continually reduce costs over a product's life, using tools such as value analysis and functional analysis.

The underlying aim of Kaizen ('continuous improvement') is to use an organisation's human resources to produce a continuous stream of improvements.

4. Total quality management (TQM)

TQM aims to get things right first time. Key principles within TQM are: striving for zero defects; focusing on customers' needs and expectations; and acknowledging that everyone in an organisation is responsible for quality.

5. Quality management and costs of quality

Costs of quality can be grouped into four categories: prevention; appraisal; internal failure costs and external failure costs. Prevention and appraisal are 'costs of conformance', while internal failure and external failure are 'costs of non-conformance'.

Traditional approaches seek to minimise the total cost of conformance costs plus non-conformance costs. Under a TQM approach, prevention is viewed as the most effective way of minimising the total costs of quality.

6. Six Sigma

Six Sigma is a technique for process improvement, whose overall aim is to ensure a very high and consistent quality of output from a process.

It is based around five key steps (known as 'DMAIC'):

- Define requirements
- Measure current performance
- Analyse the process
- Improve the process
- Control the new process

Further study guidance

Question practice

Now try the following from the Further question practice bank (available in the digital edition of the Workbook):

Q13 *Thebe*

Activity answers

Activity 1: Peach Co

1   Investment = 1,500,000 + 500,000 + 1,400,000

$\qquad$ = 3,400,000

Return required = 3,400,000 × 25%

$\qquad$ = $850,000

Profit per unit = $\dfrac{\$850,000}{100,000 \text{ units}}$ = $8.50

∴ target cost = 50 – 8.50 = $41.50

Cost gap = 44.35 – 41.50 = $2.75

2   Possible suggestions (you may have thought of others):

Materials are the largest element of the cost, so start by looking for possible reductions to these:

Bulk discounts

Cheaper materials

Less material (simplify product design/specification?)

Labour	Learning curve effects
	Training, so staff can produce y-pads more quickly
Overheads	May be linked to labour (so reducing one may reduce the other)
	Cost savings to be identified

Activity 2: Kwaly Co

	20X6		20X7	
	$'000	%	$'000	%
Prevention costs				
Quality control	40	10.1	120	39.3
Appraisal costs				
Inspection of WIP	85	21.6	70	23.0
Internal failure costs				
Rework	125		60	
Scrap	60	46.8	20	26.2
External failure costs				
Returns	35		15	
Complaints	50	21.5	20	11.5
	395	100	305	100

Total costs of quality are falling. Also more is being spent on improving conformance. Prevention costs have trebled (from $40,000 to $120,000) which might suggest Kwaly is looking to increase its effort on preventing defects as a means of reducing its total quality costs.

Costs of failure are falling. However, reduced appraisal costs could cause future failures to increase. However, this also depends on the success of Kwaly's efforts to prevent defects.

A longer period of assessment would be helpful.

If the costs were expressed as a percentage of sales that would also be more helpful, because if the company's activity levels are changing then this will have an impact on costs.

12

Performance measurement and strategic HRM issues

Learning objectives

On completion of this chapter, you should be able to:

	Syllabus reference no.
Advise on the relationship of HR management to performance measurement (performance rating) and suitable remuneration methods.	D6(a)
Advise on the link between achievement of the corporate strategy and the management of human resources (eg through the building block model).	D6(b)
Discuss and evaluate different methods of reward practices, including the potential beneficial and adverse consequences of linking reward schemes to performance measurement	D6(c)
Discuss the accountability issues that might arise from performance measurement systems.	D7(a)
Assess the statement: 'What gets measured gets done' in the context of performance management.	D7(b)
Demonstrate how management style needs to be considered when designing an effective performance measurement system (such as Hopwood's management styles).	D7(c)

Exam context

For most organisations, their performance, and their ability to successfully achieve objectives, will be strongly influenced by the skills and behaviours of their employees.

As such, human resource management (HRM) plays an important role in enabling organisations to implement their strategies successfully. The performance measurement systems used to assess employees, and the reward systems in place, are key components in the relationship between HRM and strategy because they need to motivate employees to help an organisation achieve its objectives.

In the context of an exam question, you need to be prepared to look critically at an organisation's remuneration and reward schemes and the extent to which they help an organisation implement its strategy successfully through the efforts and behaviours of its staff, and by helping the organisation recruit and retain appropriate staff.

Fitzgerald and Moon's Building Block model provides a framework for linking HRM to corporate strategy, and because the model is specifically listed in the Study Guide you should be prepared for it to be directly examined. This model is examinable in the context of HR issues such as rewards, and is also covered in syllabus section E, in Chapter 13, in the context of multi-dimensional performance appraisal.

Chapter overview

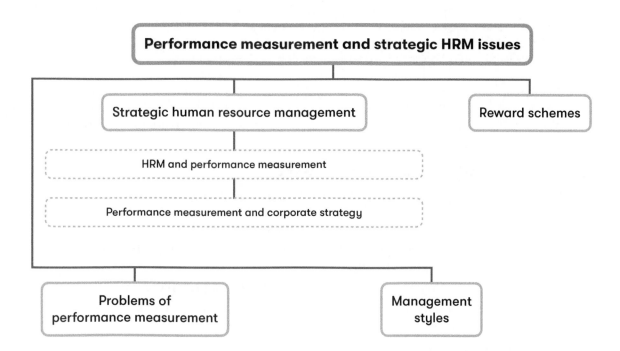

1 Strategic human resource management (HRM)

KEY TERM

Human resource management (HRM): 'A strategic approach to managing employment relations which emphasises that leveraging people's capabilities and commitment is critical to achieving sustainable competitive advantage or superior public services. This is accomplished through a distinctive set of integrated employment policies, programmes and practices, embedded in an organisational and societal context.' (*Bratton & Gold, 2012, p. 7*)

The definition of HRM highlights that employees' knowledge and skills are an important strategic resource of organisations. It is important for organisations to have the right quantity and quality of people it needs. So operational success can depend on effective **recruitment** and **retention** and **motivation** of staff.

1.1 HRM and performance measurement

Performance management requires that the strategic objectives of the organisation are broken down into layers of more and more detailed sub-objectives, so that individual performance can be judged against personal goals that support and link directly back to corporate strategy.

This hierarchy of goals and objectives was discussed in Chapter 2 earlier. **Targets** set for individuals need to be **achievable and controllable**.

Performance against targets will be reviewed as part of the **appraisal process**.

In addition to providing a performance rating, a staff appraisal scheme will:

- Set motivating **challenges;**
- Identify **training needs**;
- Provide a forum for exchanging **feedback;** and
- Identify **future aspirations** and expectations (career management).

Essential reading

See Chapter 12 Section 1 of the Essential reading for more detail about appraisals and their use in performance management.

See Chapter 12 Section 2 of the Essential reading for more detail about the selection of suitable performance indicators against which to measure employees' performance.

The Essential reading is available as an Appendix of the digital edition of the Workbook.

1.2 Performance measurement and corporate strategy

Fitzgerald and Moon (1996) focused on performance measurement in service businesses in their building block model. This framework is also known as the **results** and **determinants** framework, because it is argued that **performance dimensions** need to cover two general areas:

Fitzgerald and Moon (1996) suggest that **results** and **determinants** should be viewed over **six dimensions** (with 1–2 being 'results' and 3–6 being 'determinants').

(1) **Financial performance** (eg profitability)

(2) **Competitive performance** (eg sales growth; market share)

(3)   **Quality** – reliability, courtesy, competence and availability

(4)   **Resource utilisation** – how efficiently resources are being used to create outputs
       (eg productivity of staff)

(5)   **Flexibility** – the ability to deliver at the right time in response to customer needs
       (eg speed of delivery, responding to different customer requirements, coping with fluctuating
       levels of demand)

(6)   **Innovation** – developing new products or services to find new, more effective ways of
       satisfying customers' needs

1.2.1   Other 'building blocks'

Fitzgerald and Moon's building block model is **not** only about the dimensions over which
performance should be measured. It is also about the nature of the **standards** against which
performance is measured, and the **rewards** associated with achieving these standards. The full
model is shown below:

Building Block model (after *Fitzgerald & Moon, 1996*)

1.2.2   Standards

- The dimensions of performance should be set according to the following **standards**:

Ownership

- Employees need to participate in the creation of standards to take ownership of them, and to
  feel more motivated to achieve them.

Achievement

- The standards set must be challenging but achievable. If staff perceive standards to be set so
  high that they are unachievable, this is likely to demotivate them.

Equity (fairness)

- Each division or department must have appropriate standards set for it in order to ensure
  fairness in measurement.

1.2.3   Rewards

Achievement of standards should be supported by **rewards**. This should involve:

Clarity

- The objectives of the organisation need to be clearly understood by those whose performance
  is being assessed; they need to know what targets they are working towards.

Motivation

- Individuals need to be motivated to achieve the objectives. Goal clarity, and participation in
  target setting can contribute to higher levels of motivation to achieve targets.

Controllability

- Managers should not be held responsible for aspects of performance over which they have no control (eg managers should not be held responsible for costs they do not control).

2 Reward schemes

> **Reward scheme:** A reward scheme (or reward system) encompasses 'all of the monetary, non-monetary and psychological payments that an organisation provides for its employees in exchange for the work they perform' (*Bratton & Gold (2007), cited in Ryan, 2015(b)*).

The rewards provided for employees may be seen as **extrinsic** or **intrinsic**.

(a) **Extrinsic rewards** derive from **job context** and include pay and other material benefits as well as such matters as working conditions and management style.

(b) **Intrinsic rewards** derive from **job content** and satisfy higher-level needs, such as those for self-esteem and personal development.

An organisation's reward scheme is based on these two types of reward, but also includes the policies and processes involved in providing them.

Reward schemes should:

- Support the overall **strategy** of the organisation by aligning the **goals** of individual employees with the goals of the organisation;
- Be **affordable** (remember: reward is a cost to the employer), and **easy to administer** efficiently and correctly;
- Support **recruitment** and retention policies;
- Increase **motivation**;
- Encourage **ethical behaviour**, and promote compliance with workplace rules and expectations; and
- Be **fair** and **conform with law** (eg minimum wage legislation).

When evaluating potential reward schemes, an organisation also needs to consider:

- How do levels of pay and material benefits compare to what employees believe to be the prevailing market rate? (ie **external competitiveness** of rewards).
- Internal comparison: how do rewards earned by employees within the organisation compare to those earned by other employees in similar roles? (ie **Internal equity** (fairness) of rewards).
- If employees are dissatisfied with rewards and leave the organisation, this will lead to increased recruitment costs to find replacements.

2.1 Reward methods

Material reward may be divided into three categories:

(a) **Base pay** (basic salary)

(b) **Performance-related pay** (eg bonuses); remuneration is linked to an assessment of performance, usually measured against pre-agreed objectives

(c) **Indirect pay** (eg benefits such as pension plans; health insurance or child care; provided in addition to base pay or performance-related pay)

Essential reading

See Chapter 12 Section 3 of the Essential reading for more detail about performance-related pay, and share options as potential methods of reward.

The Essential reading is available as an Appendix of the digital edition of the Workbook.

Activity 1: Alpha division

The RRR Group (RRR) provides roof repair services to individual customers on a nationwide basis. RRR operates a number of regional divisions, each of which offers similar services. Table A shows actual results for Alpha division for 20X8 and 20X9, together with data representing an average of a number of similar competitor company divisions.

As an incentive to support the strategic goals of RRR, a set of key performance indicators (KPIs) will be introduced in 20Y0 and used on the basis of the data in Table B. Divisional staff will be paid a bonus as a percentage of salary based on the overall weighted percentage score deduced from the analysis as per Table B.

Table A: Summary of financial and other operating information

	Alpha division 20X9 $m	Alpha division 20X8 $m	Competitors 20X9 $m
Sales revenue	90.0	80.0	85.0
Less costs:			
Cost of sales	60.0	50.0	
Marketing	8.5	8.0	
Staff training	4.0	4.0	
Remedial work on orders	0.8	0.5	
Customer enquiry costs	1.5	1.4	
Customer complaint related costs	0.2	0.1	
Total costs	75.0	64.0	69.5
Net profit	15.0	16.0	15.5
Number of			
Customer enquiries	15,000	16,000	
Customer orders placed	10,000	8,800	
Orders placed requiring remedial work	300	440	
Customer complaints	100	132	

Table B: Staff bonus calculation for 20X9 using KPIs

KPI	Weighting factor (A)	KPI total score % (B)*	Weighted score % (A) × (B)
Revenue 20X9 versus previous year	0.15		
Revenue 20X9 versus competitor	0.20		
Profit 20X9 versus previous year	0.15		
Profit 20X9 versus competitor	0.20		
Quality items 20X9 vs 20X8:			
No. of orders requiring remedial work	0.075		
No. of complaints investigated	0.075		
% of enquiries converted into orders	0.15		
Total	**1.000**	Bonus (%) =	?

(B)* – each KPI score value is positive (+) where the 20X9 value shows an improvement over the previous year **or** negative (–) where the 20X9 value shows poorer performance than in the previous year.

Each KPI score value is the % increase (+) or decrease (–) in 20X9 as appropriate.

Required

1   Apply the KPI appraisal process explained in Table B, using data for 20X8 and 20X9 to show the bonus (as a percentage of salary) that would have been achieved by Alpha division for 20X9. **(12 marks)**

2   Briefly discuss potential benefits that may be derived from the application of the KPI appraisal and bonus approach, both for Alpha division and throughout the RRR Group. **(3 marks)**

(Total = 15 marks)

Solution

PER alert

Element (d) of Performance objective 14 identifies that you should 'Use review and reward systems to monitor and assess performance'.

Reward systems are not only a key part of human resource management; they can also play an important role in helping an organisation to achieve its strategy objectives (by motivating employees). Equally, however, poorly designed reward systems could have a detrimental impact on employees' behaviour and, consequently, an organisation's performance.

Issues relating to HRM more generally are also relevant to element (c) of Performance objective 5 – Leadership and management: 'Manage human... resources within your control or allocated to your department to deliver your objectives to agreed deadlines, seeking opportunities to motivate or assist in the development of others'.

2.2 Accountability

The principle of accountability requires that an agent (eg a company's managers and employees) are **motivated** to do what the principal (eg shareholders) want them to, and that their performance is **monitored**.

Reward systems have to incorporate the means of monitoring (performance measurement) and motivating the agent to do what is required of them. The following steps should be considered to help ensure accountability:

(a) Choose and make public a range of accepted performance measures;

(b) Ensure that the benefits of the performance measures have been identified;

(c) Identify and understand possible problems in the use of performance measures; and

(d) Consider ways in which to counter perceived problems in the use of performance measures.

Essential reading

See Chapter 12 Section 4 of the Essential reading for more detail about accountability and control, and the different types of control mechanisms which organisations can use to manage the performance of their staff.

The Essential reading is available as an Appendix of the digital edition of the Workbook.

3 Problems of performance measurement

3.1 What gets measured, gets done

The notion that 'What gets measured, gets done' (*Peters, 1986*) is often raised in relation to performance measured, and highlights the fact that people will typically put more effort into trying to perform well in those areas of performance which they know are being measured, compared to those which are not.

This could have **positive implications**: eg if an employee's objectives are aligned to their organisation's objectives and CSFs, then 'what gets measured, gets done' should help improve performance in relation to those key areas. (This reiterates the importance of ensuring there is congruence between employees' individual goals, and the goals of the organisation.)

3.2 Problems of performance measures

Berry, Broadbent and Otley (1995) suggest there could be a number of potential problems involved in performance measurement systems:

Problem	Explanation
Tunnel vision	'What gets measured, gets done' leads to a focus on a few specific aspects of performance or performance measures to the **detriment of others.** This could be a particular problem where the areas being focused on are not the ones which contribute most to competitive advantage or organisational success. (The issue is known as **sub-optimisation**: focusing on some objectives with the result that others – which could bring greater success – are not achieved.)
Myopia	Focusing on short-term success or goals at the expense of **longer-term** objectives and long-term success.
Measure fixation	An organisation focuses on achieving specific measures and targets, even though they may not be effective; ie the focus is on the measures themselves rather than underlying goals and objectives.
Misrepresentation	**'Creative' reporting, or deliberate manipulation of data** to make a result appear better than it actually is, or deliberate distortion of performance to secure some strategic advantage eg not finalising a new sales deal in the current period, because the sales target for the period had already been achieved, but delaying the deal will help to improve performance in the following period.
Misinterpretation	Users misunderstand performance data, eg as a result of failing to recognise the complexity of the environment in which an organisation operates and therefore the external influences on performance.
Ossification	**Unwillingness to change** the performance measure scheme once it has been set up.

Activity 2: Problems with performance management

Identify possible solutions for the problems that have been identified in the previous section.

Solution

4 Management styles

Hopwood (1974) identified three distinct management styles.

Style	How are managers assessed	Effect
Budget-constrained	Ability to meet budgets, regardless of the impact on other criteria	High tension High manipulation Poor staff relations
Profit-conscious	General effectiveness of the unit's operations in relation to an organisation's purpose	Medium tension Little manipulation Good staff relations
Non-accounting	Budgets are not important Non-financial factors are more important	Medium tension Little manipulation Good staff relations

Hopwood believed that the **profit-conscious style** was often optimal, but stressed the appropriateness of different styles depended on the organisation and its environment.

Essential reading

See Chapter 12 Section 5 of the Essential reading for more detail about Hopwood's research into management styles, and why different styles could be appropriate in different contexts.

The Essential reading is available as an Appendix of the digital edition of the Workbook.

BPP LEARNING MEDIA

Chapter summary

Performance measurement and strategic HRM issues

Strategic human resource management

- Organisations need to use people's capabilities to achieve competitive advantage
- Recruitment; retention; development
- Measuring/managing employee performance

HRM and performance measurement
- Set targets, linked back to corporate strategy
- Monitor performance vs target
- Appraisals: Feedback? Development?

Performance measurement and corporate strategy

Fitzgerald & Moon Building blocks model

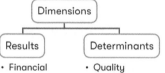

Dimensions

Results
- Financial performance
- Competitive performance

Determinants
- Quality
- Resource utilisation
- Flexibility
- Innovation

Standards
Ownership
Achievability
Equity

Rewards
Clarity
Motivation
Controllability

Reward schemes

- Need to:
  - Support overall strategy
  - Align individual's goals to organisation's
  - Be affordable
  - Support recruitment and retention
  - Increase motivation
  - Align employees' risk preferences with the organisation's
  - Encourage ethical behaviour and compliance
  - Be fair
  - Conform with law
  - Be easy to administer
- Methods:
  - Basic
  - Performance-related (individual; group)
  - Indirect

Problems of performance measurement

- 'What gets measured, gets done'
- Problems:
  - Tunnel vision
  - Sub-optimisation
  - Myopia
  - Measure fixation
  - Misrepresentation
  - Misinterpretation
  - Ossification

Management styles

- Hopwood: Three styles
  - Budget-constrained: Meet budget
  - Profit-conscious: Effectiveness
  - Non-accounting: Budgets not important

Tension	High	Medium	Low
Manipulation	Extensive	Little	Little
Staff relations	Poor	Poor	Good
Focus	Cost (short-term)	Business	Non-financial

Knowledge diagnostic

1. HRM and strategy

Employees are vital assets to organisations, so human resource management needs to be integrated with, and aligned to, an organisation's strategy.

Fitzgerald and Moon's building block model (dimensions, standards and rewards) provides a structure for designing effective reward systems, which are aligned to organisational strategy.

2. Reward systems

- Supporting the recruitment and retention of staff
- Motivating employees to high levels of performance
- Promoting compliance with workplace rules and expectations (including ethical behaviour)

Reward systems also need to ensure an employee's risk preferences are aligned to that of their organisation.

3. Reward models

Reward systems include all the monetary, non-monetary and psychological payments that an organisation provides its employees in exchange for the work they perform.

Extrinsic rewards derive from job context and include pay and benefits. Intrinsic rewards derive from job content and satisfy higher-level needs.

Monetary payments include base pay and performance-related pay. A mixture of individual and group performance incentives may be used.

Share options and performance shares can be valuable mechanisms for encouraging managers to work in the best interests of shareholders over the long term.

4. Problems of performance measurement

The notion that **'What gets measured, gets done'** suggests people will make a greater effort to perform well in activities which are being measured, compared to those which are not ('tunnel vision').

Placing too much emphasis on measuring performance can cause dysfunctional behaviour, including short-term thinking and a loss of focus on underlying goals and objectives.

5. Management styles

Hopwood defined three management styles: budget-constrained; profit-conscious; and non-accounting. He suggests the profit-conscious style is often the most effective one, but that the appropriateness of a different style depends on the context in which it is used.

Further study guidance

Question practice

Now try the following from the Further question practice bank (available in the digital edition of the Workbook):

Q14 *Connie Head*

Further reading

There are two Technical Articles available on ACCA's website about HRM and reward systems:

* *Human resource management and the appraisal system*
* *Reward schemes for employees and management*

These articles supplement the material in this chapter, and you are strongly advised to read them in full as part of your preparation for the APM exam.

The benefits of performance measures and the potential problems of performance measurement are discussed in another of the Technical Articles on ACCA's website: *The Pyramids and Pitfalls of Performance Measurement*.

You are encouraged to read this article in full as part of your preparation for the APM exam.

Activity answers

Activity 1: Alpha division

1   **Bonus as a percentage of salary for Alpha division for the year ended 30 November 20X9**

KPI	Weighting factor	KPI total score	Weighted score
Revenue 20X9 versus previous year $(90/80)	0.15	12.50	1.875
Revenue 20X9 versus competitor $(90/85)	0.20	5.88	1.176
Profit 20X9 versus previous year $(15/16)	0.15	(6.25)	(0.938)
Profit 20X9 versus competitor $(15/15.50)	0.20	(3.23)	(0.646)
Quality items 20X9 versus previous year			
Number of orders needing remedial work (W1)	0.075	31.82	2.387
Number of complaints investigated (W1)	0.075	24.20	1.815
Percentage of enquiries converted into orders (W2)	0.15	21.30	3.195
Total	1.000	Bonus %	8.864

Workings

1   The KPI score is positive if performance has improved. The quality items both show fewer remedial works or complaints in 20X9 which means the score should be positive. The calculations are 140/440 × 100% and 32/132 × 100%.

2   This is calculated as (customer orders placed/enquiries) as a percentage and compared year on year. Therefore 20X9 is 10,000/15,000 = 0.667 and 20X8 8,800/16,000 = 0.55. The percentage increase year on year is (0.667 − 0.55)/0.55 = 21.27 or 21.30%.

2   **Potential benefits from applying the KPI appraisal and bonus approach for Alpha and the Group**

Alpha. The KPI approach is clear to understand as the calculation involves a few key performance measures. The measures are both financial and non-financial, the latter based on customer service and the quality of service provided. The use of a broad range of measures provides a rounder picture of performance than if just financial measures were used.

The calculation is easy to do and the factors making up the bonus calculation are clearly shown. It is also clear where a factor adds to or reduces the bonus percentage, which will encourage staff to focus efforts in these areas. The factors are based on actual results, which can be updated over time, as they relate to comparisons over two years in some cases.

Group. The KPI measures are uniform across the divisions which allow comparisons between divisions to be made easily. The approach also minimises the possibility of bias against certain divisions or complaints being made about unfairness.

Activity 2: Problems with performance management

Problem	Solution
Tunnel vision	Considering the **dimensions** of performance Considering critical success factors and/or issues which are most important to consumers when determining performance measures Involving staff from all levels of the organisation, and from different departments/divisions when determining performance measures
Myopia	**Fostering** a long-term view/perspective amongst staff
Measure fixation	**Sensible number** of measures Flexible use of performance measures Review (or audit) the data used in performance measurement
Misrepresentation	**Do not place too much emphasis on results** **Involvement of staff** at all levels to ensure that standards are fair
Misinterpretation	Include **benchmarking** Include performance measures which take account of external factors (eg market share, as well as revenue)
Ossification	Keeping the performance measurements system under **constant review** Encourage all **staff to input suggestions** for change

Skills checkpoint 4

Critical analysis

Overview

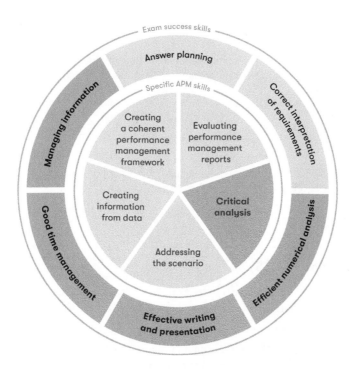

Introduction

The overall aim of the APM syllabus highlights that candidates should be able to exercise professional judgement in selecting and applying strategic management accounting techniques in different business contexts.

As such, it will reward candidates who can critically analyse the techniques that they have studied, for example to consider whether a certain technique would be appropriate for an organisation to use.

This skill requires candidates not only to understand the techniques, but also to appreciate their potential advantages or disadvantages, and to recognise that introducing a 'new' management accounting technique will not always be appropriate for an organisation. This can sometimes come as a surprise to candidates who have revised how to apply a relatively modern technique (such as economic value added, or the balanced scorecard) but have not considered that some organisations might not find these techniques useful.

Sometimes a critical analysis will be a choice that you make as a part of a question that asks for a 'discussion' or that requires 'advice' or an 'evaluation'.

The skill of '**critical analysis**' can potentially be applied to any syllabus area in APM, and can be an important ingredient in developing a discussion answer that addresses the scenario in a way that adds value. (This skill of addressing the scenario is discussed further in Skills Checkpoint 5.)

APM Skill: Critical analysis

The key steps in applying this skill are outlined below. They will be explained in more detail in the following sections, and illustrated by answering a question from a past exam.

> **STEP 1:**
>
> Analyse the scenario and requirements.
>
> Examine the requirement words and assess their meaning.
>
> Ensure that you are alert to the possibility that a critical approach to your analysis can be used to 'add value'.
>
> This will be signalled by the requirement words 'discuss', 'evaluate', 'advise' or 'critically analyse'.

> **STEP 2:**
>
> Plan your answer.
>
> Without adopting a hyper-critical approach, ensure that your answer is balanced in terms of looking at the potential use and limitations of techniques that are being employed.

> **STEP 3:**
>
> As you write your answer, try wherever possible to apply your criticisms to the scenario instead of simply writing about them in technical terms. (This is discussed further in Skills Checkpoint 5.)

Exam success skills

The following illustration is based on an extract from a past exam question, about an entertainment business called 'ENT'. This extract was worth 14 marks.

For this question, we will also focus on the following **exam success skills**:

- **Managing information.** In APM questions it is always crucial to allocate sufficient time to **carefully reading the requirements and the scenario.**

- **Efficient numerical analysis.** APM often does not require a significant amount of calculation. However, the skill you need to demonstrate will be in assessing the required approach to analysing the numbers, then applying this approach clearly and correctly.

- **Effective writing and presentation.** Make sure that your writing is concise, but not so brief that you are unable to explain the relevance of your points to the scenario.

- **Good time management.** Complete all the tasks in the time available. This means that you need to be careful not to be too ambitious in the scope of any numerical analysis that you perform.

Skills activity

STEP 1 Analyse the scenario and requirements. Examine the requirement words and assess their meaning. Ensure that you are alert to the possibility that a critical approach to your analysis can be used to 'add value'.

Required

(a) Perform a BCG analysis of ENT's business and[46] use this to evaluate the company's performance.

(7 marks)

[46] Two aspects to this question.

(b) **Critically evaluate**[47] this BCG analysis as a performance management system at ENT.

(7 marks)

(Total = 14 marks)

[47] Clear instruction to apply critical analysis.

The key action verb here is 'evaluate'. This is defined by the ACCA as 'Determine the situation in the light of the arguments for and against' so specifically means you need to consider the benefits **and** limitations/problems with a particular technique or system.

Here there will be a greater emphasis on making critical points as you are asked to 'critically' evaluate.

This is a 14-mark question so, at 1.95 minutes a mark, it should take 27 minutes. On the basis of spending approximately 20% of your time reading and planning, this time should be split approximately as follows:

- Reading and planning time – 5 minutes (take longer if needed)
- Writing up your answer – 22 minutes (11 marks per part)

Now read the scenario.

Question – ENT (14 marks)

Company background and objectives

ENT Entertainment Co (ENT) is a large, diversified entertainment business based in Teeland. The company's objective is the maximisation of shareholder wealth for its family owners. It has four divisions:

(a) Restaurants

(b) Cafés

(c) Bars

(d) Dance clubs

Recently, ENT's board has identified that there are problems in managing such a diversified company. They have employed consultants who have recommended that they should perform a Boston Consulting Group (BCG) analysis to understand whether they have the right mix of businesses. The Chief Executive Officer (CEO) has questioned[48] whether using this analysis is helpful in managing the group's performance.

[48] A clear signal that a critical approach is appropriate, but this should be employed as part of a balanced evaluation.

Revenue information for each division

A business analyst has prepared information on each division in the table below.

Revenue*	Actual 20X0 $m	Actual 20X1 $m	Forecast 20X2 $m	Forecast 20X3 $m
Restaurants				
ENT	54	56	59	62
Market sector	10,752	10,860	10,968	10,968
Cafés				
ENT	31	34	41	47
Market sector	3,072	3,348	3,717	4,051
Bars				
ENT	349	342	336	336
Market sector	9,984	9,784	9,491	9,206
Dance clubs				
ENT	197	209	219	241
Market sector	1,792	1,900	2,013	2,195

* This data will be used in the BCG evolution in part (a). Here we are required to 'create information from data' – this is a recap of Skill Checkpoint 1.

Economic context:[49]

[49] Useful data for evaluating market growth and relative market share?

In Teeland, the economy is generally growing at about 2% per annum.

The restaurant, café and bar sectors are all highly fragmented with many small operators. Consequently, a market share of more than 3.0% is considered large as that is comparable to the share of the largest operators in each sector.

There are fewer small late night dance club operators and the market leader currently holds a 15.0% market share. There have not been many new developments within the divisions except for a new wine bar format launched by the Bars Division which has surprised the board by its success.

STEP 2 Plan your answer.

Without adopting a hyper-critical approach, ensure that your answer is balanced, in terms of looking at the potential use **and** limitations of techniques that are being employed.

Answer plan

Requirement	Points / Approach to take
Perform BCG analysis*	Use the revenue data for the market to analyse market growth. (Use all data or just historical?) Use latest actuals to analyse ENT's current performance in terms of relative market share.
Use this analysis to evaluate the company's performance	Categorise and use scenario points given in the 'economic context' section of the question.
Evaluate this BCG analysis**	Again use scenario points given in the 'economic context' section of the question. How useful is the BCG matrix in helping ENT manage performance?

* Keep analysis as simple as possible as it only looks to be worth 3–4 marks (so only analyse relative market share for 20X1).

** Keep analysis as focused on the scenario as possible.

STEP 3 As you write your answer, try wherever possible to apply your criticisms to the scenario instead of simply writing about them in technical terms. (This is discussed further in Skills Checkpoint 5.)

As already noted, performing the calculations and writing up your answer should take 22 minutes.

There are many ways of laying out an answer to this question; **one approach** is shown below.

(a)

Market growth (%)*

Division	20X1	20X2	20X3	Average of annual growth rates (20X0–X3)
Restaurants	1.0	1.0	–	0.67
Cafés	9.0	11.0	9.0	9.66
Bars	(2.0)	(3.0)	(3.0)	(2.67)
Dance clubs	6.0	5.9	9.0	7.01

Market share (%)**

	ENT market share	Market leader	Relative market share
Restaurants	0.50	3.00	0.17
Cafés	1.01	3.00	0.34
Bars	3.50	3.00	1.17
Dance clubs	10.99	15.00	0.73

* The BCG model uses market growth, so this is the first calculation required.

** Given mark allocation, only shown for 20X1.

BCG analysis and evaluation of performance

Restaurants Division[50] – This division has a low market share of a market sector with low growth, making it a **dog** in the BCG classification. The Restaurant Division therefore looks a likely candidate for **divestment**, as it is in a weak position and operates in a low growth sector.

Cafés Division – The Cafés Division also has a relatively low market share, but it is operating in a market sector with high growth. It should therefore be classified as a **question mark**.

The market sector is already showing good growth, but it currently seems quite fragmented. There could be additional opportunities for ENT to grow by acquiring some rival businesses. Alternatively, if ENT does not want to invest in this way, it might consider selling its Café Division to another business looking to consolidate in the sector.

[50] Apply your technical knowledge to the numbers you have calculated to categorise and discuss each division.

Bars Division – The Bars Division is the market leader (high market share) in a market which has low (actually, negative) growth. This should be classified as a **cash cow**.

The Bars Division is currently ENT's largest division, and it contributed about 55% of the group's total revenue in 20X0. The current decline in the bars market should therefore be a concern for ENT, given the Bars Division's role as a cash cow in the group. ENT is likely to want to use the Bars Division to generate cash for the other businesses in its portfolio, but if the bars market starts declining in time this may limit the division's ability to generate cash for the rest of the group.

Dance clubs – The Dance Clubs Division has a moderately high market share (although still less than 1) in a market with reasonably high growth. This should currently be classified as a **question mark** as ENT is not yet the market leader in the sector, but it has the potential to become a star if it can achieve market leadership.

Its market share is already relatively close to the market leader's share, so with continued investment the division could grow to become the leader. The performance of this division is likely to be crucial to ENT's longer-term success, particularly if the performance of some of ENT's more mature businesses continues to decline.

(b) Context for performance[51] – The BCG provides a useful context in which to assess the performance of the different divisions. For example, it illustrates to management that they shouldn't expect the Bars Division to grow at the same rate as the Clubs Division, due to the underlying differences in the growth rates of the two sectors.

[51] An evaluation requires a balanced assessment to be made. Positive factors are therefore relevant, as well as problems and limitations

Management approach – Equally, identifying the differences in the growth potential of the different divisions identifies that different styles of management will be appropriate for the different divisions. For example, the Clubs Division may require capital investments to enable it to sustain its rate of growth, but the focus in the Bars Division (in a more mature business sector) should be on cost control.

Help set performance metrics – By helping to set expectations and approach in this way, managers can then also tailor their performance management systems and metrics to reflect the different contexts of each of the divisions. So, the metrics for the high growth divisions (cafés and clubs) should be based on profit or return on investment, while the metrics for the low growth divisions (bars and restaurants) should be focused on maintaining margins, cash control and cash generation.

Limitations of BCG approach:[52]

- **Problems of definition** – Although we have identified that the BCG matrix can be useful for providing a context for performance management, its usefulness is limited by its simplicity. For example, a business unit is only considered to have a high market share if its relative market share is greater than 1. By definition, however, this means that only the market leader can have a high market share, and therefore also there can only be one star or cash cow in each market sector.

[52] Each of the points in bold are text-book limitations of the BCG. These need to be applied clearly and concisely to the context of the scenario

- **Overlooks possible synergies** – Another issue which arises from the simplicity of the model is that it treats business units in isolation, and in doing so can overlook possible synergies between them. For example, some of ENT's bars and restaurants may be linked to its clubs, such that customers may go for a drink or a meal and then go on to a club afterwards. However, if in time the restaurants and later some of the bars are divested then this link between the business units will be lost.

- **Defining the market sector** – Another potential issue with using the BCG matrix comes from defining market sectors themselves. For example, the Bars Division has launched a new wine bar format which appears to have been successful. This suggests it has been growing, although the rest of the Bars Division has actually had negative growth. However, this raises an issue of whether the wine bar format should be treated as a separate sub-section (and as a problem child which is given the support and investment needed to grow) or whether it should be subject to cost control in the same way that the rest of the Bars Division is.

- **Portfolio analysis, not performance management** – It is also important to remember that the BCG matrix was designed for analysing a product portfolio, not as a performance management system. Therefore, while it can help to determine the appropriate performance management approach for a business, it is not in itself a performance management system.

Exam success skills diagnostic

Every time you complete a question, use the diagnostic below to assess how effectively you demonstrated the exam success skills in answering the question. The table has been completed below for the ENT activity to give you an idea of how to complete the diagnostic.

Exam success skills	Your reflections/observations
Managing information	Did you understand the 'economic context' facing ENT before starting your analysis?
Efficient numerical analysis	Did you identify your approach before starting your calculations, especially given the mark allocation for the numerical element of part (a)? Did your answer present neat workings in a format that would have been easy for a marker to follow?
Effective writing and presentation	Did you explain the meaning of your analysis clearly and concisely using sub-headings?
Good time management	Did you allow yourself time to address all requirements?
Most important action points to apply to your next question	

Summary

The APM syllabus includes a large number of performance management techniques which need to be studied and learned. However, at Strategic Professional level, you will be expected not only to be able to explain a technique, but also to appreciate the potential benefits of using it, and to be aware of what its drawbacks might be and in what circumstances its use may be inappropriate. You should not expect every technique you study to be appropriate to every scenario, and in APM **critical analysis** is encouraged (where relevant given the wording of a requirement).

However, where you are making a criticism of a theory/technique it is important that you relate this criticism to the context of the scenario wherever possible; for example, identifying the characteristics of an organisation which mean that a technique would not be appropriate for it to use.

The skill of '**critical analysis**' can potentially be applied to any syllabus area in APM, and can be an important ingredient in developing a discussion answer that addresses the scenario in a way that adds value. (This is discussed further in Skills Checkpoint 5.)

13

Alternative views of performance measurement and management

Learning objectives

On completion of this chapter, you should be able to:

	Syllabus reference no.
Apply and evaluate the 'balanced scorecard' approach as a way in which to improve the range and linkage between performance measures.	E1(a)
Apply and evaluate the 'performance pyramid' as a way in which to link strategy, operations and performance.	E1(b)
Apply and evaluate the work of Fitzgerald and Moon that considers performance measurement in business services using building blocks for dimensions, standards and rewards. (Already covered in Chapter 12)	E1(c)
Discuss and evaluate the application of activity-based management.	E1(d)
Evaluate and apply the value-based management approaches to performance management.	E1(e)

Exam context

You should already be familiar with some of the content of this chapter (for example the balanced scorecard) from your previous studies of *Performance Management*, at Applied Skills level. However, at APM level you are expected not only to know the elements of the models, but also to apply them to a practical context, and to evaluate their usefulness.

Important Note

This chapter and the following two chapters collectively cover Section E of the APM syllabus. One of the 25-mark **Section B questions** in the exam will come mainly from syllabus **Section E**, so any of the models we cover in this chapter could easily be the subject of a Section B question.

In addition to being in syllabus Section E, the balanced scorecard is also referenced in Section A, while the building block model is also mentioned in Section D. The **Section A** (50-mark) question in the exam is expected to focus on areas from syllabus Sections A, C and D. Therefore, the balanced scorecard and the building block model could feature in **either** a 50-mark **or** a 25-mark question.

Chapter overview

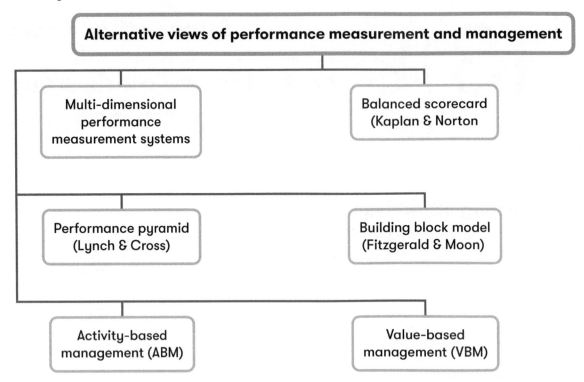

1 Multi-dimensional performance measurement systems

One of the key themes in this course is that it is no longer sufficient for organisations to measure performance solely in terms of financial results. Instead, as discussed in Chapter 10, they also need to assess the performance of the activities and operations that give rise to those financial results, and they do this by reference to non-financial performance indicators.

In this chapter, we look at three models which enable a range of performance measures to be produced and linked: the balanced scorecard (Section 2), the performance pyramid (Section 3) and the building blocks model (Section 4).

Importantly, these approaches look at 'performance' not only from a financial perspective but also from a non-financial perspective.

2 The balanced scorecard

The balanced scorecard (*Kaplan & Norton, 1992, 1996a*) emphasises the need to provide management with information about relevant areas of financial and non-financial performance.

The scorecard views the business from four perspectives and aims to establish **goals** for each perspective, together with a small number of key performance **measures**.

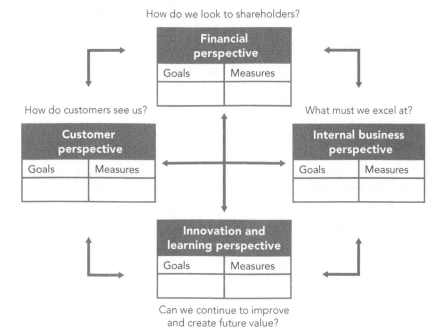

Financial measures: Successful strategies should create value for **shareholders**. Measures look at **survival** (cash flow), **success** (sales or profit) and **prosperity** (shareholder value).

Customer measures: Often focus on quality, delivery time, performance, service.

Internal business measures: For processes that are important in meeting **customer expectations** eg quality, time, cost.

Innovation and learning measures: Improving key **internal processes** and creating value for **customers**. Measures often focus on the amount of innovation and the success of innovation, and also achieving long-term targets for improving business processes.

2.1 Features/benefits of the scorecard

- It links performance measures to key elements of a company's **strategy**.
- It requires a **balanced consideration** of all **four perspectives**, to prevent improvements being made in one area at the expense of another.
- It considers **financial and non-financial** measures and goals and both **internal** and **external** factors.
- It attempts to identify the needs and concerns of customers to identify **new products and markets**.

2.2 Problems with using the scorecard

- It can be difficult to select which measures to include, and how many to include. There could be a danger of **information overload**. It is important to only include indicators because they add value, not because they are easy to measure.
- Having a number of different indicators (or too many indicators) can make **interpretation** of overall performance **difficult**. Worse performance in some areas may lead to improved performance in other areas (eg higher material costs may cause profits to fall in the short term, but could lead to higher customer satisfaction).
- The needs of internal stakeholders (particularly **staff**) are not explicitly included. Also, the scorecard doesn't take account of **corporate social responsibility** (CSR).

2.3 Information systems

If an organisation is thinking of introducing a balanced scorecard (or any of the other measurement systems covered in this chapter) it is important to consider whether the organisation's information systems can capture the data necessary to measure the key indicators selected in the scorecard.

Essential reading

See Chapter 13 Section 1 of the Essential reading for more detail about implementing and using the balanced scorecard.

The Essential reading is available as an Appendix of the digital edition of the Workbook.

Activity 1: Armstrong Stores

Armstrong Stores (Armstrong) is a listed business with a chain of 126 general department stores in South Postland. The company is known for the high quality of its products, mainly food and clothing. The majority of its goods are sourced from trusted manufacturers and branded under the company's own 'Strongarm' label.

Currently, Armstrong faces a tough competitive environment with all the major players in its market trying to secure their positions. Poor economic conditions worldwide have significantly affected South Postland. Consumer spending is falling throughout the economy and there is no immediate likelihood of a resumption of growth.

Armstrong's chief executive officer (CEO) has recently conducted a strategic review of the business in the context of the current economic recession. She has identified the following strategy as critical for Armstrong's success:

- Focus on key customers – those who are occasional shoppers but not currently loyal to the business.
- Ensure Armstrong's offering addresses their needs.
- Cut out costs that do not address these customers' priorities.
- Amend current processes to meet this new focus.
- Build for the future with a programme of sustainable development.

The company now needs to address the impact of this new strategy on its performance measurement systems. Armstrong uses a balanced scorecard to assess its strategic performance and the scorecard is used to connect the business strategy with its more detailed performance measures. The CEO has asked you to consider the implications of the new strategy for the performance measures used by the business.

Currently, Armstrong uses economic value added (EVA™), earnings per share (EPS) growth, and share price performance to monitor its financial performance. The company has supplied data in Appendix 1, which the CEO wishes to see used to assess the financial performance from the shareholders' perspective. She has asked that you explain the problems of capturing performance with these particular metrics and also how they may affect management's behaviour.

Required

1 Describe the four perspectives of the balanced scorecard showing how the new strategy of the business as outlined by the CEO links to the different perspectives. Illustrate your answer by suggesting appropriate performance measures for Armstrong for each of the detailed points within the strategy. **(8 marks)**

2 Assess the financial performance of the company using the three shareholder performance indicators. **(6 marks)**

3 Critically evaluate the use of these performance metrics and how they may affect management's behaviour. **(6 marks)**

(Total = 20 marks)

Exhibit: Appendix 1 – Financial data for Armstrong Stores

	20X8	20X9
	$m	$m
Operating profit	505.7	435.1
Interest	40.2	77.6
Profit before tax	465.5	375.5
Profit for the year	353.8	271.7
Average number of shares in issue	1,600.0	1,600.0

	20X8	20X9
EVA™	$306m	$110m

Stock market information	20X8	20X9
South Postland market index	1,115.2	724.9
Retailing sector index	2,450.7	1,911.5
Armstrong Stores (average share price)	$2.45	$2.08

Solution

---

3 The performance pyramid (Lynch and Cross)

The performance pyramid derives from the logic of the Anthony hierarchy (Chapter 1), and the idea that planning and control operates at different levels: strategic, tactical and operational.

The pyramid identifies the areas to focus upon at each level, in a way which links an organisation's overall strategic vision to day-to-day operations.

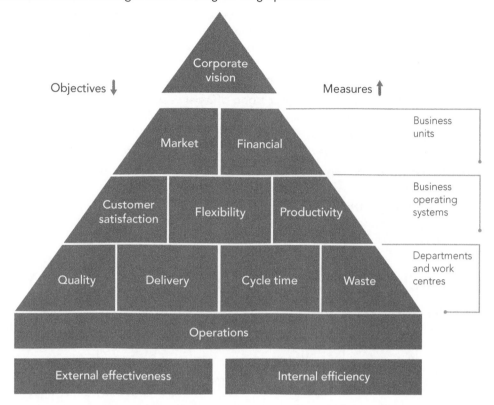

Performance Pyramid (after Lynch and Cross, 1991, p. 65)

At the top of the pyramid, **vision** is about how long-term corporate success is to be achieved.

Market and financial **objectives** then need to be set in accordance with an organisation's vision.

At the **strategic business unit level**, strategies are developed to achieve these market and financial objectives.

- Meeting customer expectations (**customer satisfaction**) and the responsiveness of the business operating system (**flexibility**) help to achieve **market objectives**.
- **Flexibility** and **productivity** (management of resources, such as labour and time) enable **financial objectives** to be achieved.

Operational level strategies then need to be developed to support business unit strategies.

- **Quality** and **delivery** contribute to **customer satisfaction**.
- **Delivery** and **cycle time** provide **flexibility**.
- Improving **cycle time** and **waste** should ensure rising **productivity**.

Features of the pyramid	Comment
Highlights linkages between measures and objectives	Each level is linked to, and supports, the ones **above it**. Linking operational performance measures to strategic objectives should help to ensure goal congruence. Objectives cascade 'top down' through the organisation; measures and information flow 'bottom up'.
The model ensures that internal and external aspects of performance are both considered	The **left-hand side** of the pyramid focuses on **external measures** ('external effectiveness'). The **right-hand side** focuses on **internal efficiency**.

Features of the pyramid	Comment
Focuses on value creation	Highlights the importance of focusing business activities on the requirements of the **customer**, and creating value for the customer.

Potential issues with applying the pyramid

- **Measures could conflict** (eg potential trade-offs between quality and cost). This could demotivate managers if they feel they are caught in 'no win' situations.
- An organisation should measure the factors which are most important to achieving its objectives. But these **may be difficult or expensive to measure**.
- **Management effort** (which could otherwise be spent running the business) could be used devising performance measures.
- The pyramid **concentrates on** two main groups of stakeholders: **customers and shareholders** (financial performance). But organisations may also need measures which reflect the interests of other stakeholders.

4 The building block model (Fitzgerald and Moon)

The building block model was designed for performance measurement in **service businesses**. Fitzgerald and Moon (1996) identify that the three 'building blocks' of **dimensions, standards** and **rewards** can be used to create effective performance measurement systems for service businesses.

We have **already introduced the building block model in Chapter 12.**

4.1 Potential benefits of the model

- The model **looks beyond performance measures** and explains how to encourage employee participation in setting budgets and standards, and links these to the reward system.
- The model highlights a range of financial and non-financial dimensions, similar to the balanced scorecard but tailored specifically for **service industries**.

4.2 Potential problems with the model

- Although employees are encouraged to take part in budget setting, it may not be clear how the overall objectives of the organisation relate to the budgets. The model does not emphasise the **hierarchy** of performance like the performance pyramid does.

5 Activity-based management (ABM)

Activity-based management is the use of activity-based costing for improving cost management and value engineering.

KEY TERM

> **Activity-based management (ABM):** 'The entire set of actions that can be taken, on a better informed basis, with activity-based cost information. ABM enables the organisation to accomplish its outcomes with fewer demands on organisational resources; that is, the organisation achieves the same outcomes at a lower total cost.' (*Kaplan & Cooper, 1998; p. 4*)

5.1 Activity-based costing (ABC)

Traditional cost analysis analyses costs by type for each responsibility centre (eg function). Activity-based costing (ABC) analyses costs on the basis of activities and therefore provides information on **why** costs are incurred and on the **output** of the **activity** in terms of **cost drivers**.

The total costs of an organisation can be controlled or reduced by controlling or reducing cost drivers. Cost drivers operate at different levels in organisations:

Classification level	Cause of cost	Examples of cost	Necessity of cost
Unit level	Production of a single unit of product or delivery of single unit of service	Direct materials Direct labour	Once for each unit produced
Batch level	A group of things being made in a single production run	Purchase orders, set-ups, inspection	Once for each batch produced
Product/process level	Development, production and sale of individual product line	Equipment maintenance Product-specific R&D and marketing	Supports a product type or a process
Organisational/ facility	Existence of facility	Building depreciation and maintenance Organisational advertising	Supports the overall production or service process

These costs need to be allocated to products in order to obtain an accurate estimate of product or service cost (and therefore product profitability).

Unit level costs are allocated over number of units produced, batch level costs over the number of units in the batch, and product level costs over the number of units produced by the product line.

However, organisational level costs are not product related, and so should simply be deducted from net revenue.

5.2 ABM

ABM uses ABC information to focus management attention on key value-adding activities, key customers and key products, in order to maintain or increase competitive advantage.

However, the extent to which activity-based approaches can be applied depends on an organisation's ability to identify its main activities and their associated cost drivers.

ABM views the business as a set of linked activities that ultimately add value to the customers, and focuses on managing the business on the basis of these activities. Activities create costs, so managing activities and cost drivers will enable costs to be managed.

The goal of ABM is to enable customer needs to be satisfied while making fewer demands on organisational resources.

ABM information can be used for a variety of business applications, including cost reduction, benchmarking and business process re-engineering and total quality management.

One of the key ways ABM can help in relation to cost reduction is by encouraging managers to distinguish between **value added** activities and **non-value added** activities, because the latter provide an opportunity for cost reduction without reducing customers' perception of a product or service.

The diagram below summarises some of the main ways ABM could be used in an organisation:

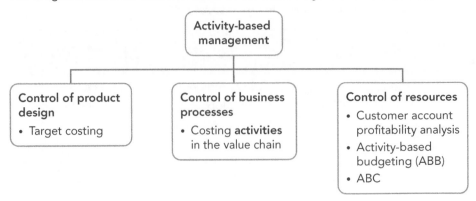

5.2.1 Levels of ABM

ABM can be useful at two levels:

- **Operational**: 'doing things right'. ABM can be used to help make an organisation more efficient, by reducing the cost of activities or increasing the productivity of resources (eg by eliminating activities which do not add value).
- **Strategic**: 'doing the right thing'. ABM can help to determine which products or markets to focus on over the long term, based on an analysis of product and customer profitability.

5.3 Benefits and limitations of activity-based management

ABM focuses on managing the activities in the organisation that ultimately bring **value to the customer**. It encourages managers to focus on key value-added activities, to help an organisation maintain or increase its competitive advantage.

More specifically, ABM could be useful to organisations in helping to:

(a) Design products and services that meet or exceed customers' expectations and can be produced and delivered at a profit

(b) Identify where improvements (either continuous, or one-off transformations) are required in quality, efficiency and speed

(c) Negotiate with customers about prices, product features, quality, delivery and service

However, ABM should not be seen as a solution for all the problems an organisation might be facing:

(a) **ABM will not, by itself, reduce costs**. It can help organisations understand their costs better but action steps still have to be identified to redesign activities to reduce costs.

(b) The **amount of work** required to set up the ABC system and in data collection must be considered, to assess if the cost of setting up the system outweighs the benefits of having it.

(c) **Organisational and behavioural consequences**. Selected activity cost pools may not correspond to the formal structure of cost responsibilities within the organisation (eg the purchasing activity may spread across purchasing, production, stores, administrative and finance departments) and so determining 'ownership' of the activity can be difficult. Also, it can sometimes be difficult to find out what costs apply to a particular activity. Some areas of activity overlap and may be difficult to separate. (This is a weakness of ABC in general).

Activity 2: Costing systems

MNOP plc is an IT consultancy that provides IT advice to a range of clients.

MNOP classifies its customers into four main categories.

	M	N	O	P
	$'000	$'000	$'000	$'000
Sales value	1,000	3,000	850	1,200

MNOP employs ten full-time IT specialists who each deliver 1,500 chargeable hours per year and who are paid $60,000 per year.

MNOP has estimated its other costs as follows:

	Costs
	$'000
Telephone support	1,000
After-sales service	1,500
Client meetings	280
	2,780

MNOP has reviewed its existing client database and determined the following four average profiles of typical clients:

	M	N	O	P	Total
	'000	'000	'000	'000	'000
Number of telephone queries	20	480	50	250	800
Number of visits	3	21	4	8	36
Number of meetings	70	90	20	100	280
Chargeable hours	4	6	2	3	15

Previously MNOP used a single cost rate of $200 per hour for both in-house profit reporting and quotations for new contracts.

Required

1   Prepare calculations to show the profit attributed to each customer group using the current system of attributing costs.   **(2 marks)**

2   Prepare calculations to show the profit attributed to each customer group using an activity-based system of attributing costs.   **(4 marks)**

3   Discuss the differences between the costs attributed using ABC and those attributed by the current system and advise whether the change to the ABC system should be adopted.
                                                                                          (4 marks)

                                                                                          (Total = 10 marks)

Solution

6 Value-based management (VBM)

6.1 Principles of VBM

The **underlying principle** behind value-based management (VBM) is that the value of a company is measured by its **discounted future cash flows**, and value is only greater when the capital which companies invest generates returns which are greater than the cost of that capital.

Management decision making needs to focus on the activities that **create value for shareholders** (ie activities should only be undertaken if they create value for shareholders).

However, VBM is not just a set of performance measures. When making decisions, managers need **the right information and incentives** to ensure those decisions create value. Underlying this, senior managers must have a good understanding of the company's strategy for creating value and their role within this (ie the key value drivers in their department/business unit).

The VBM approach aligns strategic, operational and management processes so that **they all work together** to create value.

6.2 Implementing VBM

There are **four essential management processes** involved in implementing VBM:

Step 1   A company or business unit **develops a strategy** to maximise value which is communicated to managers. Critical **value drivers** are identified.

Step 2 This strategy is translated into short-term and long-term **performance targets throughout the organisation** defined in terms of the key value drivers.

Targets are likely to involve a structured **mix of financial and non-financial key performance indicators (KPIs)** (eg balanced scorecard, performance pyramid, building block models), where non-financial goals are used if they are important influences on the amount of value created (eg customer satisfaction or product innovation).

VBM requires an organisation to move away from traditional, profit-based financial performance measures (eg profit margin, ROCE) as these **do not focus sufficiently on value creation**. Instead, financial performance targets need to be set in terms of value creation.

A key financial measure is likely to be **EVA**™ (because this embeds the weighted average cost of capital into the performance measure).

Step 3 **Plans** are drawn up to define the steps that will be taken to achieve the performance targets.

Step 4 Finally, **performance metrics and incentive systems** are set up to monitor performance against targets and to encourage employees to meet their goals.

VBM will only be effective if **all decision makers** in a company (not just senior managers) adopt value-based thinking.

Essential reading

See Chapter 13 Section 2 of the Essential reading for more detail about implementing value-based management in a company, and the implications of value-based management.

The Essential reading is available as an Appendix of the digital edition of the Workbook.

Chapter summary

Alternative views of performance measurement and management

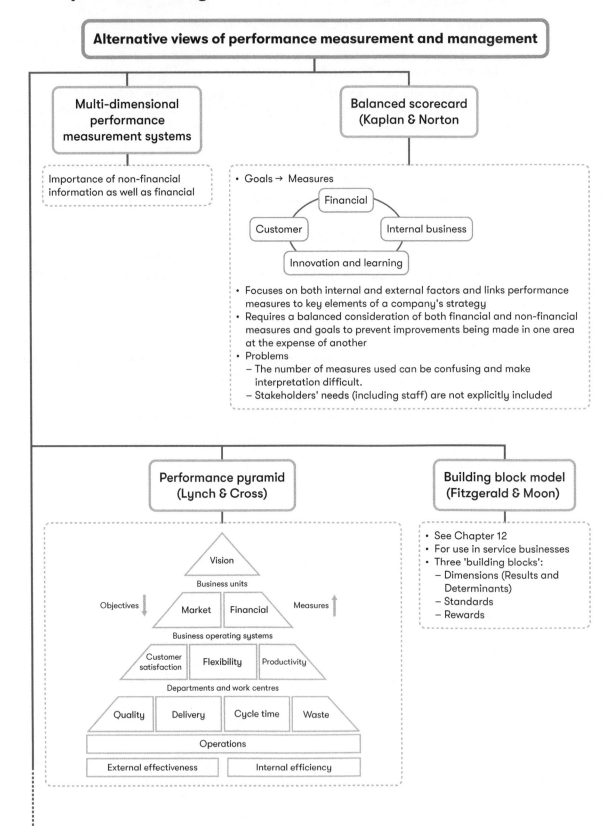

Multi-dimensional performance measurement systems

Importance of non-financial information as well as financial

Balanced scorecard (Kaplan & Norton

- Goals → Measures

  - Financial
  - Customer
  - Internal business
  - Innovation and learning

- Focuses on both internal and external factors and links performance measures to key elements of a company's strategy
- Requires a balanced consideration of both financial and non-financial measures and goals to prevent improvements being made in one area at the expense of another
- Problems
  - The number of measures used can be confusing and make interpretation difficult.
  - Stakeholders' needs (including staff) are not explicitly included

Performance pyramid (Lynch & Cross)

- Vision
- Business units
- Objectives ↓
- Market
- Financial
- Measures ↑
- Business operating systems
- Customer satisfaction
- Flexibility
- Productivity
- Departments and work centres
- Quality
- Delivery
- Cycle time
- Waste
- Operations
- External effectiveness
- Internal efficiency

Building block model (Fitzgerald & Moon)

- See Chapter 12
- For use in service businesses
- Three 'building blocks':
  - Dimensions (Results and Determinants)
  - Standards
  - Rewards

```
                                ┌─────────────────────┐         ┌─────────────────────┐
                                │   Activity-based    │         │    Value-based      │
                                │  management (ABM)   │         │  management (VBM)   │
                                └─────────────────────┘         └─────────────────────┘
```

Activity-based management (ABM)

- Is the use of activity-based costing for improving cost management and value engineering
- Goal is to enable customer needs to be satisfied using fewer resources and reducing costs
- Need to distinguish between value added and non-value added activities
- Two levels of ABM:
  - (1) Operational – reduce cost or increase productivity of existing activities
  - (2) Strategic – determine which products or markets to focus on longer term, based on product and customer profitability

Value-based management (VBM)

- Managers need to focus on creating value for shareholders. Activities should only be undertaken if they add value.
- Value is measured by discounted future cash flows, not simply current profit.
- Decisions should be made with reference to **value drivers** (financial, and non-financial).
- Four-stage implementation process:
  - (1) Develop **strategy** to maximise value
  - (2) Translate strategy into **targets** defined in terms of key value drivers
  - (3) **Plan** the steps required in order to achieve targets
  - (4) **Performance metrics** and **incentive systems** to monitor performance

Knowledge diagnostic

1. Balanced scorecard

The balanced scorecard approach to performance measurement focuses on four different perspectives: financial, customer, internal business process and innovation and learning.

By including a combination of non-financial indicators alongside financial ones, the scorecard highlights the role that non-financial aspects of performance play in shaping an organisation's financial performance.

2. Performance pyramid

The performance pyramid highlights the importance of linkages across the performance hierarchy, from an organisation's corporate vision to its functional objectives.

Performance at each of the different levels in the pyramid needs to support the other levels, in order for an organisation to achieve its corporate vision successfully. The pyramid identifies key areas of performance to monitor at different levels.

3. Building block model

The building blocks – dimensions, standards and rewards – attempt to overcome the problems associated with performance measurement in service businesses. The 'dimensions' building block is split into 'results' and the 'determinants' which affect those results (quality of service, flexibility, resource utilisation and innovation).

4. Activity-based management (ABM)

ABM aims to **meet customer needs** while using fewer resources, by eliminating activities which do not added value for customers, and performing value-added activities more efficiently. An important element of ABM is distinguishing between **value added** and **non-value added activities**.

Activity-based costing supports ABM.

5. Value-based management (VBM)

VBM focuses on **value drivers**, and highlights that companies create value by generating returns in excess of their cost of capital.

An important implication of this for performance measurement is that companies should focus on future cash flows rather than on profit.

Further study guidance

Question practice

Now try the following from the Further question practice bank (available in the digital edition of the Workbook):

Q15 *Hampton*

Q16 *Bettaserve*

Further reading

The Technical Article on ACCA's website called *Activity-based management* discusses the elements of activity-based management (ABM), including the way that activity-based costing (ABC) information is used in ABM. The article also looks at the way ABM can be used to improve performance in organisations, and it includes an illustrative example of the way ABC information can be used in ABM, based on a past exam question. You are strongly advised to read this article as part of your preparation for your exam.

There is also a Technical Article available on ACCA's website called *Performance measures to support competitive advantage* which explores the way companies could use the balanced scorecard to help maintain their competitive edge.

Finally, there is also a Technical Article available on ACCA's website called *Demystifying value-based management*, which aims to demystify the topic of VBM by looking into its background, key ideas, problems, and steps for implementation.

Activity answers

Activity 1: Armstrong Stores

Marking guide		Marks	
1	0.5 marks per explanation of each perspective, up to 2 marks	2	
	1.5 marks for comments discussing each of the performance measures including the link to the new objectives, up to 6 marks	6	
			8
2	Comments: 1 mark per point up to a maximum of 2 on EPS and share price (together) and a maximum of 2 on EVA (maximum of 4)	4	
	Workings: 1 mark for calculation on EPS and 0.5 each other calculation, up to maximum of 2	2	
			6
3	Up to 2 marks on each metric and 2 marks on impact on management behaviour (maximum of 6)	6	
			6
Total			20

1   The four perspectives of the balanced scorecard are:

- **Financial** – how do we create value for our shareholders?

- **Customer** – how should we present ourselves to our customers? What do our customers (both existing and new) want from us?

- **Internal business process** – what processes are critical to achieving our financial and customer goals and how can we optimise these?

- **Innovation and learning** – how do we ensure we continue to improve, and are able to create value in the future?

The new strategy addresses these perspectives in different ways. Ultimately all of the perspectives will have financial effects whether in the short- or long-term interests of our shareholders.

Focus on key customers: This directly addresses the **customer perspective** and will require the collection of the profiles and needs of these customers in order to generate market growth and so improve our financial position. Suitable performance measurement would segment our market (for example, by customer age or gender) and identify our changing market share within each segment.

Ensuring we meet key customer needs: This again addresses the **customer perspective** but will also have an impact on the products/services that Armstrong offers and so affect the **internal business process** perspective. Suitable performance measures from the customer perspective would be levels of repeat business (measured as repeat visits per customer, for example) and customer satisfaction scores. In relation to the business process perspective, Armstrong will measure its product range and quality. Range would be measured by comparing Armstrong's product range against competitors, while the level of customer complaints or returns could provide an indication about the quality of products. Customer satisfaction scores could also provide some insight in quality (eg if product quality declines, customer satisfaction scores might also fall).

Cost cutting: This connects to the **business process** perspective as it seeks to focus the business on value-added activities. (By doing so, and reducing avoidable costs, a targeted cost-cutting programme should also help to support the financial perspective of the scorecard.) Suitable performance measures would be efficiency savings generated by removing or reducing unnecessary processes/products. Armstrong could possibly look to simplify its supply chain by cutting the number of suppliers with which it deals.

Amend current processes to meet the new focus: Clearly, the **process perspective** and measurement of this objective will be by way of the achievement of goals in a specific change programme to assist the other objectives.

Programme of sustainable development: This objective looks to the future and so could be linked to the innovation and learning perspective. However, one of the criticisms sometimes made against the balanced scorecard is that the perspectives don't specifically take account of social responsibility and sustainability. Suitable measures for this area would include the company's carbon footprint (its CO_2 output), the efficiency of energy use of the business, and the level of packaging waste generated.

2   **Armstrong's financial performance**. The year-on-year performance of Armstrong has declined, with **earnings per share** falling by 23% (see Workings). Normally, this would imply that the company would be heavily out of favour with investors. However, the share price seems to have held up relatively well, with a decline of only 15% compared to a fall in the retail sector of 22% and the South Postland stock market as a whole of 35%.

The sector comparison is the more relevant to the performance of Armstrong's management as the main market index will contain data from manufacturing, financial and other industries. Shareholders will be encouraged by the implication that the market views Armstrong as one of the better future prospects for investment within the retail sector.

This view is substantiated by the positive **EVA™** for 20X9 ($110m), which Armstrong generated. EVA™ has fallen by 64% from 20X8 but it has remained positive and so the company continues to create value for its shareholders even in the poor economic environment.

3   **Evaluating the financial metrics**. The indicators each have strengths and weaknesses. EVA™ is a widely used indicator, which aims to capture the increase in **shareholder wealth** that the company generates. To do this, it makes a number of amendments to traditional profit-based information in order to approximate the net present value method of appraising an investment. In this way, EVA™ provides a clear focus on the major objective of most commercial entities. However, its calculation requires a large number of adjustments to the traditional accounting figures, for example the need to calculate the economic rather than accounting depreciation, the need to distinguish between cash flow and accruals, and to distinguish between expense and investment. This makes the method less easily understood than the two other measures currently used by Armstrong.

EPS growth is important to shareholders as it relates to dividend growth which is a fundamental variable used in the calculation of share value (dividend valuation method). It is a widely used measure by equity analysts and so is a key driver of share prices. However, it is based on accounting profit and only captures year-on-year change and so can be subject to short-term manipulation if the trend over a number of years is not considered.

Share price performance reflects the capital performance of an investment but tends to be volatile and subject to significant fluctuations outside of the control of management. It will be the figure that most shareholders turn to in order to get a quick impression of their investment performance but it can lead to judgements being formed on the basis of that short-term volatility which are more appropriate for speculators rather than investors. The use of an average share price in this instance should help to ameliorate such problems but the averaging method and time period should be further investigated.

Working

		20X8	*20X9*	
1	*Economic value added (EVA™)*	$306m	$110m	(down 64%)
2	*EPS (profit for year/av no of shares)*	0.221	0.170	(down 23%)

	20X8	20X9	
3 Stock market information			
Main market index	1,115.2	724.9	(down 30%)
Retail sector index	2,450.7	1,911.5	(down 22%)
Armstrong Stores share price	$2.45	$2.08	(down 15%)

Activity 2: Costing systems

1 Current cost system ($'000)

	M	N	O	P	Total
Sales ($'000)	1,000	3,000	850	1,200	
Less $200/hour	(800)	(1,200)	(400)	(600)	3,000
Margin from customer	200	1,800	450	600	
Net margin/$ sales	20%	60%	52.9%	50%	

2 ABC system ($'000)

	M	N	O	P
Sales ($'000)	1,000	3,000	850	1,200
Less customers' specific costs:				
Direct costs (W1)	160	240	80.0	120.0
Telephone support (W2)	25	600	62.5	312.5
After-sales service (W3)	125	875	166.7	333.3
Client meetings (W4)	70	90	20.0	100.0
Total cost	380	1,805	329.2	865.8
Net margin from customer	620	1,195	520.8	334.2
Net margin/$ sales	62%	39.8%	61.2%	27.9%

Workings

1 **Direct costs**

$$\frac{10 \text{ staff} \times \$60,000}{10 \times 1,500 \text{ hours}} = \$40/\text{hour}$$

2 **Telephone support**

Telephone support ÷ telephone queries: OAR = 1,000/800 = 1.25 per query

3 **After-sales service**

After-sales service ÷ no. of visits: OAR = 1,500/36 = 41.667 per visit

4 **Client meetings**

Client meetings ÷ no. of meetings: OAR = 280/280 = 1 per meeting

3   The ABC system highlights that:

  • M and O are more profitable than believed. M costs less than previously thought because M customers require little support.

  • N and P are less profitable than believed, due to higher costs as they use a high proportion of support services, especially expensive after-sales service visits.

Also the previous system has recovered only $3,000 of costs from a total of $3,380. Any under-recovery could lead to losses, especially if this cost is used to set prices and quotations.

ABC systems provide better cost analysis, both for reporting of profitability and for decision making. The ABC system should be adopted.

Strategic performance issues in complex business structures

Learning objectives

On completion of this chapter, you should be able to:

	Syllabus reference no.
Discuss the problems encountered in planning, controlling and measuring performance levels, eg productivity, profitability, quality and service levels, in complex business structures.	E2(a)
Discuss the impact on performance management of the use of business models involving strategic alliances, joint ventures and complex supply chain structures.	E2(b)

Exam context

One of the themes of APM is that performance management plays an important role in directing and supporting the performance of employees and departments so that they work efficiently and effectively, and that their goals are aligned to the organisation's overall goals and strategy.

However, one of the key issues which can arise in relation to complex business structures (such as joint ventures) is deciding what the organisation's goals and objectives are. The decision-making process can be particularly difficult if the strategic partners involved have different approaches – for example, if one partner in a joint venture wants to pursue a high-risk, high-return approach to growth, while the other would prefer a more cautious approach.

Similarly, if different aspects of performance are important to the venture partners in a joint venture, this could make it difficult to decide what the performance metrics for the venture should be.

We will discuss these issues in this chapter, and we will also discuss some of the practical considerations around how to manage performance in complex structures. For example, if a company outsources areas of its business to third-party service providers, how can it control the service provider's performance?

Remember, as we noted in the introduction to the previous chapter, the Study Guide for APM identifies that one of the Section B questions in the exam will come mainly from syllabus Section E, which is partly covered by this chapter.

Chapter overview

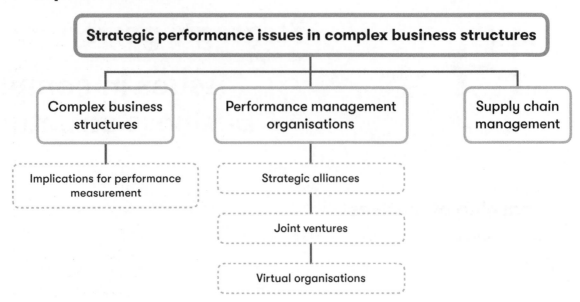

1 Complex business structures

Traditional performance management activities, and performance indicators, focus on the internal activities within an organisation, to maximise the value that organisation generates.

However, it is increasingly common for organisations to form relationships with other organisations; ie to create networks of business relationships.

These could take a variety of forms (which are covered in detail in Section 2):

(a) Strategic alliances

(b) Joint ventures

(c) Virtual organisations

In these structures, a wider range of stakeholders and activities (both internal and external) contribute to performance. This means that performance measurement can no longer focus on a single organisation's own internal operations, but needs to take account of all the different organisations (ie the overall system) which are involved in the value network (for example, in relation to their productivity or the quality of their output).

Building trust and developing relationships between partner organisations also now becomes an important part of performance management.

Real world example

Most Nike shoes never see the inside of a Nike factory because they are manufactured by outsourced suppliers. The flow of information between Nike and the suppliers is critical:

*   From Nike, to identify the design and quantity of shoes required; and

*   From the suppliers to identify the progress of the orders.

However, the productivity of the suppliers and the quality of the shoes they produce are still vital aspects of performance that Nike needs to manage. For example, if there is a problem with the quality of the shoes, it is Nike's brand reputation with customers which will be damaged.

1.1 Implications for performance measurement

Planning – the core organisation needs to be sure that suppliers have capacity to meet potential demand. This may be complicated if the core organisation cannot forecast demand accurately.

However, the core organisation can seek to ensure that the system has sufficient flexibility and capacity to meet potential demand.

Control – the core organisation needs to measure the performance of its partners in key areas. These are often **non-financial**: for example, quantity and quality of goods or services supplied; quality of customer service; reliability of delivery times; ethical behaviour (eg working conditions for employees).

1.1.1 Service level agreements

Contracts or **service level agreements** should be used to specify what is expected of each partner (eg customer orders to be fulfilled within a certain time). Actual performance can then be assessed against the target level.

In some cases, partners may be eligible for an element of profit share or a bonus if they meet or exceed the target level, to motivate them to perform well.

1.1.2 Ethical behaviour

The reputation of the core organisation could be damaged if its partners behave unethically (for example, using child labour, or not safeguarding the health and safety of employees).

Service level agreements may require partners to comply with a corporate code of ethics, and to allow inspections and audits to be performed by the core organisation.

Control issues could also relate to **data security** and confidentiality. The core organisation could be sharing sensitive information with partners (for example, names and addresses of customers) and so needs assurance over the **security** of partners' **information systems**.

1.1.3 Reliability of data

When assessing performance (eg against service level agreements) it is important that both parties agree the figures being used.

Information systems are crucial for measuring the performance of partner organisations. Having a single database used by all partners should improve communication and co-ordination between them.

This should also reduce scope for disagreements (for example, if different systems show partners have produced different levels of output), and give the core organisation greater control over the security of the data.

Essential reading

Our main focus in this chapter is on complex business structures involving multiple companies. However, individual companies also face challenges in measuring and managing performance when they operate in multiple countries (ie they are multinational).

See Chapter 14 Section 1 of the Essential reading for more detail about performance measurement in multinational companies.

The Essential reading is available as an Appendix of the digital edition of the Workbook.

2 Performance management

2.1 Strategic alliances

Strategic alliances are formed by two or more businesses when they wish to **share their resources and activities to pursue a particular strategy**. They decide to do this rather than set up a new company or buy access to resources and competences.

The organisations in the alliance remain independent organisations, so will retain their own internal procedures, culture and objectives. But if cultures and objectives vary between alliance partners, this could lead to differences in the focus of their performance measurement and control.

Also, the alliance partners may have different management information systems. This could make it difficult to collate, and compare, performance information.

The 'loose' nature of the alliance structure means that communication and collaboration are crucial. There isn't a formal set of goals and objectives which can be disseminated as in a single organisation. Nonetheless information needs to be shared efficiently across the network to allow stakeholders to identify bottlenecks in a production process (for example) or opportunities to improve process efficiency.

It will also be important to identify which alliance partner is accountable for which outcomes.

2.2 Joint ventures

Joint venture: Two (or more) firms combine resources for manufacturing, financial and marketing purposes, and each has a share in both the equity and the management of the joint business.

Potential issues	Comments
Co-ordination and control	Ensuring co-ordination and control among the venture partners (eg deciding who will produce the management information for the venture). Problems could arise if there is no clear pattern for decision making, or a lack of overall leadership.
Attitudes to risk	Problems could also arise if the partners have different attitudes to risk (eg when choosing between strategic options, a risk taker might select a different option than someone who is risk averse).
Establishing goals and objectives	If the partners have different goals and objectives for the venture, this could mean that different aspects of performance will be important to them (eg if one partner is interested in short-term profit, and the other is interested in longer-term growth, it could be difficult to agree on the key performance metrics for the venture).
Culture and management styles	If there are significant differences between the cultures of the venture partners, this could reduce the chances of the venture being successful.
Accountability	Is it clear who is responsible for which activities? (If not, disagreements could arise over who is accountable when things go wrong.) How will performance be managed, if the areas one partner is responsible for are performing better than the areas another partner is responsible for?
Reciprocity	The issue of how much one partner is contributing relative to another could be a source of tension (if one partner feels that the other is damaging the overall performance of the venture – eg through poor quality output.) The performance of the venture affects the results of both partners.

Another potential issue in joint ventures is that the partners need to share information and intellectual property. However, venture partners may be reluctant to share too much about their own business with their partners (to protect their own competitive position).

Developing the strength of the relationship between the venture partners and the **trust** between them could be very important for the success of a joint venture.

Activity 1: Autoplus

Autoplus is a car manufacturer, based in Essland, specialising in environmentally friendly 'hybrid' cars (powered jointly by electric batteries and petrol.) Autoplus has invested heavily in developing its hybrid engines, and is now looking to expand. Although it is a relatively young company, it has already developed a favourable reputation for the quality and reliability of its cars. The majority of Autoplus shares are owned by two venture capitalist firms who are supporting its growth plans.

The board of Autoplus is considering entering into a joint venture with Carman, with each owning a 50% share of the venture.

Carman is a large, well-established car manufacturer based in Veeland, a neighbouring country to Essland with a rapidly growing market for environmentally friendly cars. Carman does not currently manufacture any hybrid vehicles, but it has spare capacity in its factory. Carman's shareholders have been concerned about the company's performance, with safety issues adversely affecting sales of two of its more popular models of cars in recent years.

Required

Discuss the potential problems with managing the performance of the joint venture if it goes ahead.   **(8 marks)**

Solution

2.3 Virtual organisations

Virtual organisations use the capabilities of other organisations to create and distribute product and services, without being physically linked to the other organisations.

Key features include geographical dispersion, and IT being central to the production process.

Amazon is perhaps the best-known example of a virtual organisation. Customers place their orders on Amazon's website, but these are fulfilled by a huge number of different suppliers who send the goods directly to the customers.

The 'core' organisation (eg Amazon) co-ordinates the activities of the partners it works with. However, because the 'core' organisation depends on multiple partners across different locations to deliver its products and services, the ability to **capture information about partners** and to **share information with them** is likely to be crucial in performance management.

2.3.1 Implications for performance management

The 'core' organisation also has to manage the performance of its partners, because they are crucial in delivering value to its customers. Managing these relationships, and ensuring that partner organisations are motivated to ensure the success of the whole organisation, becomes an important capability in its own right (eg ensuring network partners deliver the **quantity** and **quality** of goods required, and do so on **time**).

However, the 'core' organisation does not typically own the partners, so has no legal right to manage or control them. This reinforces the importance of having a contract or service level agreement in place, specifying the obligations of both parties (eg standards required of the partners; payment terms for the 'core' organisation).

The agreements may also describe reporting requirements, meaning the partners have to report their performance against key metrics (eg, percentage of deliveries on time).

2.3.2 Remote working

Some of the issues which virtual organisations face may also apply to managing remote workers (or home workers). Remote workers (freelance workers or in-house home workers) cannot be monitored in the same way that in-house staff can, where managers can see what their staff are doing. Instead, performance needs to be managed in terms of results and output (including quantity and quality).

IT can be used to monitor remote employees (for example, when they log on and off from a system and logging their output).

It is also important that managers provide remote employees with clear goals and expectations for their work (in order to evaluate actual performance against the goals).

3 Supply chain management

Some of the issues faced by virtual organisations can be faced by companies more generally, where they have chosen to outsource certain functions to external suppliers and concentrate on their 'core competences' where they add most value.

> **Supply chain management:** 'Encompasses the planning and management of all activities in sourcing and procurement, conversion, and all logistics management activities. Importantly, it also includes coordination and collaboration with channel partners, which can be suppliers, intermediaries, third party service providers, and customers. In essence, supply chain management integrates supply and demand management within and across companies.'
>
> *(Council of Supply Chain Management Professionals, 2017)*

Managing the supply chain requires information/knowledge about:

- Customer demand patterns (eg seasonal variations in demand). This could be assisted by data analytics (eg in relation to predicting demand)
- Service level requirements (eg speed of delivery; quality expectations)
- Distance considerations (location and logistics)
- Cost (eg of orders fulfilled by different suppliers)

IT plays an important role in ensuring information is shared quickly and efficiently across a supply chain.

Real life example

'When a customer makes a purchase online from Amazon, the supply chain includes, among others, the customer, Amazon's website, the Amazon warehouse, and all of Amazon's suppliers and their suppliers. The website provides the customer with information regarding pricing, product variety, and product availability. After making a product choice, the consumer enters the order information and pays for the product. The customer may later return to the website to check the status of the order. Stages further up the supply chain use customer order information to [fulfil] the request. That process involves an additional flow of information, product, and funds among various stages of the supply chain' *(Chopra & Meindl, 2016, p.14)*.

We discussed in Chapter 6 the ways IT can affect management accounting systems, but these could also be relevant in managing the supply chain:

- **Electronic data interchange (EDI)** – enabling instantaneous, paperless purchase orders with suppliers.
- **Enterprise resource planning system (ERPS)** – integrating an entity's systems thereby helping managers co-ordinate production, procurement, inventory, customer orders and sales.
- **Radio frequency identification (RFID)** – RFID tags attached to materials or inventory enable them to be tracked more accurately. A company knows what is being delivered when, and what is already in stock.

A key issue for successful supply chain management is the **speed** with which activities can be carried out and customer demands met. If a firm, helped by its suppliers and sub-suppliers in the chain, can **respond quickly and flexibly** to customer requirements, it will benefit from **lower inventories, lower operating costs, better product availability and greater customer satisfaction.**

Chapter summary

Strategic performance issues in complex business structures

Complex business structures

- Networks of business relationships between organisations
- Performance management needs to take account of all organisations across a value network (rather than a single organisation)

Implications for performance measurement

- Planning: flexibility and capacity to meet demand
- Control: need to measure quantity; quality; reliability in partner companies
- Service level agreements (SLA): set standards and targets to measure performance against
- Importance of ethical behaviour across whole network / supply chain
- Data: reliability (single database?); security (cyber security?)

Performance management organisations

Strategic alliances

Potential issues:

- How to collate and compare performance information (across different systems)
- Differences in cultures, procedures, objectives?

Joint ventures

Potential issues:

- Co-ordination and control
- Attitudes to risk
- Agreeing goals and objectives
- Culture and management styles
- Accountability
- Reciprocity
- Information sharing

Virtual organisations

- Importance of managing relationships with network partners
- Ensuring they meet quantity/quality requirements; and on time
- Need for SLA
- Importance of information sharing with partners

Supply chain management

- Integrating supply and demand management within, and across, companies
- Responding to customer demand patterns
- Managing service level expectations (speed; quality)
- Applications of IT to help manage supply chain: (EDI; ERPS; RFID)

Knowledge diagnostic

1. Performance measurement

In business structures which include more than one company (strategic alliances, joint ventures, virtual organisations) performance measurement needs to include all of the different companies involved in the value network, in order to plan and control their performance (eg quantity/ productivity; quality; reliability; ethical behaviour).

It is important that all the companies are using the same performance information, to avoid disputes over actual levels of performance.

2. Service level agreements

Service level agreements (SLAs) can be used to identify expected levels of performance and behaviour; enabling actual performance to be measured against the standards and targets in the SLA.

3. Performance management

Collaborative arrangements (eg strategic alliances; joint ventures; virtual organisations) have the advantage of being flexible, and allowing each company in a network to work together using their individual areas of expertise.

However, these arrangements can create a number of challenges for performance management, including: slow decision making (while consensus is reached between partners); differing objectives between partners; different culture and management styles; and concerns about sharing (commercially sensitive) data.

4. Virtual organisations

In collaborative organisations, the core enterprise needs to manage the performance of its partners in order to deliver value to customers.

5. Supply chain management

Companies need to manage their supply chains in order to be able to respond efficiently to patterns of customer demand. IT can play a key role in managing the supply chain (eg through data analytics to predict demand, and use of EDI, ERPS and RFID for communicating and sharing information).

Further study guidance

Question practice

Now try the following from the Further question practice bank (available in the digital edition of the Workbook):

Q17 *CHN Retail Chain*

Further reading

There is a Technical Article on ACCA's website called *Complex Business Structures* which looks at some of the main issues involved in managing performance across complex business structures.

The article highlights some of the problems the 'core enterprise' might face in relation to planning and control, and it highlights the important role IT can play in performance management.

You are strongly advised to read this article as part of your preparation for your exam.

Activity answers

Activity 1: Autoplus

Goals and objectives – Autoplus' goals and objectives for the venture will be linked to achieving growth, and expanding into a new market (Veeland). Carman's motive for the venture appears to be based more on a desire to use spare capacity, resulting from a potential decline in sales following safety issues. However, if the partners have different objectives, it may be difficult to agree the ventures' goals, and to develop performance metrics to support those goals.

Quality – The partners may also have different expectations of the level of quality of products being produced. Autoplus has developed a favourable reputation for the quality of its cars, but Carman has recently been affected by safety issues with some of its cars. If Autoplus' cars are more of a premium brand than Carman's, then disagreements around acceptable levels of quality (and other non-financial aspects of performance) may damage the performance of the joint venture.

Culture – Autoplus is a relatively young company, backed by venture capitalists, while Carman is a much larger, well-established company. As such, it is likely they will have different management styles and organisational cultures. This could cause problems not only in setting strategy and objectives for the company, but also at operational level if the management styles of the venture partners conflict.

Decision making – One of the problems in joint ventures is that there needs to be a consensus among the venture partners when making decisions. This could be a particular problem in this venture since both partners will own 50%, meaning it will be very difficult to make any decisions in situations where there is any disagreement between the partners.

Sharing information – Another problem with JVs is that they require the venture partners to share information and intellectual property with each other. If the venture means Autoplus cars are to be manufactured in Carman's factory, Autoplus will need to share commercially sensitive details about the designs of the cars and their engines with Carman. However, Autoplus may be reluctant to share too much information, in case (for example) Carman subsequently decides to develop its own range of hybrid cars.

Predicting and preventing corporate failure

Learning objectives

On completion of this chapter, you should be able to:

	Syllabus reference no.
Discuss how long-term survival necessitates consideration of life cycle issues.	E3(a)
Assess the potential likelihood of corporate failure, utilising quantitative and qualitative performance measures and models (such as Z scores and Argenti).	E3(b)
Assess and critique quantitative and qualitative corporate failure prediction models.	E3(c)
Identify and discuss performance improvement strategies that may be adopted in order to prevent corporate failure.	E3(d)
Identify and discuss operational changes to performance management systems required to implement the performance improvement strategies.	E3(e)

Exam context

This chapter completes syllabus Section E – Performance Evaluation and Corporate Failure.

As we have mentioned in the previous chapters, **one of the Section B 25-mark questions will come mainly from syllabus Section E** and therefore could cover corporate failure.

This is an area that is often neglected by students, probably because it is the last chapter(!). However, this is unwise not only because you know a question from syllabus Section E will be examined, but also because all the questions are compulsory, so if corporate failure is tested you will have to attempt the question.

There are a number of ways the topics in this chapter could be tested, but there are two key angles to be aware of. On the one hand, you could be asked to assess the different **models** of corporate failure, their strengths and weaknesses, and their usefulness in predicting corporate failure in a given scenario. On the other hand, you could be asked to use the models to assess the likelihood of an **organisation** suffering a corporate failure.

This is a relatively short chapter, with a fairly limited technical content. However, after assimilating the technical models, you then need to practise the skill of applying them to the scenario-based questions; so question practice on this area is also important.

Chapter overview

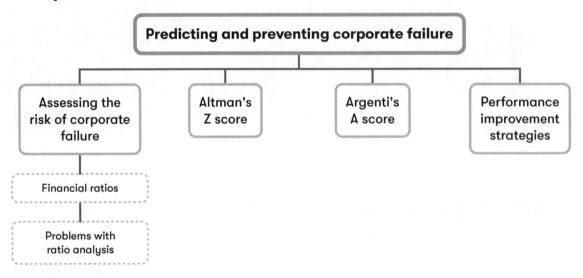

Predicting and preventing corporate failure

- Assessing the risk of corporate failure
  - Financial ratios
  - Problems with ratio analysis
- Altman's Z score
- Argenti's A score
- Performance improvement strategies

1 Assessing the risk of corporate failure

1.1 Financial ratios

A number of financial ratios can be compared against industry averages to analyse potential financial instability or risk.

1.1.1 Current ratio

Formula to learn

$$\text{Current ratio} = \frac{\text{Current assets}}{\text{Current liabilities}}$$

The current ratio can be calculated by dividing the most liquid assets in the business (receivables, inventories and cash) by the business's payables.

1.1.2 Quick ratio

Formula to learn

$$\text{Quick ratio} = \frac{\text{Current assets (excluding inventory)}}{\text{Current liabilities}}$$

The quick ratio excludes inventory as this is often not a liquid asset in a failing business.

It is sometimes suggested that a company with a current ratio well below 2:1 or a quick ratio well below 1:1 might be considered illiquid and in danger of failure. However, when looking at a company's ratios it would also be useful to benchmark them against other companies in the same industry (or an industry average) because some industries are typically more liquid than others.

Essential reading

See Chapter 15 Section 1 of the Essential reading for an overview of other basic working capital ratios.

The Essential reading is available as an Appendix of the digital edition of the Workbook.

1.1.3 Interest cover

Formula to learn

$$\text{Interest cover} = \frac{\text{Profits before interest and tax}}{\text{Interest payable}}$$

As a general guide, an interest coverage ratio of **less than three times** is considered low, indicating that profitability is too low given the company's level of debt.

1.1.4 Financial gearing

Formula to learn

$$\text{Financial gearing ratio} = \frac{\text{Long - term debt (prior charge capital)}}{\text{Long - term debt} + \text{equity (shareholders' funds)}}$$

Financial gearing is an attempt to quantify the **degree of risk** involved in holding equity shares in a company, both in terms of the company's ability to remain in business and in terms of expected ordinary dividends from the company.

The more geared the company is, the **greater the risk** that little (if anything) will be available to distribute by way of dividend to the ordinary shareholders. Interest and preference dividends on debt must continue to be paid regardless of the company's profits. A high financial gearing therefore means the company is more vulnerable to poor trading conditions.

Gearing ultimately measures the company's ability to **remain in business**. A high-geared company has a large amount of interest to pay annually. If those borrowings are 'secured' in any way (and bonds in particular are secured), then the holders of the debt are perfectly entitled to force the company to realise assets to pay their interest if funds are not available from other sources. Clearly, the more highly geared a company, the more likely this is to occur if and when profits fall.

1.1.5 Operational gearing

Operational gearing measures the ratio of fixed costs to its variable costs. High operational gearing is risky because if revenue falls, fixed costs will not. Operational gearing can be a very useful indicator of a firm's ability to survive a reduction in sales (and therefore helps to measure business risk).

> **Formula to learn**
>
> $$\text{Operating gearing ratio} = \frac{\text{Fixed costs}}{\text{Variable costs}}$$

Note. Other definitions of operational gearing are possible.

1.2 Problems with ratio analysis

Ratios are based largely on published financial data so they enable comparisons to be made relatively easily. However, analysis of individual financial ratios has been shown to be an **unreliable indicator** of corporate failure.

Problems with financial ratios:

- Financial statements may be up to a year in the past
- Industry averages do not provide an adequate benchmark for analysing the risk of failure
- Ignore non-financial issues (see Argenti's A score model later)

1.3 Prediction models

Moving beyond basic ratio analysis, many models have been developed from research into failed businesses to help predict future corporate failures. Two of the best-known prediction models are:

(a) Altman's **Z score**

(b) Argenti's **A score**

These are the key corporate failure models for the APM exam.

2 Altman's Z score

2.1 Quantitative model

Quantitative models for predicting business failure are based on a statistical analysis of financial ratios to understand the danger signals that flag the likelihood of company failure. There are many such models, but the best known is the Altman Z score model (*Altman, 1968*).

Altman researched **the financial results** of manufacturing businesses in the USA in the 1960s, some of which had failed, and some of which had survived. From this, he used statistical analysis to determine five key indicators of success or failure.

The model emerged as:

$$Z = 1.2X_1 + 1.4X_2 + 3.3X_3 + 0.6X_4 + 1.0X_5$$

Wherein:

Factor	Calculation	Measure of
X_1	Working capital/total assets	Liquidity
X_2	Retained earnings/total assets	Cumulative profitability
X_3	Earnings before interest and tax/total assets	Solvency
X_4	Market value of equity/book value of total debt	Gearing
X_5	Revenue/total assets	Revenue-generating capacity

Note. If required, this formula will be provided in an exam question.

2.2 Key values

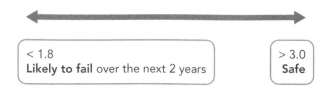

| < 1.8 | > 3.0 |
| **Likely to fail** over the next 2 years | **Safe** |

Between 1.8 – 3.0 there is a 'grey area' where the eventual failure or non-failure of an organisation could not be predicted with certainty.

Altman also adapted this **quantitative model** to allow relative scoring from 0 to 100. A score of 75, for example, would indicate that 25% of companies have higher Z scores than the company under consideration. Relative measurement over time permits trends to be identified more easily.

2.3 Weaknesses of quantitative models

There are a number of weaknesses of this type of approach to analysing corporate failure, including:

(a) It is based on visible factors so **fails to include internal weaknesses not apparent in financial information**

(b) **It ignores** the risk of a change in **environmental factors**.

2.3.1 Additional weaknesses of Z score model

In addition to the previous section, the Altman model can also be criticised because:

(a) It is based on a sample of companies from the **USA.**

(b) The analysis was performed in the **1960s.**

(c) The sample it used consisted of **manufacturing companies**, so it may not be appropriate to use on non-manufacturing companies without some modification.

(d) It requires a market value for equity which **limits its use to quoted companies.**

(e) In capital-intensive industries, additional investment (eg in new machinery) will, according to Z score analysis, make failure more likely because sales/total assets will worsen. This is **counter-intuitive.**

Activity 1: Zorro

Zorro is a manufacturer of fancy dress costumes. It has expanded rapidly in the last few years under the leadership of its autocratic chair and chief executive officer, Sally Maysmith.

The company has developed a major new product range linked to the relaunch of a major film franchise, which has necessitated a large investment in new equipment. However, the recent share price performance has caused concern at board level and there has been comment in the financial press about the increased gearing and the strain that this expansion is putting on the company.

A junior analyst in the company has correctly prepared a spreadsheet calculating the Z scores as follows:

		20X8	20X9	20Y0
X_1	Working capital/Total assets	−0.28	−0.25	−0.20
X_2	Retained earnings/Total assets	0.12	0.21	0.21
X_3	Profit before interest and tax/Total assets	0.16	0.09	0.05
X_4	Market value of equity/Total long-term debt	1.62	0.95	0.60
X_5	Revenue/Total assets	1.50	0.72	0.84
	Z score	**2.832**	**1.581**	**1.419**

Required

Comment on the results in the junior analyst's spreadsheet.

Note. The formula would be provided if you were required to calculate a Z score.

Solution

3 Argenti's A score

3.1 Qualitative model

Qualitative models are based on a judgement of the risk of failure that includes both financial and non-financial factors. This approach stems from research which identified that corporate decline was often due to **non-financial factors** such as:

- Frequent changes of management
- Falling market share
- Lack of planning
- Weak culture, eg crisis denial, blame culture - leading to inaction
- Ineffective scrutiny by non-executive directors

The key qualitative model for the APM exam is Argenti's A score model (*Argenti, 1976*).

Argenti argued that symptoms such as worrying financial ratios were only obvious in the later stages of failure and failure could be better predicted by looking at **root causes**, which he believed lay in the ability of management to lead a business. Thus failure follows a predictable system.

A score is given to each weakness, with a score of **zero** meaning that the weakness is **not present**:

Factor		Illustration	Score if present
Defects	Management	Chief Executive is an autocrat	8
		Chief Executive is also the Chairman	4
		Passive board of directors	2
		Unbalanced skills in board of directors	2
		Weak Finance Director	2
		Lack of management in depth	1
		Poor response to change	15
	Accounting	No budgets or budgetary controls	3
		No cash flow forecasts, or out of date	3
		No costing system; don't know costs and contribution from each product or service	3
Total			<u>43</u>

Factor		Illustration	Score if present
Mistakes	Overtrading	Company expanding faster than funding; capital base too small or unbalanced	15
	High gearing	Inability to service debt levels	15
	Failure of a big project	The failure of which would cause the company to fail	15
Total			<u>45</u>
Symptoms	Deteriorating ratios	Financial analysis (eg poor Z score)	4
	Creative accounting	Gaming and misrepresentation	4
	Declining morale and quality	Uncleaned and untidy offices or factory, high staff turnover, rumours	4
Total			<u>12</u>

3.2 Key values

In order for a firm to be considered not at risk, it needs to score **below** a certain level.

Factor	Maximum permitted score
Defects	10
Mistakes	15
Symptoms	<u>0</u>
Total permitted	25

Companies not at risk often score between 0 and 18, while those at risk usually score well above 25 (often 35–70).

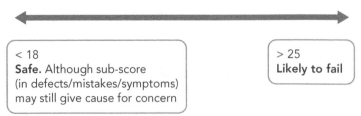

> < 18
> **Safe.** Although sub-score (in defects/mistakes/symptoms) may still give cause for concern

> > 25
> **Likely to fail**

3.3 Advantages

The A score model incorporates financial (eg gearing) and non-financial factors, giving a more holistic assessment of the likelihood of corporate failure, rather than just looking at financial factors.

It identifies factors that can often be seen in organisations before they reach a terminal state, providing the opportunity to improve performance and turn the organisation around.

3.4 Weaknesses

The main problem with this approach is the **judgement** involved in assessing the risk of failure, so the scores chosen are **subjective**. It is also important to remember that one or two defects/mistakes on their own do not necessarily constitute terminal decline for a business.

In addition the Argenti model can also be criticised because:

(a) Lack of formal testing to prove the model's validity.

(b) Lack of industry considerations

(c) Focuses mainly on internal factors and fails to consider the importance of broader environmental factors

4 Performance improvement strategies

In the exam if you are asked to recommend which actions a company will need to take to increase their chances of survival then the key issue will be to say something practical about the 'underlying causes' of the company's problems.

4.1 Insights from qualitative models

One of the benefits of qualitative models such as the A score model is that they analysis **the root cause** of the risk of failure and therefore allow targeted action to be taken (eg the A score may indicate the need to improve controls around project management to reduce the risk of a big project causing the failure of a company).

4.2 Other issues

4.2.1 Industry/life cycle issues

In order to increase the likelihood of survival, life cycle factors need to be considered.

Industries reach the end of their life cycle when overtaken by new products or suffer temporary difficulties due to economic factors.

As the competitive environment changes, pressure is placed on margins. Unless a company has the lowest cost base, a superior advantage or a loyal niche of customers, it is likely to lose market share.

Essential reading

See Chapter 15 Section 2 of the Essential reading for a more detailed look at life cycle issues.

The Essential reading is available as an Appendix of the digital edition of the Workbook.

4.2.2 Broader environmental factors

Changes in general environmental factors (as considered in Chapter 1) need to be carefully monitored, eg if an economic downturn is expected then the company will have to plan how to adapt to this in order to survive.

Essential reading

See Chapter 15 Section 3 of the Essential reading for some further discussion of performance management issues in relation to performance improvement strategies.

The Essential reading is available as an Appendix of the digital edition of the Workbook.

Chapter summary

Predicting and preventing corporate failure

Assessing the risk of corporate failure

Financial ratios
- Liquidity
- Gearing
- Poor indicators of failure

Problems with ratio analysis
- Historical financial statements
- Industry averages inadequate
- Ignore non-financial issues

Altman's Z score

- Quantitative model
- **Less than 1.8:** likely to fail
  - Ignores non-financial issues
  - Ignores environmental issues
  - Based on US manufacturing companies in 1960s
- Working capital
- Retained earnings
- Productivity
- EBIT/assets
- Market value of equity/book value of debt

Argenti's A score

- Qualitative model
- **More than 25:** likely to fail
  - Subjective scores
  - Ignores environmental issues
- Defects
  - Management
  - Board
  - Accounting
- Mistakes
  - Overtrading
  - Gearing
  - Project failure
- Symptoms
  - Deteriorating ratios
  - Creative accounting
  - Falling morale and quality

Performance improvement strategies

- Direct at underlying cause
- Aims to **prevent corporate failure**
  - Address life cycle issues
  - Address environmental issues
  - Strengthen management
  - Provide financial stability
  - Address other performance management issues

Knowledge diagnostic

1. Quantitative models

Use objective financial ratios to measure the risk of corporate failure. An example is Altman's Z score model.

2. Qualitative models

Use subjective assessment to measure the risk of corporate failure. An example is Argenti's A score model, which looks at defects, mistakes and symptoms.

3. Key values for Z score

For the Z score model, the **lower** the score, the higher the risk. A score of below 1.8 indicates failure (more than 3 is safe).

4. Key values for A score

For the A score model, the **higher** the score, the higher the risk of failure. A score of above 25 indicates failure (less than 18 is safe).

Further study guidance

Question practice

Now try the following from the Further question practice bank (available in the digital edition of the Workbook):

Q18 *NewsPrint Co*

Further reading

There is a Technical Article on ACCA's website entitled *Business Failure*. This article covers the main models in this chapter and gives other useful background information about corporate failure, so you should read it as part of your preparation for the APM exam.

Activity answers

Activity 1: Zorro

The Z score for Zorro in 20Y0 is 1.419, which is below the danger level of 1.8 and so suggests the company is at risk of failing. Moreover, the Z score has fallen significantly over the past three years from 2.832 to 1.419.

The most dramatic decline in the Z score arises from variable X_4 which has fallen from 1.62 to 0.60, or 63%. This represents the market value of equity to total long-term debt. This is due to the increase in gearing (debt) coupled with falls in the share price. If the adverse comments in the financial press continue, these could lead to further falls in the share price.

The other variables that have seen a significant decline are X_5 (Revenue/TA) and X_3 (PBIT/TA). These will both have been affected by the large investment in new equipment (increasing the value of total assets). However, this investment has not been matched by a similar increase in revenue and operating profit, causing the ratios to decline. However, it is possible that these ratios may improve in future periods as revenue (and associated profit) is earned from the new investment.

It is likely at the early stage of the project that costs will be high and revenues low. So a longer-term view needs to be taken before concluding the company is definitely failing.

Skills checkpoint 5

Addressing the scenario

Overview

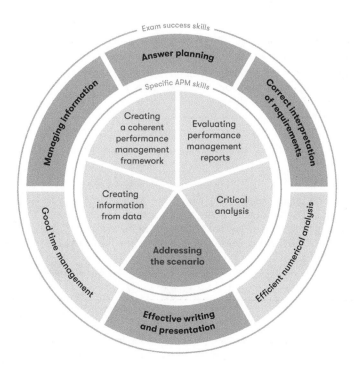

Introduction

All of the questions in the APM exam will be scenario-based. In Section A of the exam (50 marks) you can expect the scenario to be approximately three pages in length, and in the shorter (25 mark) Section B question scenarios will each normally be about one page long, although the exact length of the scenarios varies from exam to exam, depending on the type of information included in it (text, figures, diagrams etc).

The scenarios are there for a reason! It is vital to spend time reading and assimilating the scenario as part of your answer planning. It is important for you to use the information in the scenario to validate that the discussion points that you are making in your answer are 'relevant'. The discussion parts of the question – applying your knowledge to the scenario – will normally account for the majority of the marks available.

As you get into the habit of addressing the scenario, you will be less likely to make the mistake of including **too much repetition of theory** in your answers. There are a large number of APM theories, and it is **important that you have a good broad knowledge** of these, because they often examined. However, you are primarily being tested on your **ability to apply** your theoretical knowledge to the scenario in question, not your ability to simply recite it. The APM ACCA Examining Team often comment that candidates **repeating** memorised material 'will probably score only between 20% and 30%...' A good, professional-level answer will go beyond the mere repetition of how a technique works and will focus on relating it to the entity's specific environment, as identified in the question scenario.

It goes without saying that, if you don't have the underlying theoretical knowledge, you won't be able to apply it! So, there is a need to develop a sound knowledge of APM theories. However, the key point is that to be successful in the exam you need to do more than simply recite 'rote learned' theories in your answers.

The skill of **'addressing the scenario'** is the most important of the APM specific skills, as it is relevant to all syllabus areas and **every question** in the APM exam.

APM Skill: Addressing the scenario

A step-by-step technique for ensuring that your discussion points are relevant to the scenario is outlined below. Each step will be explained in more detail in the following sections, and illustrated by answering a requirement from a past exam question.

STEP 1:

Allow at least 20% of your allotted time for analysing the scenario and requirements; don't rush into starting to write your answer.

Assuming 1.95 minutes per mark this means about 20 minutes of analysis and planning for a 50-mark question (1.95 minutes × 50 marks × 20%) and about 10 minutes for a 25-mark question.

STEP 2:

Prepare an answer plan using key words from the requirements as headings (ie a mind map or a bullet-pointed list). Complete your answer plan by working through each paragraph of the question identifying specific points that are relevant to the scenario (and requirement) to make sure you generate enough points to score a pass mark (ACCA marking guides typically allocate 1–2 marks per relevant well-explained point).

STEP 3:

As you write your answer, explain what you mean in one (or two) sentence(s) and then in the next sentence explain why it matters here (in the given scenario). This should result in a series of short punchy paragraphs containing points that address the specific content of the scenario.

Write your answer in a time-efficient manner.

Exam success skills

The following illustration is based on an extract from a past exam question, about a developer and manufacturer of medical drugs, called 'PT'. This extract was worth 18 marks.

For this question, we will also focus on the following **exam success skills**:

- **Managing information.** It is easy for the amount of information contained in scenario-based questions to feel overwhelming. To manage this, focus on the requirement first – underline the key exam verbs to ensure you answer the question properly. Then read the rest of the question, underlining and annotating important and relevant information from the scenario.

- **Correct interpretation of requirements.** At first glance, it looks like part (b) of the following question just contains one requirement. However, on closer examination you will discover that it contains two; this is very common in the APM exam.

- **Answer planning.** Everyone will have a preferred style for an answer plan. For example, it may be a mind map, bullet-pointed lists, or simply annotating the question scenario. Choose the approach that you feel most comfortable with or, if you are not sure, try out different approaches for different questions until you have found your preferred style.

- **Effective writing and presentation**. It is often helpful to use key words from the requirement as headings in your answer. You may also wish to use sub-headings in your answer – you could use a separate sub-heading for each paragraph from the scenario in the question which contains an issue for discussion. Underline your headings and sub-headings, and write in full sentences, ensuring your style is professional.

Skills activity

STEP 1 Allow at least 20% of your allotted time for analysing the scenario and requirements; don't rush into starting to write your answer.

Start by analysing the requirements so that you know what you are looking for when you read the scenario.

Required

Evaluate[53] the performance measure proposed for PT's[54] balanced scorecard.

(10 marks)

Briefly describe[55] a method of analysing stakeholder influence **and**[56] analyse the influence of **four different external**[57] stakeholders on the **regulator (BDR)**[58].

(8 marks)

(Total = 18 marks)

[53] Verb – refer to ACCA definition.

[54] So, no need to invent new ones.

[55] First requirement of a two-part question. Be brief as instructed.

[56] 2nd part of the two-part question.

[57] Ie, only external stakeholders.

[58] On BDR not on PT!

The first key action verb is 'evaluate'. This is defined by the ACCA as: 'Determine the situation in the light of the arguments for and against'. As discussed in Skills Checkpoint 4, an evaluation should include a balanced debate.

The other key action verb is 'analyse'. This is defined by the ACCA as 'Break into separate parts and discuss, examine, or interpret each part'. This is clearly more important than the brief description required in the first part of part (b). So your analysis of the stakeholders' influence needs to include more detail than your 'brief description' of the method.

This is an 18-mark question and at 1.95 minutes a mark, it should take 35 minutes.

On the basis of spending approximately 20% of your time reading and planning, this time should be split approximately as follows:

- Reading and planning time – 7 minutes (longer if needed)

- Writing up your answer – 28 minutes (approximately 16 minutes for part (a) and 12 for part (b))

In the real exam, these requirements would have been part of a larger question (eg this was part of a 25-mark Section B question) and the planning time would take place at the start of the question and would involve planning for all of the question's requirements (so 10 minutes of planning for the whole question).

Some flexibility may be required, and if a question contains a substantial number of discussion issues (as here) then more reading and planning time may be needed.

However, it's still too early to start drawing up an answer plan at this stage. In some questions, particularly in Section A of the exam, the scenario will contain extra information about what is meant by the requirements.

So, now move on to reading the scenario, and identifying the key pieces of information provided in it. From reading the requirements, you should know the key issues or clues you are looking for in the scenario.

Question – PT (18 marks)

Company background:[59]

Pharmaceutical Technologies Co (PT) is a developer and manufacturer of medical drugs in Beeland. It is one of the 100 largest listed companies on the national stock exchange. The company focuses on buying prospective drugs (which have shown initial promise in testing) from small bio-engineering companies. PT then leads these drugs through three regulatory stages to launch in the general medical market.

The three stages are:

(1) To confirm the safety of the drug (does it harm humans?), in small-scale trials;

(2) To test the efficacy of the product (does it help cure diseases?), again in small-scale trials; and

(3) Finally, large-scale trials to definitively decide on the safety and efficacy of the product.

[59] The company background is always worth noting. It will influence the validity of the proposed performance measures. Also hints at some important stakeholders.

The drugs are then marketed through the company's large sales force, to healthcare providers and end users (patients). The healthcare providers are paid by either health insurance companies or the national government dependent on the financial status of the patient.

Industry regulator:[60]

The Beeland Drug Regulator (BDR) oversees this testing process and makes the final judgement about whether a product can be sold in the country. Its objectives are to protect, promote and improve public health by ensuring that:

- Medicines have an acceptable balance of benefit and risk;

- The users of these medicines understand this risk-benefit profile; and

- New beneficial product development is encouraged.

The regulator is governed by a board of trustees appointed by the government. It is funded directly by the government[61] and also through fees charged to drug companies when granting licences to sell their products in Beeland.

Balanced scorecard:

PT has used share price and earnings per share as its principal measures of performance to date. However, the share price has underperformed the market, and the health sector, in the last two years. The Chief Executive Officer (CEO) has identified that these measures are too narrow, and is considering implementing a balanced scorecard approach to address this problem.

A working group has drawn up a suggested balanced scorecard. It began by identifying the objectives[62] from the board's medium-term strategy:

- Create shareholder value by bringing commercially viable drugs to market.

- Improve the efficiency of drug development.

- Increase shareholder value by innovation in the drug approval process.

[60] Clues about stakeholders affecting BDR (part (b)) are given here.

[61] The government looks to be another key stakeholder.

[62] Strategic objectives are always important and worth noting. The measures in the balanced scorecard should support these.

The working group then considered the stakeholder perspectives[63]:

- Shareholders want a competitive return on their investment.

- Payers/purchasers (governments, insurers and patients) want to pay a reasonable price for the drugs.

- Regulators want an efficient process for the validation of drugs.

- Doctors want safe and effective drug products.

- Patients want to be cured.

[63] Summary list of stakeholders for use in part (b). Be careful only to use external stakeholders (and to assess their influence on BDR, not PT).

Finally, this leads to the proposed scorecard of performance measures[64]:

- Financial – share price and earnings per share.

- Customer – number of patients using PT products.

- Internal business process – exceed industry standard on design and testing; time to regulatory approval of a product.

- Learning and growth – training days undertaken by staff; time to market of new product; percentage of drugs bought by PT that gain final approval.

[64] These are the proposed measures that need to be evaluated.

The balanced scorecard now needs to be reviewed to ensure that it will address the company's objectives and the issues that it faces in its business environment[65].

[65] An important hint about how to tackle part (a).

STEP 2 Now you should be ready to prepare an answer plan using key words from the requirements as headings. This could take the form of a mind map or a brief bullet-pointed list.

Complete your answer plan by working through each paragraph of the question identifying specific points that are relevant to the scenario and requirement to make sure you generate enough points to score a pass mark (ACCA marking guides typically allocate 1–2 marks per relevant well-explained point).

Completed answer plan

Having worked through each paragraph, an answer plan can now be completed. A possible answer plan is shown here. This uses the wording of the requirement and the initial ideas that have been noted in the margins as shown earlier.

Part (a)	Ideas
Evaluate: pros and cons*	As proposed: **Financial: 1. share price 2. eps** Good balance, but ignores dividends/cash flow? **Customer: 3. number** Only considers end-user? **Internal: 4. standards and 5. time to approval** Supports objectives but ignores quality **Learning: 6. training days, 7. time to market, 8. % approval** No consideration of innovation (key objective)?

* There are eight measures to evaluate. A few preliminary thoughts are noted here. Main point of the plan is to establish the **structure** of the answer.

Part (b)	Ideas
Briefly describe	Mendelow's matrix
Analyse influence of FOUR different EXTERNAL stakeholders affecting BDR	Drug companies** Doctors and healthcare providers** Patients** Government** Use power/influence as per Mendelow

** There are four external stakeholders mentioned – again the plan mainly sets up the **structure** as opposed to the content of the answer.

STEP 3 As you write your answer, explain **what you mean** – in one (or two) sentence(s) – and then in the next sentence explain **why it matters here** (in the given scenario). This should result in a series of short, punchy paragraphs that **address the specific context of the scenario.**

Note, however, that addressing the specific context of the scenario does not simply mean repeating the wording in the question. You should **avoid doing this; and instead try to explain why your point matters.**

Be concise (don't waffle, given that any one point is normally unlikely to be worth more than 2 marks) and especially **avoid reciting theory at length** (although briefly defining your terms is often an easy way of scoring a mark).

Finally, write your answer in a time-efficient manner. If 20% of your time has been used for planning/analysis this means that when you are writing the 1.95 minutes per mark becomes 1.95 × 0.8 = 1.56 minutes per mark of writing time.

Suggested solution

(a) Financial measures[66]

The financial perspective has not been altered from the existing measures of strategic performance. These are appropriate to address the objectives of enhancing shareholder wealth[67], although it has been argued that measures such as economic value added or shareholder value added are better long-term measures of this topic. Also, it is more common to use share price and dividend per share to reflect total shareholder return.

Although it is important to look at earnings and profits, PT's financial measures overlook the importance of cash flow and liquidity[68], which will be essential to its survival especially given the long lead-times for introducing new products.

Customer perspective

PT has two different types of customer: users (healthcare providers and patients) and the people who fund the drug use (insurance companies or government). The measure currently proposed seems to focus mainly on the end users. However, their concerns may not always be same as those who are paying for a course of treatment. For example, the healthcare providers and patients are likely to focus primarily on how effective the product is as a cure. However, the funding bodies will also be interested in the cost of the treatment in comparison to PT's competitors.

Internal business processes

One of the objectives from the medium-term strategy is to improve the efficiency of drug development[69]. Performance measures designed to improve the standard of design and testing, and to reduce the time to gain regulatory approval, should help achieve this objective.

[66] Do not start your answer with a lengthy description of the balanced scorecard – this is not relevant here.

[67] Each perspective of the balanced scorecard will be worth 2–3 marks, so keep your answer concise and focused on the scenario.

[68] Don't get drawn into suggesting new measures as this is beyond the scope of the question.

[69] Add value by relating the measure to the objectives as given in the scenario, and also by thinking about consistency with financial measures.

These measures also help support the financial objectives. If PT can reduce the time it takes to get new drugs approved by the regulator, it will also be able to start selling those drugs more quickly, thereby increasing sales and earnings.

Learning and growth

The third of the objectives from the medium-term strategy highlights the importance of innovation in the drug approval process[70]. The measures in the learning and growth perspective of the scorecard should therefore directly help PT to achieve this objective.

We are not told anything about the relative importance or ranking of any of the measures in the scorecard, but it is debatable whether the number of training days attended is the main measure of learning and growth[71]. Reducing the time to market of new products, and increasing the percentage of drugs that gain final approval, are likely to be more directly strategically important.

Measurement issues

Although the measures suggested seem largely appropriate in relation to PT's objectives, the management will also need to consider how practical it will be to collect data for some of the non-financial measures[72]. For example, an assessment of whether PT has exceeded industry standard on design and testing is likely to be subjective, unless there are industry-wide quality audits which formally assess companies against a common set of criteria.

Conversely, measures should not be chosen because they are easy to measure. The number of training days undertaken by staff will be easy to measure by staff. However, there may be a danger that staff will simply end up going on training days simply to achieve a target number of days. Training will only be valuable to PT and its staff if it is relevant and appropriate for the people attending.

[70] Again, add value by relating the measure to the objectives as given in the scenario.

[71] An evaluation should involve critical points too.

[72] Data to support performance measures is often a relevant area to comment on, and involves thinking across to different syllabus areas.

(b) Stakeholder influence[73]

A stakeholder's influence over an organisation can be analysed in relation to the stakeholder's power and interest, using Mendelow's matrix.

Power identifies the extent to which a stakeholder (or group of stakeholders) has the power to influence a decision or situation. The level of interest reflects the likelihood that a stakeholder will exercise their power in relation to any given decision or situation.

This approach can be used to analyse the four key external stakeholders affecting the regulator (BDR)[74].

Drug companies:[75]

- **Interest** – likely to have a **high interest** in BDR, because it makes the final judgement about whether a product can be sold in the country.

- **Power** – **little power** to influence BDR. BDR's responsibility is to the public and to public health, therefore BDR needs to be (and be seen to be) independent of the drug companies.

Government:

- **Power** – **high power** because it appoints the board of trustees and also directly funds BDR.

- **Interest** – will have a keen interest in public health overall, but their direct interest in BDR is likely to be **relatively low**. The government has appointed the trustees to manage BDR on its behalf so it is unlikely to intervene in decision making at BDR.[76]

Healthcare providers:

- **Interest** – will have a **high level of interest** in the approval process, because they will want to be confident that any new drugs approved are safe for use. They will also have an interest in BDR's role in encouraging the development of beneficial new drugs.

[73] A brief description will only be worth a small number of marks (2 marks here) so keep this brief.

[74] Answer planning ensures that part (b) has been interpreted correctly. Focus on BDR, not PT.

[75] Now the easy bit (hopefully) – short pararaphs, using the theory, and addressing the question requirements.

[76] Having stated the level of power or interest, you then need to explain (briefly) why you think this is the case.

- **Power** – likely to have **low power** over the approval process because BDR is an independent regulator (but may be able to exert some power by lobbying government).

Patients:

- **Interest** – will have a **high level of interest in** the drug approval process because they will want to be reassured that any drugs approved are safe; also will have an interest in potential new cures being available on the market quickly.

- **Power** – as with healthcare providers, **patients also only have low power** over any decisions made at BDR.

Other points to note:

- **Very occasionally** the requirement will allow for a general answer that is **not** linked to the scenario. This will be the case if the name of the company/any specific reference to the scenario **is not** made in the requirement. This was not the case here.

Exam success skills diagnostic

Every time you complete a question, use the diagnostic below to assess how effectively you demonstrated the exam success skills in answering the question. The table has been completed below for the PT activity to give you an idea of how to complete the diagnostic.

Exam success skills	Your reflections/observations
Managing information	Did you identify the strategic objectives of PT and think how they could influence the choice of measures in the balanced scorecard?
Correct interpretation of requirements	Did you identify that part (b) was about **external** stakeholders only? Did you identify that part (b) concerned the stakeholders of BDR, **not** PT?
Answer planning	Did you draw up an answer plan using your preferred approach (eg mind map, bullet-pointed list)? Did your plan help to create a structure for your answer?
Effective writing and presentation	Did you use headings (key words from requirements)? Did you use full sentences? And most importantly – **did you explain why your points related to the scenario?**
Most important action points to apply to your next question	

Summary

All the questions in the APM exam are scenario-based. It is therefore essential that you try to create a practical answer that is relevant to the scenario, and/or addresses the issues identified in the scenario, instead of simply repeating rote-learned, technical knowledge.

APM is positioned as a Masters level qualification. It is not easy to address your points to the scenario, but it is important to realise that this is a fundamental skill that is being tested at this stage in your qualification.

As you move into practising questions as part of your final revision, you will need to practise assimilating information from a scenario quickly (using active reading), accurately understanding the requirements, and creating an answer plan and a final answer that concisely and accurately addresses the requirements in the context of the scenario.

This is not to suggest that theoretical knowledge is unimportant, because often scenario-based questions will involve applying theories to the scenario. In order to pass the exam, you need to develop a sound knowledge of APM theories, **but equally you need to apply this knowledge to the question scenarios** (for example to address problems or issues raised in the scenario). Simply reciting your knowledge will not be sufficient to pass the exam.

Appendix 1: Mathematical tables

Present Value Table

Present value of 1 ie $(1+r)^{-n}$

Where r=discount rate; n=number of periods until payment

Periods (n)	1%	2%	3%	4%	Discount rate (r) 5%	6%	7%	8%	9%	10%
1	0.990	0.980	0.971	0.962	0.952	0.943	0.935	0.926	0.917	0.909
2	0.980	0.961	0.943	0.925	0.907	0.890	0.873	0.857	0.842	0.826
3	0.971	0.942	0.915	0.889	0.864	0.840	0.816	0.794	0.772	0.751
4	0.961	0.924	0.888	0.855	0.823	0.792	0.763	0.735	0.708	0.683
5	0.951	0.906	0.863	0.822	0.784	0.747	0.713	0.681	0.650	0.621
6	0.942	0.888	0.837	0.790	0.746	0.705	0.666	0.630	0.596	0.564
7	0.933	0.871	0.813	0.760	0.711	0.665	0.623	0.583	0.547	0.513
8	0.923	0.853	0.789	0.731	0.677	0.627	0.582	0.540	0.502	0.467
9	0.914	0.837	0.766	0.703	0.645	0.592	0.544	0.500	0.460	0.424
10	0.905	0.820	0.744	0.676	0.614	0.558	0.508	0.463	0.422	0.386
11	0.896	0.804	0.722	0.650	0.585	0.527	0.475	0.429	0.388	0.350
12	0.887	0.788	0.701	0.625	0.557	0.497	0.444	0.397	0.356	0.319
13	0.879	0.773	0.681	0.601	0.530	0.469	0.415	0.368	0.326	0.290
14	0.870	0.758	0.681	0.577	0.505	0.442	0.388	0.340	0.299	0.263
15	0.861	0.743	0.642	0.555	0.481	0.417	0.362	0.315	0.275	0.239

(n)	11%	12%	13%	14%	15%	16%	17%	18%	19%	20%
1	0.901	0.893	0.885	0.877	0.870	0.862	0.855	0.847	0.840	0.833
2	0.812	0.797	0.783	0.769	0.756	0.743	0.731	0.718	0.706	0.694
3	0.731	0.712	0.693	0.675	0.658	0.641	0.624	0.609	0.593	0.579
4	0.659	0.636	0.613	0.592	0.572	0.552	0.534	0.516	0.499	0.482
5	0.593	0.567	0.543	0.519	0.497	0.476	0.456	0.437	0.419	0.402
6	0.535	0.507	0.480	0.456	0.432	0.410	0.390	0.370	0.352	0.335
7	0.482	0.452	0.425	0.400	0.376	0.354	0.333	0.314	0.296	0.279
8	0.434	0.404	0.376	0.351	0.327	0.305	0.285	0.266	0.249	0.233
9	0.391	0.361	0.333	0.308	0.284	0.263	0.243	0.225	0.209	0.194
10	0.352	0.322	0.295	0.270	0.247	0.227	0.208	0.191	0.176	0.162
11	0.317	0.287	0.261	0.237	0.215	0.195	0.178	0.162	0.148	0.135
12	0.286	0.257	0.231	0.208	0.187	0.168	0.152	0.137	0.124	0.112
13	0.258	0.229	0.204	0.182	0.163	0.145	0.130	0.116	0.104	0.093
14	0.232	0.205	0.181	0.160	0.141	0.125	0.111	0.099	0.088	0.078
15	0.209	0.183	0.160	0.140	0.123	0.108	0.095	0.084	0.079	0.065

Annuity Table

Present value of an annuity of 1 ie $\dfrac{1-(1+r)^{-n}}{r}$

Where r=discount rate; n=number of periods

Periods (n)	\multicolumn{10}{c}{Discount rate (r)}

Periods (n)	1%	2%	3%	4%	5%	6%	7%	8%	9%	10%
1	0.990	0.980	0.971	0.962	0.952	0.943	0.935	0.926	0.917	0.909
2	1.970	1.942	1.913	1.886	1.859	1.833	1.808	1.783	1.759	1.736
3	2.941	2.884	2.829	2.775	2.723	2.673	2.624	2.577	2.531	2.487
4	3.902	3.808	3.717	3.630	3.546	3.465	3.387	3.312	3.240	3.170
5	4.853	4.713	4.580	4.452	4.329	4.212	4.100	3.993	3.890	3.791
6	5.795	5.601	5.417	5.242	5.076	4.917	4.767	4.623	4.486	4.355
7	6.728	6.472	6.230	6.002	5.786	5.582	5.389	5.206	5.033	4.868
8	7.652	7.325	7.020	6.733	6.463	6.210	5.971	5.747	5.535	5.335
9	8.566	8.162	7.786	7.435	7.108	6.802	6.515	6.247	5.995	5.759
10	9.471	8.983	8.530	8.111	7.722	7.360	7.024	6.710	6.418	6.145
11	10.368	9.787	9.253	8.760	8.306	7.887	7.499	7.139	6.805	6.495
12	11.255	10.575	9.954	9.385	8.863	8.384	7.943	7.536	7.161	6.814
13	12.134	11.348	10.635	9.986	9.394	8.853	8.358	7.904	7.487	7.103
14	13.004	12.106	11.296	10.563	9.899	9.295	8.745	8.244	7.786	7.367
15	13.865	12.849	11.938	11.118	10.380	9.712	9.108	8.559	8.061	7.606

(n)	11%	12%	13%	14%	15%	16%	17%	18%	19%	20%
1	0.901	0.893	0.885	0.877	0.870	0.862	0.855	0.847	0.840	0.833
2	1.713	1.690	1.668	1.647	1.626	1.605	1.585	1.566	1.547	1.528
3	2.444	2.402	2.361	2.322	2.283	2.246	2.210	2.174	2.140	2.106
4	3.102	3.037	2.974	2.914	2.855	2.798	2.743	2.690	2.639	2.589
5	3.696	3.605	3.517	3.433	3.352	3.274	3.199	3.127	3.058	2.991
6	4.231	4.111	3.998	3.889	3.784	3.685	3.589	3.498	3.410	3.326
7	4.712	4.564	4.423	4.288	4.160	4.039	3.922	3.812	3.706	3.605
8	5.146	4.968	4.799	4.639	4.487	4.344	4.207	4.078	3.954	3.837
9	5.537	5.328	5.132	4.946	4.772	4.607	4.451	4.303	4.163	4.031
10	5.889	5.650	5.426	5.216	5.019	4.833	4.659	4.494	4.339	4.192
11	6.207	5.938	5.687	5.453	5.234	5.029	4.836	4.656	4.486	4.327
12	6.492	6.194	5.918	5.660	5.421	5.197	4.988	4.793	4.611	4.439
13	6.750	6.424	6.122	5.842	5.583	5.342	5.118	4.910	4.715	4.533
14	6.982	6.628	6.302	6.002	5.724	5.468	5.229	5.008	4.802	4.611
15	7.191	6.811	6.462	6.142	5.847	5.575	5.324	5.092	4.876	4.675

Index

U

Uncertainty, 99

Unified corporate databases, 122

V

Value for money, 202

Value-based management (VBM), 278

Virtual organisations, 294

W

What gets measured, gets done, 248

Z

Zero-based budgeting, 52

Bibliography

ACCA (2015) Not-for-profit organisations – Part 1. *ACCA Technical Articles*. [Online]. Available from: www.accaglobal.com/gb/en/student/exam-support-resources/professional-exams-study-resources/p5/technical-articles/nfp-organisations1.html [Accessed 1 October 2020].

Altman, E. (1968) Financial Ratios, Discriminant Analysis and the Prediction of Corporate Bankruptcy. *Journal of Finance*, 23 (4), 589–609.

American Society for Quality (ASQ) (2018) *Cost of quality* [Online]. Available from: https://asq.org/quality-resources/cost-of-quality [Accessed 1 October 2020].

Anthony, R. N. (1965) *Planning and Control Systems: A Framework for Analysis*. Boston, Division of Research, Harvard Business School.

Argenti, J. (1976) *Corporate Collapse: The Causes and Symptoms*. New York, McGraw Hill.

Beaver, W. H. (1966) Financial Ratios as Predictors of Failure. *Journal of Accounting Research*, Vol 4, Empirical Research in Accounting: Selected Studies, 71–111.

Berry, A. J., Broadbent, J. and Otley, D. T. (1995) *Management Control: Theories, Issues and Practices*. London, Macmillan.

Berry, A. J., Broadbent, J. and Otley, D. T., (2005) *Management Control: Theories, Issues and Performance*. 2nd edition. Basingstoke, Palgrave Macmillan.

Boston Consulting Group, (1970) The Growth Share Matrix. [Online] Available from: https://www.bcg.com/en-gb/publications/2014/growth-share-matrix-bcg-classics-revisited[Accessed 1 October 2020].

Boston Consulting Group, (1973) The experience curve – reviewed IV. The growth share matrix or the product portfolio. *BCG Perspectives*. [Online]. Available from: www.bcg.com/documents/file13904.pdf [Accessed 1 October 2020].

Bratton, J. and Gold, J. (1999) *Human Resource Management: Theory and Practice*. Basingstoke, Palgrave Macmillan.

Bratton, J. and Gold, J. (2007) *Human Resource Management: Theory and Practice*. 4th edition. Basingstoke, Palgrave Macmillan.

Bratton, J. and Gold, J. (2012) *Human Resource Management: Theory and Practice*. 5th edition. Basingstoke, Palgrave Macmillan.

Brown, G. (1994) Management Accounting and Strategic Management. *ACCA Student Newsletter*. March

Burns, J. and Baldvinsdottir, G. (2007) The changing role of management accountants, in Hopper, T., Northcutt, D. and Scapens, R. *Issues in Management Accounting*. 3rd edition. Harlow, Pearson, pp117–132.

Burns, J. and Scapens R. (2000) *The changing nature of management accounting and the emergence of 'hybrid' accountants*. International Federation of Accountants, New York.

Buytendijk, F. (1 March 2009) Organization as network: A modern approach to performance management. *Business Finance*. [Online]. Available from: www.frankbuytendijk.com/download.html [Accessed 1 October 2020].

Campbell, A., Devine, M. and Young, D. (1990) *A sense of mission*. London, Economist Books/Hutchinson.

Campbell, D. J. and Lee, C. (1988) Self-appraisal in performance evaluation: Development versus evaluation. *Academy of Management Review*. 13, 302–14.

Chopra, S. and Meindl, P. (2016) *Supply Chain Management: Strategy, Planning and Operation*. 6th edition. Harlow, Pearson.

CIMA, (2005) *CIMA Official Terminology*. Oxford, CIMA Publishing/Elsevier.

CIMA (2014) *Big Data: Readying business for the big data revolution*. London, CIMA.

Council of Supply Chain Management Professionals (2017) *CSCMP Supply Chain Management Definitions and Glossary*. [Online]. Available from: https://cscmp.org/imis0/CSCMP/Educate/SCM_Definitions_and_Glossary_of_Terms/CSCMP/Educate/SCM_Definitions_and_Glossary_of_Terms.aspx?hkey=60879588-f65f-4ab5-8c4b-6878815ef921 [Accessed 1 October 2020].

Daugherty, P. and Wilson, H. (2018) *Human + Machine*. Boston, HBR.

Davenport, T. H. and Short, J. E. (1990) The New Industrial Engineering: Information Technology and Business Process Redesign. *Sloan Management Review*. 31 (4), 11–27.

Denison, D. (1990) Toward a theory of organizational culture and effectiveness. *Organization Science*. 6 (2), 204–223.

DHL, (December 2013) *Big Data in Logistics: A DHL perspective on how to move beyond the hype*. [Online]. Available from: www.dhl.com/content/dam/downloads/g0/about_us/innovation/CSI_Studie_BIG_DATA.pdf [Accessed 1 October 2020].

Dunk, A. and Perera, H. (1997) The incidence of budgetary slack: a field study exploration. *Accounting, Auditing & Accountability Journal*. 10 (5), 649–664.

Drury, C. (2004) *Management and Cost Accounting*. 6th edition. London, Thomson Learning.

Fitzgerald, L., Johnston, R., Brignall, S., Silvestro, R. and Voss, C. (1991) *Performance Measurement in Service Businesses*. London, CIMA.

Fitzgerald, L. and Moon, P. (1996) *Performance Measurement in Service Businesses: Making it Work*. London, CIMA.

Gartner (2018) *IT glossary*. [Online]. Available from: www.gartner.com/it-glossary/big-data/ [Accessed 18 December 2018].

Hamel, G. and Prahalad, C. K. (1990) The core competence of the corporation. *Harvard Business Review*. 68 (2), 79–91.

Hammer, M. (1996) *Beyond Reengineering: How the Process-Centred Organisation is Changing Our Work and Our Lives*. New York, Harper Collins.

Hammer, M. and Champy, J. (2001) *Reengineering the Corporation: A manifesto for Business Revolution*, (Revised edition). New York, Harper Collins.

Harmon, P. (2014). *Business Process Change: A Business Process Management Guide for Managers and Process Professionals*. 3rd edition. Waltham, MA, Morgan Kaufmann.

Harrigan, K. R. (1980) Strategies for Declining Industries. *Journal of Business Strategy*. 1 (2), 20–34.

Harrigan, K. R. and Porter, M. E. (1989) End-game Strategies for Declining Industries, in Asch, D. and Bowman C., (eds). *Readings in Strategic Management*. Basingstoke, Macmillan, 219–233.

Hicks, B. J. (2007) Lean information management: Understanding and eliminating waste. *International Journal of Information Management*. 27 (40, 233–249. [Online]. Available from: www.sciencedirect.com/science/article/pii/S0268401206001435 [Accessed 1 October 2020].

Hopwood, A. (1974) *Accounting and Human Behaviour*. London, Haymarket Publishing.

Imai, M. (1986) *Kaizen: The key to Japan's competitive success*. New York, McGraw-Hill.

Imai, M. (2012) *Gemba Kaizen: A commonsense approach to a continuous improvement strategy*. 2nd edition. New York, McGraw-Hill.

International Integrated Reporting Council (IIRC), (2013) *The International <IR> Framework*. [Online]. Available from: http://integratedreporting.org/wp-content/uploads/2013/12/13-12-08-THE-INTERNATIONAL-IR-FRAMEWORK-2-1.pdf [Accessed 1 October 2020].

International Integrated Reporting Council (IIRC), (no date) *Integrated Reporting: A Force for Financial Stability and Sustainability*. [Online]. Available from: www.iasplus.com/en/resources/sustainability/iirc [Accessed 1 October 2020].

International Organisation for Standardisation (ISO) (2005) *International Standard ISO 9000*. 3rd edition. Geneva, ISO.

International Organisation for Standardisation (ISO) (2016) *Selection and use of the ISO 9000 family of standards.* [Online]. Available from: www.iso.org/files/live/sites/isoorg/files/store/en/PUB100208.pdf [Accessed 1 October 2020].

Jobber, D. (2010) *Principles and Practice of Marketing.* 6th edition. Maidenhead, McGraw-Hill.

Johnson G., Whittington, R., Scholes, K., Angwin, D. and Regnér, P. (2017) *Exploring Strategy: Text and Cases.* 11th edition. Harlow, Pearson Education Limited.

Johnson, S. (no date) Environmental Management Accounting. *ACCA Technical articles.* [Online]. Available from: www.accaglobal.com/gb/en/student/exam-support-resources/professional-exams-study-resources/p5/technical-articles/environmenta-management.html [Accessed 21 October 2020].

Johnson, S. (2005) The pyramids and pitfalls of performance measurement. *ACCA Technical articles.* [Online]. Available from: www.accaglobal.com/gb/en/student/exam-support-resources/professional-exams-study-resources/p5/technical-articles/the-pyramids.html [Accessed 1 October 2020].

Kaiser Associates (1988) *Beating the competition: a practical guide to benchmarking.* Washington, DC, Kaiser Associates.

Kaplan, R. and Cooper, R. (1998) *Cost and Effect: Using Integrated Cost Systems to Drive Profitability and Performance.* Cambridge MA, Harvard Business School Press.

Kaplan, R. and Norton, D. (1992) The Balanced Scorecard: Measures that Drive Performance. *Harvard Business Review.* 70 (1), 71–79. [Reprint available Online]. Available from: https://hbr.org/1992/01/the-balanced-scorecard-measures-that-drive-performance-2 [Accessed 1 October 2020].

Kaplan, R. and Norton, D. (1996a) *The Balanced Scorecard: Translating Strategy into Action.* Boston, Harvard Business School Press.

Kaplan, R. and Norton, D. (1996b) Using the Balanced Scorecard as a Strategic Management System, *Harvard Business Review.* 74 (1), 75–85.

Kaplan, R. and Norton, D. (2004) *Strategy Maps: Converting Intangible Assets into Tangible Outcomes.* Boston, Harvard Business School Press.

Koller, T. (1994) What is value-based management? *McKinsey Quarterly.* August [Online]. Available from: www.mckinsey.com/business-functions/strategy-and-corporate-finance/our-insights/what-is-value-based-management [Accessed 1 October 2020].

KPMG, (2012) *Integrated Reporting: Performance insight through better business reporting.* Issue 2. [Online]. Available from: http://https://integratedreporting.org/wp-content/uploads/2012/06/KPMG-Integrated-Reporting-Performance-Insight-Through-Better-Business-Reporting-Issue-2.pdf [Accessed 1 October 2020].

Liker, J. (2004) *The Toyota Way: 14 Management Principles from the Word's Greatest Manufacturer.* New York, McGraw Hill.

Lucey, T. (2005) *Management Information Systems.* 9th edition. Andover, Cengage Learning.

Lynch, R. L. and Cross, K. F. (1991) *Measure up! Yardsticks for Continuous Improvement.* Malden, MA, Blackwell.

McKinsey & Company (2011) *Big data: The next frontier for innovation, competition, and productivity.* [Online]. Available from: www.mckinsey.com/business-functions/business-technology/our-insights/big-data-the-next-frontier-for-innovation [Accessed 1 October 2020].

Mendelow, A. (1991) *Stakeholder Mapping.* Proceedings of the 2nd International Conference on Information Systems. Cambridge, MA.

Merchant, K. A. (1988) *Modern Management Control Systems: Text and Cases.* New Jersey, Prentice Hall.

Meyer, H. H., Kay, E. and French J. R. (1965) Split Roles in Performance Appraisal. *Harvard Business Review*. 43 (1), 123–9. [Reprint online]. Available from: https://hbr.org/1965/01/split-roles-in-performance-appraisal [Accessed 1 October 2020].

Mintzberg, H. (1979) *The Structuring of Organisations*. New Jersey, Prentice Hall.

Monden, Y. and Lee, J. (1993) How a Japanese auto maker reduces costs. *Management Accounting*. 75 (2), 22–26.

Morgan, G. (2008) Accounting and Organisational Cultures. *ACCA Technical Articles*. Originally published in *ACCA Student Accountant*, November/December, 44–46. [Online]. Available from: www.accaglobal.com/content/dam/acca/global/PDF-students/2012/sa_novdec08_morgan.pdf [Accessed 1 October 2020].

National Institute of Standards and Technology (NIST) (2011) *The NIST Definition of Cloud Computing* (SP 800–145). [Online]. Available from: www.nist.gov/news-events/news/2011/10/final-version-nist-cloud-computing-definition-published [Accessed 1 October 2020].

OECD (2017) OECD *Transfer Pricing Guidelines for Multinational Enterprises and Tax Administrations 2017*. Paris, OECD Publishing.

Ohno, T. (1988) *Toyota Production System: Beyond Large-Scale Production*. New York, Productivity Press.

Otley, D. T. (1978) Budget use and managerial performance. *Journal of Accounting Research*. 15 (1), 122–49.

Ouchi, W. G. (1979) A conceptual framework for the design of organizational control mechanisms. *Management Science*. September, 833–48.

Peters, T. J. (1986) *What gets measured gets done*. [Online]. Available from: http://tompeters.com/columns/what-gets-measured-gets-done/ [Accessed 22 September 2019].

Peters, T. J. and Waterman, R. H. (1982) *In Search of Excellence*. New York, Harper and Row.

Pogue, M. (2008) Business Failure: Prediction and Prevention. *ACCA Technical Articles*. [Online]. Available from: www.accaglobal.com/gb/en/student/exam-support-resources/professional-exams-study-resources/p5/technical-articles/business-failure.html [Accessed 22 September 2017]. (Originally published in *Student Accountant*, June/July 2008, pp 54–57).

Porter, M. E. (1980) *Competitive Strategy: Techniques for Analyzing Industries and Competitors*. New York, Free Press.

Porter, M. E. (1985) *Competitive Advantage: Creating and Sustaining Superior Performance*. New York, Free Press.

PwC, (no date) *Data building blocks*. [Online]. Available from: www.pwc.co.uk/data-analytics/data-building-blocks.html [Accessed 14 September 2018].

Rockart, J. (1979) Chief Executives Define Their Own Data Needs. *Harvard Business Review*. 57 (2), 81–93. Reprint available online from: https://hbr.org/1979/03/chief-executives-define-their-own-data-needs [Accessed 1 October 2020].

Ryan, N. (2011a) Economic Value Added versus Profit-Based Measures of Performance – Part 1. *ACCA Technical Articles*. [Online]. Available from: www.accaglobal.com/gb/en/student/exam-support-resources/professional-exams-study-resources/p5/technical-articles/economic-value-added-part1.html [Accessed 1 October 2020].

Ryan, N. (2011b) Economic Value Added versus Profit-Based Measures of Performance – Part 2. *ACCA Technical Articles*. [Online]. Available from: www.accaglobal.com/gb/en/student/exam-support-resources/professional-exams-study-resources/p5/technical-articles/economic-value-added-part2.html [Accessed 1 October 2020].

Ryan, N. (2015a) Human resource management and the appraisal system. *ACCA Technical Articles*. [Online]. Available from: www.accaglobal.com/gb/en/student/exam-support-resources/professional-exams-study-resources/p5/technical-articles/human-resource-management-and-the-appraisal-system.html [Accessed 1 October 2020].

Ryan, N. (2015b) Reward schemes for employees and management. *ACCA Technical Articles*. [Online]. Available from: www.accaglobal.com/gb/en/student/exam-support-resources/professional-exams-study-resources/p5/technical-articles/reward-schemes-for-employees-and-management.html [Accessed 1 October 2020].

Ryan, N. (no date) Lean enterprises and lean information systems. *ACCA Technical Articles*. [Online]. Available from: www.accaglobal.com/gb/en/student/exam-support-resources/professional-exams-study-resources/p5/technical-articles/lean.html [Accessed 1 October 2020].

Slatter, S. (1984) *Corporate Recovery*. London, Penguin Books.

Slatter, S. and Lovett, D. (1999) *Corporate Turnaround*. London, Penguin Books.

Stern Value Management, (2019) *Proprietary Tools*. [Online]. Available from: http://sternvaluemanagement.com/intellectual-property-joel-stern/proprietary-tools-value-creation/ [Accessed 1 October 2020].

Van den Berg, G. and Pietersma, P. (2016) *Key Management Models: The 75+ models every manager needs to know*. 3rd edition. Harlow, FT/Pearson.

Womack, J. P. and Jones, D. T. (2003) *Lean Thinking: Banish Waste and Create Wealth in Your Corporation*. 2nd edition. London, Simon & Schuster.

Zeithaml, V., Parasuraman, A. and Berry, L. (1990) *Delivering Quality Service: Balancing Customer Perception and Expectation*. New York, Free Press.

Tell us what you think

Got comments or feedback on this book? Let us know.
Use your QR code reader:

Or, visit:
https://bppgroup.fra1.qualtrics.com/jfe/form/SV_9TrxTtw8jSvO7Pv